AF349969

One Hundred Poems
from Old Japan

Compiled *by* **Fujiwara no Teika**
Translated *by* **Michael Freiling**

TUTTLE Publishing

Tokyo | Rutland, Vermont | Singapore

Contents

Introduction

IF YOU WERE to make a list of those rare periods in human history that saw a flowering of art and culture so remarkable that it left its imprint on the world stage for centuries after, what episodes would make your list? The Athens of ancient Greece, I wager, along with Renaissance Italy. Elizabethan England, perhaps. The salons of Paris during the Enlightenment. Or maybe the revolution in classical music that took place in Vienna during the reign of Maria Theresa.

Chances are that however long your list, the Kyoto of the Heian period would not appear. And yet, for many reasons, this remarkable period is just as worthy of our appreciation and understanding. As early as the seventh century, Japan was developing a tradition of poetry that rivals some of the best ever written.

This tradition developed to such a degree that by the high point of the Heian period in the tenth and eleventh centuries, every member of the upper class, male or female, was expected to be an accomplished poet. As Ivan Morris points out in his portrait of court life in ancient Japan, *The World of the Shining Prince*, a gentleman of the period who was unable to produce a passable poem on the occasions when they were needed (and there were many) "labored under at least as great a handicap as would a gentleman in the court of Henry VIII who could not mount a horse."

More remarkably, as great as the expectations were for men, they could be even greater for women. The most accomplished writers of the period were women, expected to hold their own in poetic exchanges with their male counterparts, or even better them. Many of the best poems of the time were written by Lady Murasaki, author of *The Tale of Genji*, and Sei Shonagon, author of the *Pillow Book*.

The poetic compilations of this period run to thousands and thousands of pages, from the early *Man'yoshu* (some time after 759), to the imperial anthologies beginning with the *Kokinshu* (905), to hundreds of later collections. Heian-period poetry is deeply appreciated in Japan, even today. Nara Prefecture, for example, has an entire museum dedicated to the poems of the *Man'yoshu*, and an arboretum with the plants referred to those poems. The city of Uji, near Kyoto, contains a museum dedicated to what is perhaps the greatest literary product of that period, Lady Murasaki's *Tale of Genji*.

The Hyakunin Isshu

This welter of complexity clearly poses a problem for English-speaking poetry lovers who wish to acquaint themselves with the poems of this period—where does one get started? The question has a simple answer—with the one hundred poems contained in this book, the translation of an anthology entitled *Hyakunin Isshu* in Japanese, meaning "one hundred poets; one poem each."

This is one of the best-known poetry collections in Japan, in part because it concisely captures a history of classical Japanese poetry, from the seventh to the early thirteenth century. It also introduces many of the greatest poets of that period.

One reason for the enduring popularity of the *Hyakunin Isshu* is that it forms one of the foundational pillars of literary education in Japan. Students are usually exposed to its poems in elementary school as an introduction to the *tanka* poetic form (see page 10). In middle school and high school, they will analyze the poems and memorize some of them. Many adults are still able to recite one or two of their favorite poems years later.

The popularity of this anthology is also reinforced by a card game based on the poems that is traditionally played at New Year's.

Fujiwara no Teika

The poems in the *Hyakunin Isshu* were selected in the early thirteenth century by Fujiwara no Teika (1162–1241), also known as

Fujiwara no Sadaie. He was a minor court official under Emperor Go-Toba (1180–1239), but his literary skills as a poet, critic and compiler of anthologies earned him the latter's patronage. As one of the six compilers of the eighth imperial anthology of poetry, the *Shin Kokinshu*, and the initial sole compiler of the ninth anthology, the *Shinchokusen Wakashu*, he was the first person ever to have worked on the compilation of two imperial poetry anthologies, giving him immense influence in the poetic world of his time.

There are two accounts of how and why Fujiwara no Teika decided to compile the *Hyakunin Isshu*. The first is that around 1230, when Teika was nearly seventy, he was asked by his son to select the poems for screens to be installed in a new house being built by the son's father-in-law on Mount Ogura. In this account, Teika's preference was for poems with vivid imagery, possibly so they could be matched with artwork depicting the scenes. This is why the collection is often referred to as the *Ogura Hyakunin Isshu*.

The second account has to do with Teika's concern for his legacy as an arbiter of poetic taste. In this account, Teika's primary concern was to create a collection that could serve as a comprehensive survey of the poetic themes and styles that had been employed in different eras, beginning with Emperor Tenchi (626–671) and ending with Emperor Juntoku (1197–1242).

Court Life in the Heian Period

To better understand the poems, we need to know a little about court life in Heian Kyo (modern-day Kyoto) during this period. Life revolved around the court of the emperor, with successors chosen from among the sons of that emperor. Consequently, able sons from other noble clans were excluded from any chance of reaching the throne.

However, one enterprising clan, the Fujiwara—of whom Fujiwara no Teika was a member—managed to insert themselves into the imperial bloodline by marrying their daughters off to the emperor in successive generations, so as to guarantee a favored position at court. By "relieving" the emperor of the burdens of the day-to-day tasks of governance, the Fujiwara eventually became the de facto rulers of the country, reducing the emperor's role to one that was largely spiritual and symbolic. Cementing control over the imperial family, they would often force the emperor to "retire" at a relatively early age (usually around thirty, just as they were coming into full adulthood), and make way for the crown prince to ascend the throne as a child. His regent would invariably be a Fujiwara.

Noble families typically owned various domains outside of Heian Kyo, from which they received the income to sustain their own existence in the capital. Even that was often done by proxy, due to complex tax rules that made it advantageous to have one's estates managed by another, more powerful clan, with the Fujiwara of course being at the top of this pecking order.

As with the emperor, whose role was largely symbolic, most of the ministerial posts in the nominal government structure were also symbolic, although they were no less highly prized for the income and grants which accompanied them. Since these posts were allocated by a Fujiwara-controlled bureaucracy, most of the aspiring young men tended to eschew serious scholarly training. The real path to advancement in this society was recognized to run through advantageous marriages, aesthetic reputation, and good looks, roughly in that order.

What passed for scholarly education at the time was limited to the Chinese classics, especially Confucius. Though not necessarily considered classics, the poets of the T'ang period, especially Po Chu-I, were popular, and the one concession that Heian gentlemen were likely to make to education was to learn enough of these poems to be able to quote them and recognize quotations in return.

As a result, the principal occupation of the nobility, from the imperial household on down, became the pursuit of aesthetic and sensory pleasures. Poetic ability was arguably the most important, since court life presented frequent occasions on which the aspiring courtier, male or female, was expected or even required to compose a poem on the spot. Calligraphy was also critical, since many of these poems need to be sent as soon as they were composed. Good handwriting was considered to be a sign of good character. Other artistic pursuits, such as the ability to play a musical instrument, were highly regarded.

All of these aesthetic endeavors were taken seriously, and court life abounded with competitions and "judgments" in which a group might discuss and evaluate the merits of various works, or the talents of various courtiers. As might be expected under such circumstances, the level of taste and the quality of the poetry became extraordinarily refined, at a time when Europe was still struggling to emerge from the Dark Ages, and the Renaissance was five or six centuries in the future.

The Merry-go-Round of Love

One of the key factors that contributed to the development of poetry in the Heian period was the somewhat unusual arrangement of relations between men and women in the court life of those days. Heian society, at least at the court level, was essentially polygamous, but as in many polygamous societies, there was an inherent structure to the polygamy.

Most men had a principal wife, whom they married at an early age. The principal wife was likely to be chosen by the family, and interests of social or political advantage were paramount. She was often several years older than her husband. Typical of many polygamous societies, the aim of this marriage was the production of offspring, personal happiness almost never being a consideration.

To satisfy his own needs and desires, a man might take additional secondary wives or concubines. These were publicly sanctioned relationships, conducted openly. "Official" relationships, in turn, could be supplemented by various and often numerous "casual" relationships, of long or short duration. Occasionally, but not always, such a casual relationship could blossom to the point where the man might choose to place the woman into a formal relationship.

None of this structure is particularly unusual when compared to societies organized along similar lines. What made relationships far more intricate in Heian Japan was the degree of freedom accorded to the women themselves. A woman could inherit, keep and manage her own property. She would often have her own household and live separately, even when married.

In fact, an unmarried woman's prospects for advancement were often much brighter than those of her brothers. Potentially, at least, she could marry into a more powerful family, or even be taken as a concubine of the imperial court, with the possibility of becoming mother or grandmother to a prince, or even a future emperor. Daughters, especially clever ones, were highly prized by those families concerned with advancing their status.

Historically, Japanese culture did not place undue emphasis on virginity, in contrast with China or the West. A woman's fidelity was more or less "expected" once she had entered into a formal relationship, but fidelity was far from universal. As long as the relationship had not been made official, a woman could dismiss her lover at any time, for any reason, including his poor aesthetic judgment, or his inability to produce elegant responses on demand. Such may have been the fate of poor Yukinari, for example, the butt of Sei Shonagon's harsh jibe in poem 62.

What prevented this amorous activity from degenerating into a tawdry free-for-all were the ironclad rules of taste and decorum to be followed. A man might signal his intention to visit by sending a poem, which left the woman free to refuse by sending a poem in response telling her suitor not to bother. As well as Shonagon's poem of dismissal, other examples of this genre include poem 67 by Lady-in-Waiting Suwo and poem 72 by Lady Kii.

When a man came to call, he would not actually see the woman he called upon, at least initially. She would be seated behind a large curtain through which they would converse. This threshold could not be crossed without the woman's invitation, or at least tacit permission. If he was successful in winning her favor, he might spend the night, slipping out just before dawn. The woman's household would turn a blind eye to these goings-on.

But immediately upon returning home, he had additional obligations to fulfill, especially if he had any hopes of continuing the liaison. He must write a morning-after poem, in his best penmanship, typically protesting his undying love for the lady, his inexpressible pain on having to part from her, and his desire to meet her again, as seen in poem 50 by Fujiwara no Yoshitaka.

Not every Heian dandy was a top-of-the-line poet, and over time these protestations tended to become stylistic, the metaphors employed often conventional, for example, the notion that one's sleeves had become soaked with dew from excessive crying, a sentiment that is found in poem 1 by Emperor Tenchi.

But it was the elegance of the poem that counted, especially if the erstwhile lover could summon up an allusion to one the earlier Japanese poetry anthologies, such as the *Man'yoshu* or the *Kokinshu*, or better yet to a well-known Chinese poem. Emperor Tenchi's poem resembles an early poem from the *Man'yoshu* which may originally have been a chant sung by farmers as they hauled in their crops.

The poem was delivered by messenger, often attached to a flower or cutting from a tree which related to the poem's message. The lady was expected to respond in like fashion, expanding on the metaphors employed or alluding to a subsequent verse in the poem referred to by her lover. Many of the poems of the *Hyakunin Isshu* have the form of these morning-after poems, although some of them were actually written for poetry competitions rather than as "real time" responses to romantic episodes, such as poem 72 by Lady Kii.

The Poems of the Hyakunin Isshu

The poems that make up this collection have a syllabic structure of 5-7-5-7-7 as compared with the more familiar 5-7-5 haiku, which evolved at a later date. The form of these poems is referred to as *tanka* ("short poems") or *waka* ("Japanese poems"), although the latter term often encompasses other poetic forms as well. A poet might often use the first three 5-7-5 lines as the preface to set a scene, and the final 7-7 couplet to deliver a "punchline" with dramatic or emotional impact that reveals the poem's true intent.

This structure can be seen in the Japanese versions of the poems in this book, but I have not attempted to replicate the Japanese syllable count in my English translations.

The scenes depicted in the poems are frequently in or near Heian Kyo. On occasion, reference may be made to more remote locations, such as Naniwa (near modern day Osaka), but to the stay-at-home populace of Heian Kyo, ventures to such far-off locations were considered dangerous. Some place names may sound familiar, but do not necessarily refer to the places that first spring to mind. The "Nara" of poem 98 does not refer to the ancient capital, but to a location near Kamigamo Shrine, while the "Nara" of poem 61 does in fact refer to that city. Similarly, the "Osaka" of poems 10, 25, and 62 does not refer to the modern-day city, but to a popular trysting spot southeast of Heian Kyo. To avoid confusion, this location is spelled "Ausaka" in the romanized versions of the poems.

The language of these poems tends primarily to the native Japanese language before its encounter with Chinese. Words of Chinese origin almost never appear. There are no words in katakana, the syllabary whose primary use is to spell out foreign loan words. Chinese kanji characters are often employed by the poets, but they are either given a Japanese reading, or used as *ateji*—stand-ins for a Japanese sound.

These linguistic features explain why some of the best poets of the period were women—more than twenty are included in this anthology. Men of the Heian period were educated to write a formal style with heavy use of Chinese characters, while women would write almost exclusively in the newly developed hiragana syllabic script, mostly using words of Japanese origin.

Images and Expressions

Quite a few of the poems relate to romantic entanglements—either as morning-afters, or refusals, or poems of reproach when a relationship comes to an end. The feelings expressed in them are often quite conventional, although there is a tendency toward overstatement when it comes to protests of undying love, or the desolation and despair at being parted from one's erstwhile lover.

Others are simple nature poems, although sometimes what appears to be a nature poem on the surface might in fact include some secretly coded message to a lover.

Sometimes a setting is augmented by an auditory image such as the cry of a deer, for example, in poems 5 or 83; or the song of a bird as in poems 78 and 81.

Some of the poems, especially the ones composed by Buddhist clergy, who represent about a tenth of the poets in the anthology, deal with themes particular to Buddhism, especially the evanescence of life and the impermanence of all things. Poem 82, by the monk Doin, is an excellent example, as he analyzes the conflict between his human tendencies and his religious beliefs.

The poems of the *Hyakunin Isshu* contain many symbols and allusions. Some of the popular ones are listed below:

CHERRY BLOSSOMS Cherry blossoms are among the best known images in Japanese art and literature. Their sudden appearance in early spring creates an explosion of beauty as intense as it is short-lived. Poetry and cherry blossoms are tied together intimately by the tradition of *hanami* ("flower-watching") parties, where plenty of sake is consumed and guests might write their own meditation on this year's blossoms. An interesting example is poem 33 by Ki no Tomonori, which begins as a conventional paean to a gorgeous spring day, only to be derailed by the almost willful demise of the cherry blossoms.

ABSENT FRIENDS Poems that dwell on the theme of aging or the impermanence of things can also often refer to the absence of friends, such as poem 66 by Archbishop Gyoson, in which he commiserates with an old cherry tree about their friendless status.

WAVES The tossing about of waves is a classic image in Japan for passion and desire. In poem 18, Fujiwara no Toshiyuki uses the wave image to symbolize a loving and passionate embrace, although, as one might expect, in his poem this embrace is denied him.

WET SLEEVES One of the most common tropes is that one's sleeves are soaking wet, presumably drenched with unstoppable tears. Emperor Tenchi and Lady Kii employ the typical use of this image in poems 1 and 72. Poem 65 by Lady Sagami offers an interesting contrast, as she uses the image to make it clear what the Heian courtiers feared more than any loss of love—the ridicule of their peers.

The Poets of the Hyakunin Isshu

At least a quarter of the poems in this collection were composed by members of Fujiwara no Teika's own clan. Teika also included poets who shared a line of descent, perhaps thinking that these might illustrate certain forms of stylistic evolution, for example Izumi Shikibu (poem 56) and her daughter Koshikibu (poem 60). He selected several poems from his contemporaries, such as Emperor Go-Toba (poem 99) and Minamoto no Sanetomo (poem 93). Interestingly, Teika saw fit to include his own poem in the collection (poem 97), in which he adopts the voice of a woman, for an entry in a poetry contest.

The poets whose verses make up this collection vary widely in talent or reputation. Nonetheless it is fair to state that among them are the best poets of the period, and others who are quite interesting in their own right. Below are listed are a few of the most notable.

LADY MURASAKI SHIKIBU (973–1014), poem 57. Arguably the greatest writer of the period, Murasaki is best known as the author of *The Tale of Genji*, considered by many to be the first novel written anywhere in the world. But she was also a prolific poet, even within the novel itself, which contains nearly eight hundred tanka poems.

Murasaki married in her twenties, but was widowed a few years later. As her literary reputation grew, she was eventually invited to court as a lady-in-waiting to Empress Shoshi. This gave her a ringside seat from which to enjoy the goings-on at court, and many of the escapades she witnessed would be reflected in her writing.

Lady Murasaki was something of an exception to the rule that women did not make heavy use of the Chinese language. She was born into a highly literate family and trained in the Chinese classics, unusual for a woman of the time. This skill often made her a target of scorn among her jealous contemporaries.

LADY SEI SHONAGON (966–1017), poem 62. Shonagon is considered by many to be the second-greatest writer of the period. Her *Pillow Book* deals with court life in great detail. Her writing, as well as her poetry, tends to be more acerbic and less genteel than Lady Murasaki's, which makes for interesting reading.

At court, Shonagon served as lady-in-waiting to Empress Sadako, the principal wife of Emperor Ichijo, which in some respect placed her on a higher rank than Murasaki, since Empress Shoshi was only Ichijo's "second" wife. Murasaki and Shonagon were fierce rivals, and both were known to take potshots at the other in their work.

SUGAWARA NO MICHIZANE (845–903), poem 24. Michizane was one of the more complex characters of the Heian period. Born into a family of well-known scholars, he built himself an illustrious career as a scholar, educator and poet.

While serving a term as a provincial governor, he became embroiled in a dispute between the emperor and a high-ranking member of the Fujiwara clan. His support for the emperor was rewarded by further advancement at court, and eventually he was appointed ambassador to the T'ang court in China.

The Fujiwara did not forget this insult. Some years later they managed to implicate him in a scandal regarding the imperial succession, and had him banished to Kyushu, an incredibly long distance from the court, which was the near equivalent of a death sentence. In fact, Michizane died some two years later.

But the scholar was to have the last laugh, posthumously at least. Shortly after his death, a series of calamities struck Heian Kyo. The emperor's sons died in quick succession. The palace itself was struck by lightning, and a plague spread throughout the capital. In an attempt to appease Michizane's vengeful spirit, his court rank was restored and he was eventually deified as the patron of scholarship, poetry, and calligraphy. Large shrines were erected in his honor, both in the capital and in Dazaifu, the Kyushu city to which he had been exiled. Michizane is still revered today. His shrines are found throughout the country. Every year at exam time, students flock to them to pray for success.

ARIWARA NO NARIHIRA (825–880), poem 17. In many ways, Narihira was the epitome of the Heian gentleman. He was born into a high-ranking family (both his grandfathers were emperors), was believed to be exceptionally good looking, and his love affairs made him the subject of legend, even in those amorous times. He was also exceptionally well-traveled, compared with other gentlemen of his day and was reputed to have traveled at least three hundred miles along the legendary Tokaido, the coastal road that runs from modern-day Kyoto to Tokyo.

His poetry was famous for being complex and rife with additional meanings, which often required long footnotes in some of the anthologies of the day. But he is best remembered for his adventures as a lover, some of which appear to have entailed a great degree of risk. Rumors about his affairs abounded, though not all have been substantiated. These included dalliances with Ono no Komachi, another *Hyakunin Isshu* poet; with a consort of the emperor; and even with the high priestess of the Great Shrine of Ise, despite the near-sacrilegious implications of this latter affair.

One legend claims his liaison with the imperial consort resulted in a son who became Emperor Yozei, and that it was a desire to avoid the presumably dire consequences of this misbehavior which was the cause of his self-imposed exile along the Tokaido road.

KI NO TSURAYUKI (872–945), poem 35. As well as an acclaimed poet, Tsurayuki was also a compiler, editor and critic of other poets of the period. He was appointed editor-in-chief of the *Kokinshu*, the first anthology of Japanese poetry compiled under the imperial sponsorship of Emperor Daigo. This collection was assembled some 120 to 130 years after the *Man'yoshu* poetry anthology.

Tsurayuki's preface to the *Kokinshu* is seen as the first critical essay on waka poetry. In it, he renders judgment on previous poets, including Ariwara no Narihira (see page 15), whom he named as one of his "six immortal poets," although the latter did not escape criticism for "trying to express too much content in too few words," according to Helen McCullough in her book *Kokin Wakashu: The First Imperial Anthology of Japanese Poetry*.

He also served in administrative posts around the country. He is believed by many to be the author of *The Tosa Diary*, a work composed in hiragana script, a form of writing that was generally the province of women in those days. It purports to be a woman's description of her trip from Tosa Province to Heian Kyo, taking some fifty-five days. His purpose in writing this anonymous work from a woman's perspective remains a subject of debate.

Tsurayuki was also considered a great poet in his own right. He was included (along with Narihira) in an expanded list of "thirty-six immortal poets" compiled by Fujiwara no Kinto in the eleventh century. Lady Murasaki, who tended to mix historical figures in with her fictional creations, saw fit to recognize him as a master of the waka form in her *Tale of Genji*, even reporting that Emperor Uda had commissioned him to inscribe his poems on panels to decorate the imperial palace.

Enjoying the Hyakunin Isshu

The poems in this book are given in English, in Japanese script and in romanized Japanese, so they can be enjoyed without knowledge of the Japanese language. Here are some suggestions for additional steps you might take to gain a deeper appreciation of the poems.

The tanka poetic form originally evolved to be sung or chanted. The *ka* in tanka for instance, means "song." Even today, Japanese people will often refer to the poems of the *Hyakunin Isshu* as "songs." The best have a lyrical and rhythmic quality that reflects this ancient usage. A set of online recordings allow you listen to the poems and appreciate their lyrical structure. See the link on page 20.

Once you've listened to the rhythm a few times, you might try reciting a poem yourself to see if you can capture the rhythm in your own feelings. You don't need to be able to read Japanese—you can use the romanization. The rhythms of Japanese tanka do tend to be a bit different from the rhythms we are accustomed to in English poetry. However, some poems have a rhythm that comes close to our own. Poem 10 by Semimaru is a good place to start.

To deepen your appreciation further, try looking at the Japanese text itself. It is written in two different scripts, the syllabic hiragana; and the ideographic kanji, which are essentially Chinese characters imported into Japan. There are forty-six basic hiragana, and there are many Internet sites that give charts showing hiragana readings.

As you peruse the various poems, you'll likely find yourself becoming familiar with several of the kanji. Just knowing a few will give you a clue as to the emotional impact of the poem. Here are some very common ones, all of which are still in use today.

心	*kokoro*	heart, mind, soul
花	*hana, ka*	flower
袖	*sode*	sleeve (drenched with tears)
哀	*aware*	sadness, melancholy
思	*omou*	to think, feel
月	*tsuki*	moon
明	*ake*	brightness, light
有	*yu*	evening
山	*yama*	mountain

About the Illustrations in This Book

The woodblock print illustrations in this book are from the series *The Ogura Imitations of One Hundred Poems by One Hundred Poets* (*Ogura nazorae hyakunin isshu*), by three of Japan's renowned nineteenth-century woodblock print artists: Utagawa Hiroshige, who created thirty-five of the prints; Utagawa Kuniyoshi, who created fifty-one of the prints; and Utagawa Kunisada, who created fourteen of them. The print series was made specially to illustrate this volume of poems, and the imagery in each print is based on scenes from Kabuki theater that relate to the theme of each poem.

Modern Kyoto and the Hyakunin Isshu

If you ever get a chance to visit Kyoto, you may enjoy visiting some spots associated with the poems or the poets of the *Hyakunin Isshu*. Here are a few of my favorites, listed in alphabetical order.

DAIKAKU-JI A Buddhist temple in the northwestern area of Kyoto, the setting for poem 55.

HASE-DERA A temple near Mount Hatsuse near Nara, the setting for poem 74.

HEIAN SHRINE For another perspective on what the imperial palace may have looked like in the Heian period, this shrine is a scaled-down reproduction of the original palace. The present shrine was constructed in 1895 for an industrial exposition being held in Kyoto.

ISHIYAMA-DERA This lovely hillside temple in Otsu, near the shores of Lake Biwa, is easily reached from downtown Kyoto on the local Keishin train line. Legend has it that Lady Murasaki stayed at this temple in 1004, and that the beauty of the full moon inspired her to begin writing *The Tale of Genji*. Several statues of Lady Murasaki dot the grounds.

KAMIGAMO SHRINE Just below Kamigamo Shrine, two streams meet, the setting for poem 98 by Fujiwara no Ietaka, describing a group of men performing the Shinto purification ritual of *misogi*, which involves bathing or standing in ice-cold water. A stone monument on the west bank commemorates the poem.

KITANO TEMMANGU Located along Imadegawa Avenue just east of Nishioji-dori Street, this was the first shrine in Japan dedicated to Sugawara no Michizane, author of poem 24, revered as the patron of the scholarly arts—academic studies, poetry and calligraphy. For more on Michizane, see page 14.

KURAMA SHRINE This shrine, along the Keifuku rail line to Arashi-yama, has rows of vermillion posts recording the names of well-known entertainers, both present and past. Sei Shonagon, author of poem 62 is enshrined here as a patron of the arts. For more on Sei Shonagon, see page 14.

KYOTO IMPERIAL PALACE Commonly referred to as the Gosho, the current building was erected in 1855 as a residence for the emperor, just a few years before the imperial residence was moved to Tokyo at the time of the Meiji Restoration in 1868. The original Heian-period palace was located somewhat to the west of the current location. Over the years, the palace has been destroyed and rebuilt some eight times. The current design represents an attempt to replicate the original structure.

SEKISEMIMARU SHRINE AND THE AUSAKA STONE A Shinto shrine located near the Keishin Otani railway stop where Semimaru, the blind poet of poem 10, is enshrined. Nearby, along the current Tokaido Highway, about 100 yards east of Otani Station, is a memorial stone marking the estimated spot of the original Ausaka Barrier, mentioned in poems 10 and 62. The Ausaka Barrier was a checkpoint along the old Tokaido Road that separated the capital,

Heian Kyo, from outlying districts. Citizens of Heian Kyo would often meet arriving guests at this location, or accompany departing guests this far, and the inherent drama of these encounters is conveyed in poem 10 by Semimaru. Sei Shonagon's poem 62 treats this location as a metaphor for a gate through which her unwelcome suitor may not pass.

Sumiyoshi Taisha A Shinto shrine on the southern edge of Osaka, near Osaka Bay, famous for its picturesque arched bridge. This is the setting for poem 18.

Tale of Genji Museum Located near the center of Uji, just outside Kyoto, this museum contains many artifacts and dioramas depicting life during the Heian period.

How to access the audio recordings for this book:

1. Check to be sure you have an Internet connection.
2. Type the URL below into to your web browser.

https://www.tuttlepublishing.com/one-hundred-poems-from-old-japan

For support you can email us at info@tuttlepublishing.com.

The Poems

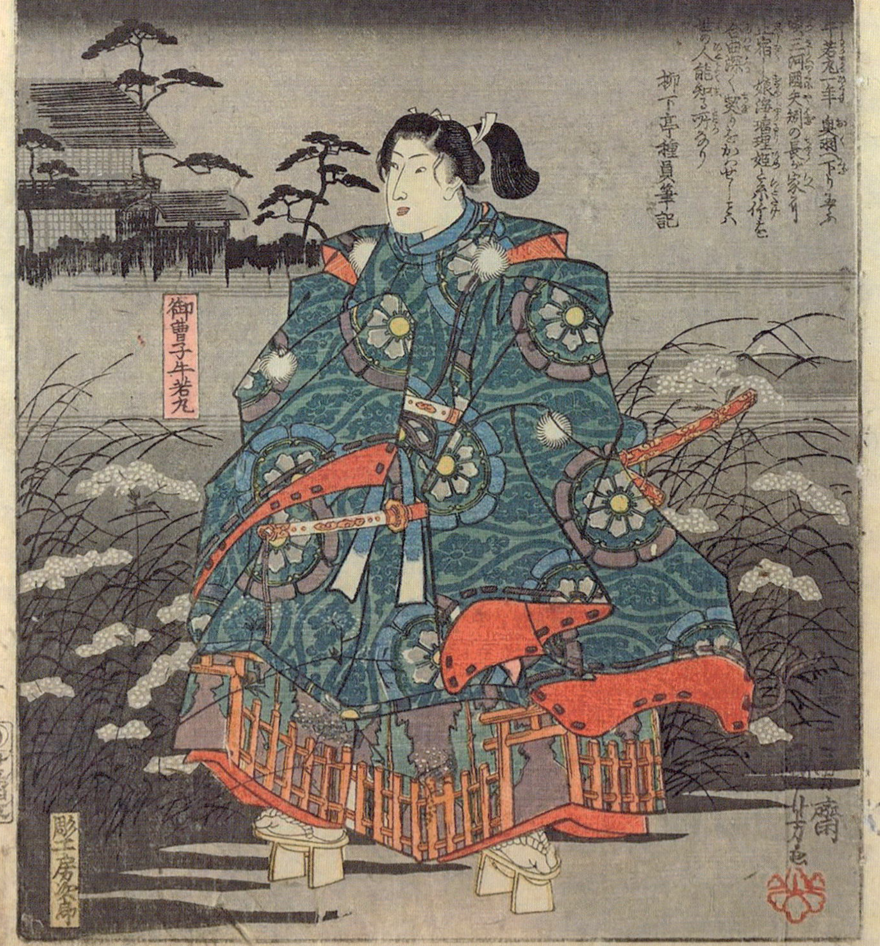
小倉擬百人一首
天智天皇
秋の田の
かりほの
庵の苫を
あらみ
わが衣手は
露にぬれつつ
御曹子牛若丸
柳下亭種員筆記
伊場仙板
彫工房次郎
芳艶画

1

Emperor Tenchi

A makeshift hut
in an autumn field
with coarse and leaky thatch—

the sleeves of my fine robes
drenched constantly with dew.

秋の田の
かりほの庵の
苫を荒み
わが衣手は
露にぬれつつ

aki no ta no
kariho no io no
toma wo arami
waga koromode wa
tsuyu ni nuretsutsu

2

Empress Jito

The passing spring
yields to summer—

blinding white
the robes of Amaterasu
so close to heaven on Kaguyama.

春過ぎて
夏来にけらし
白妙の
衣ほすてふ
天の香具山

haru sugite
natsu ki ni kerashi
shirotae no
koromo hosu cho
ama no kaguyama

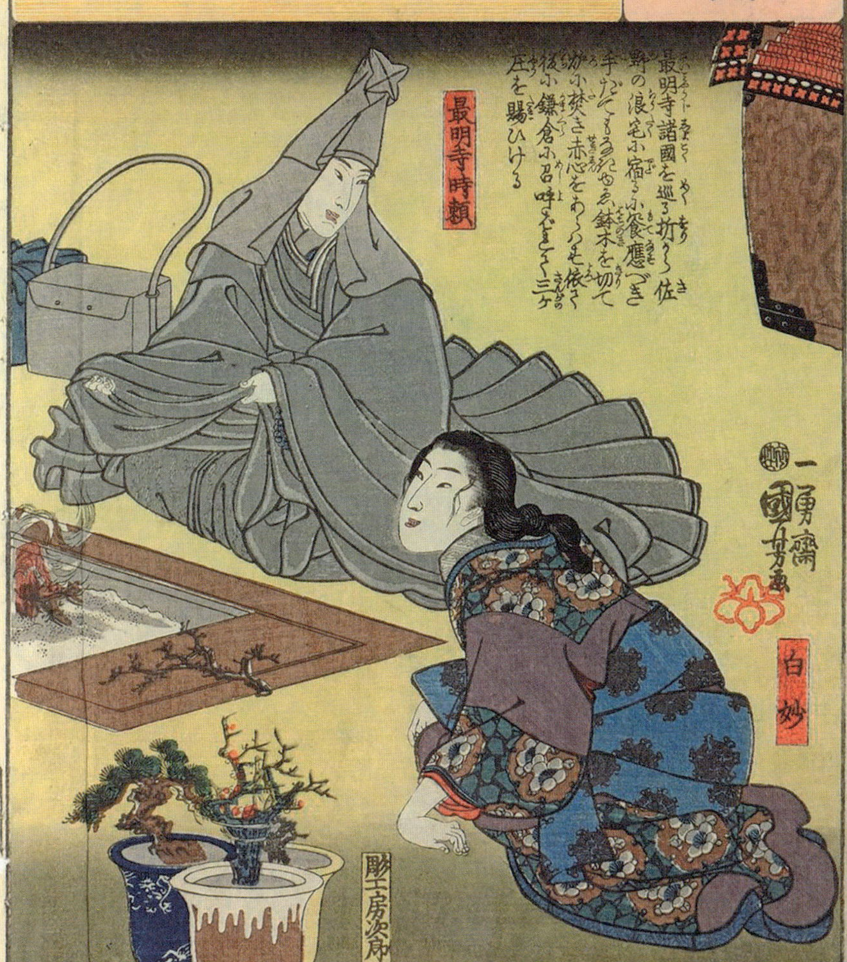
小倉
擬百人一首

持統天皇

春すぎて
夏来にけらし
白妙の
衣ほすてふ
あまの
かぐ山

最明寺時頼

白妙

一勇齋
國芳画

彫工房次郎

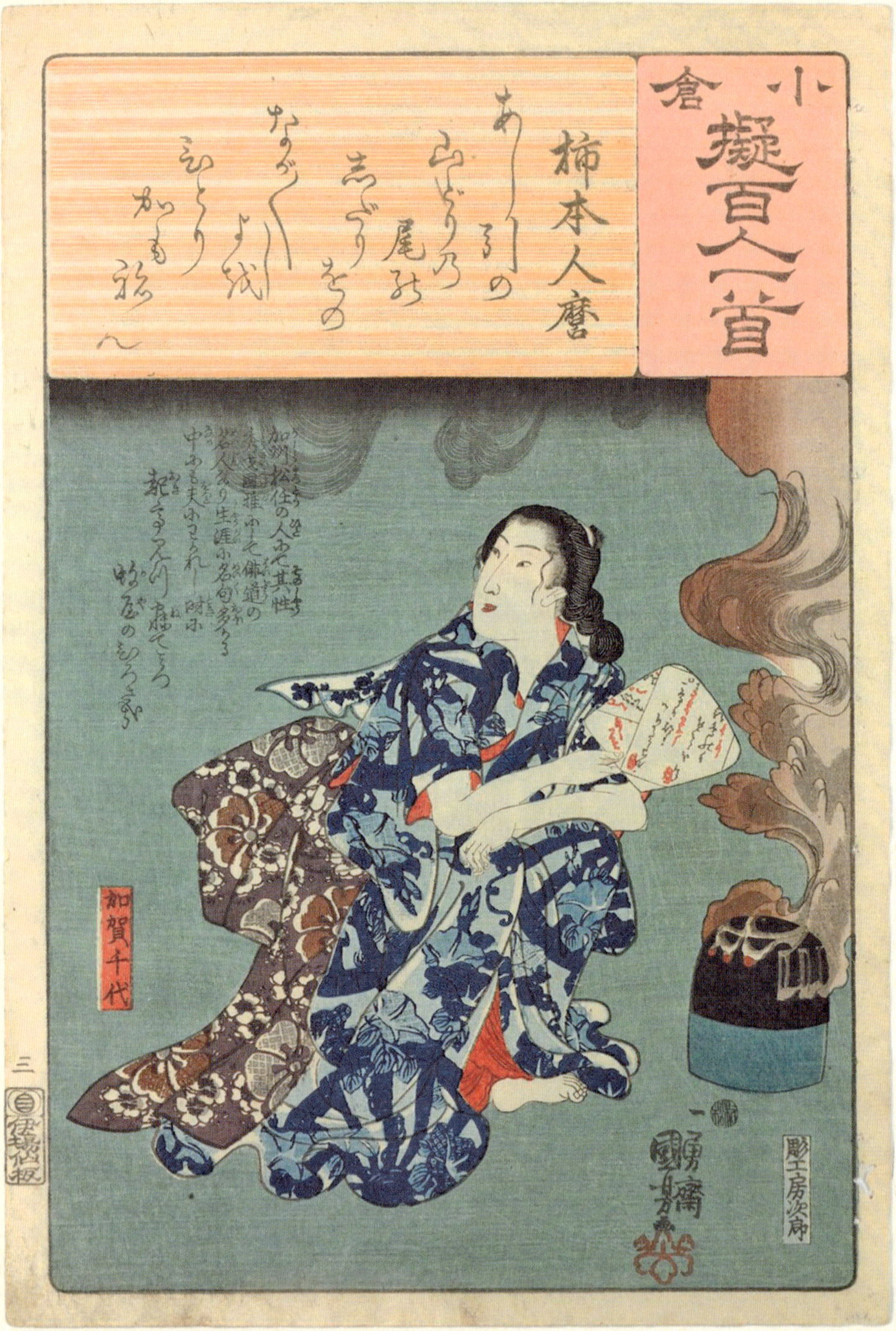

小倉擬百人一首

柿本人麿

あし引の
山どりの尾の
しだり尾の
ながながし夜を
ひとり
かも
ねん

加賀千代

一勇斎國芳画

彫工房次郎

3

Kakinomoto no Hitomaro

Interminable in length
the mountain pheasants' tails
they drag along behind them—

so long, so long this night
I must lie sleepless and alone.

足引の
山鳥の尾の
しだり尾の
ながながし夜を
ひとりかもねむ

ashibiki no
yamadori no o no
shidari o no
naganagashi yo wo
hitori ka mo nen

4

Yamabe no Akahito

Walking out on Tago Beach
when suddenly I'm face-to-face
with a sheet of solid white—

the towering peak of Fuji
crowned by snow, still falling now.

田子の浦に
打ち出でてみれば
白妙の
富士の高嶺に
雪は降りつつ

tago no ura ni
uchi idete mireba
shirotae no
fuji no takane ni
yuki wa furi tsutsu

小倉

擬百人一首

山邊赤人

田子れ
うち出て
見れば
白妙の
ふじの
たか松に
雪をふりはつ

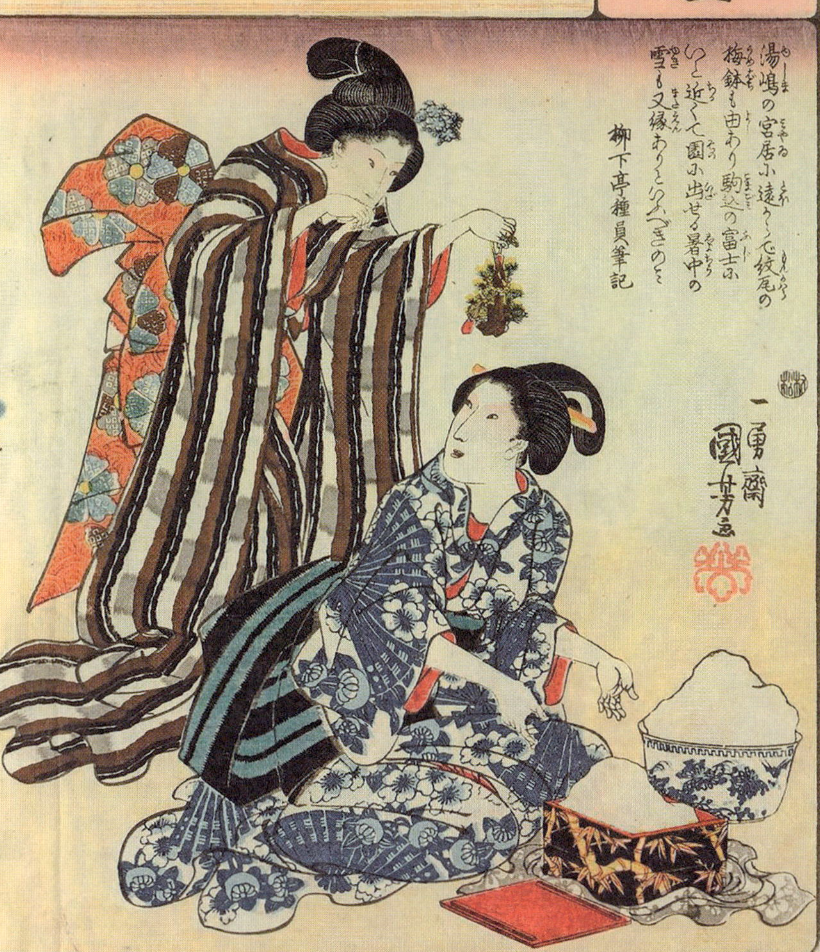
湯嶋の宮居小遠ろゝで紋尾の
梅鉢も由あり駒込の富士小
に近くて園小出せる暑中の
雪も又縁ありとうつぎのを

柳下亭種員筆記

一勇齋
國芳画

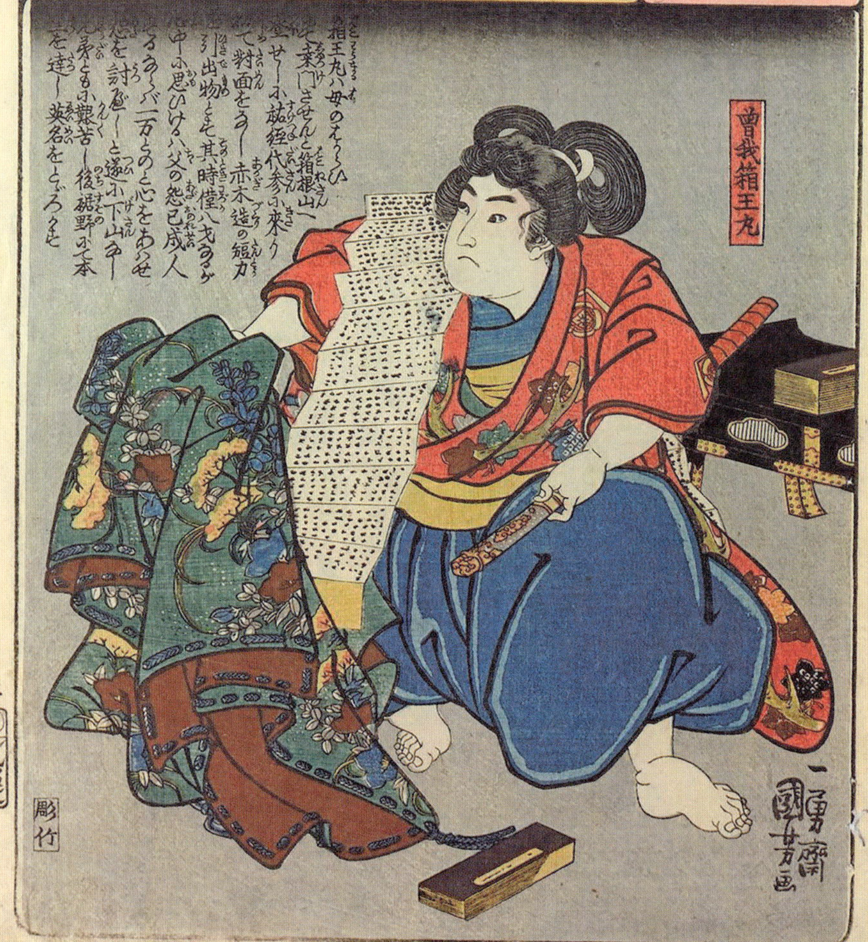

小倉擬百人一首
猿丸大夫
奥山に
もみぢ
ふみわけ
なく鹿の
こゑきく
とぎぞ
秋は
かなしき
曽我箱王丸
一勇齋國芳画
彫竹
伊場仙板
五

5

Sarumaru

Deep in the mountain woods
deer cry out pitifully,
trampling through the fallen leaves—

the crackle of these skeletons
of autumn makes me shiver.

奥山に
紅葉ふみ分け
鳴く鹿の
声聞く時ぞ
秋は悲しき

okuyama ni
momiji fumiwake
naku shika no
koe kiku toki zo
aki wa kanashiki

6

Otomo no Yakamochi

White frost settles
along this bridge that magpies cross,
pursuing their secret journeys—

its glowing whiteness tells me
night is nearly gone.

鵲の
渡せる橋に
置く霜の
白きを見れば
夜ぞ更けにける

kasasagi no
wataseru hashi ni
oku shimo no
shiroki wo mireba
yo zo fuke ni keru

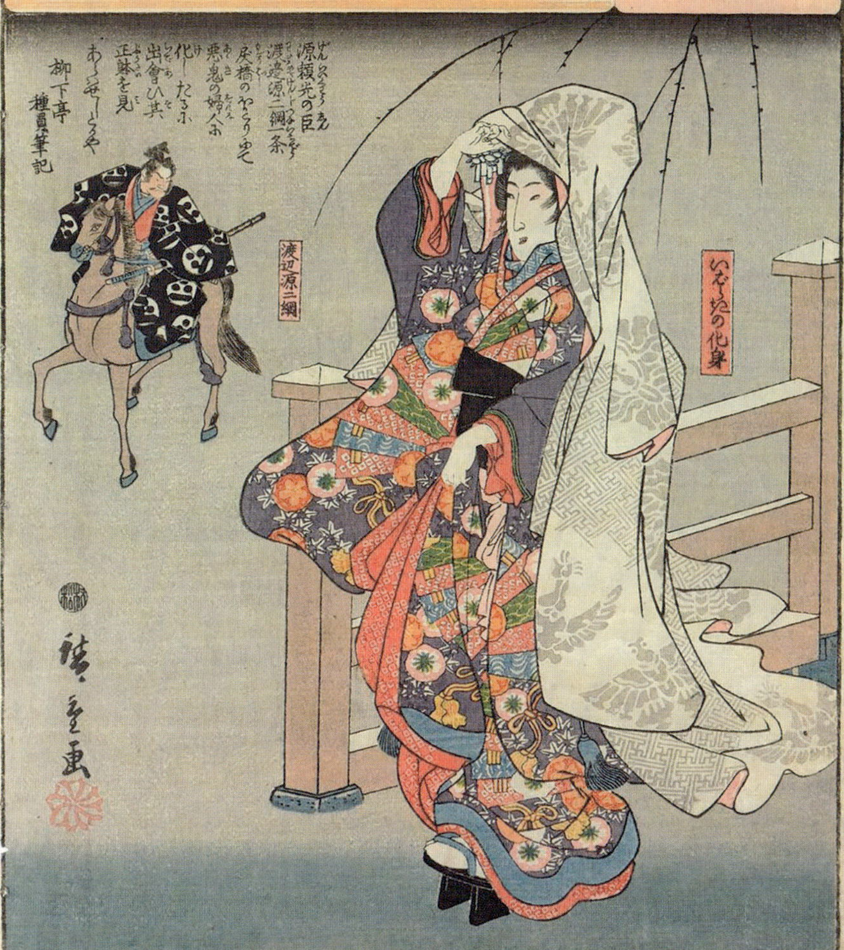
小倉
擬百人一首

中納言家持

鵲の
わたせる
おく霜の
志路きを
見れバこそ
夜ぞ
ふけに
ける

渡辺源二綱

いぞ坂の化身

源頼光の臣
渡邊源二綱ハ
庭橋のやぐらにて
悪鬼の婦人ふ
化し─たるふ
出會ひ其
正躰を見
あらはせしとや
柳下亭
種員筆記

広重画

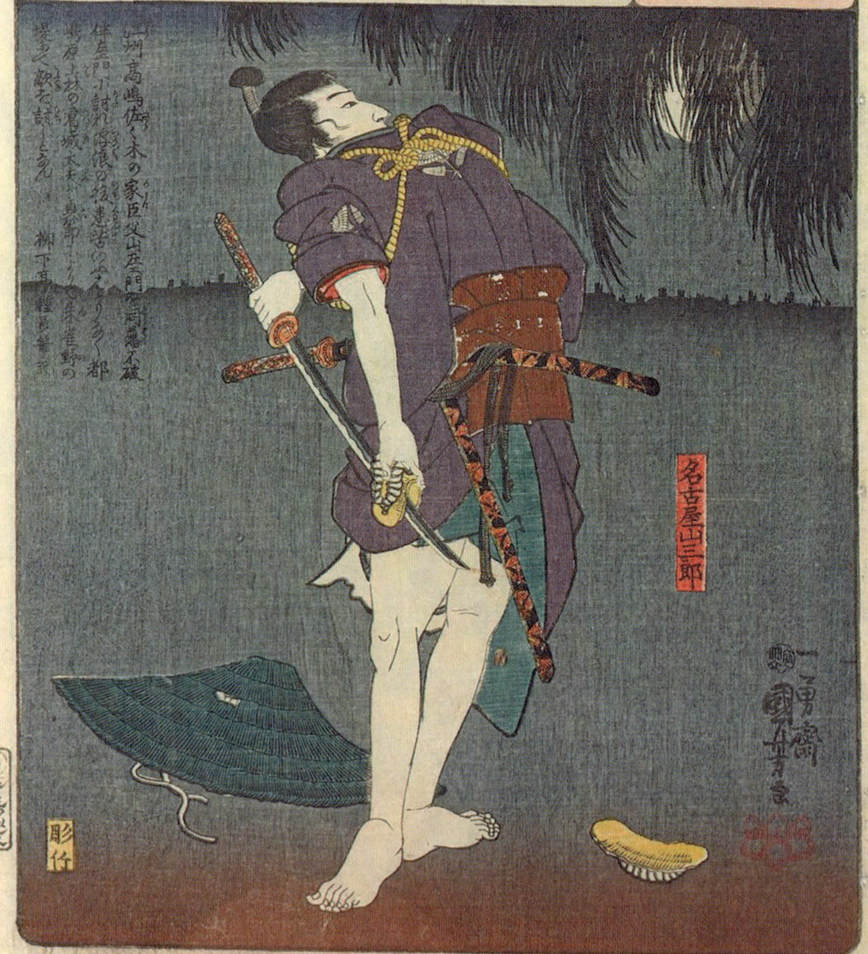
小倉擬百人一首
安陪仲麿
あまの原
ふりさけ
みれば
かすが
なる
みかさの
山に
いでし
月かも
名古屋山三郎
一勇齋國芳画
伊場仙板
彫竹
七

7

Abe no Nakamaro

Gazing at that far-off moon
across heaven's vast expanse—
can it be the same moon I once saw

at Kasuga Shrine as it rose over Mount Mikasa
while I was praying for safe passage?

天の原
ふりさけ見れば
春日なる
三笠の山に
出でし月かも

ama no hara
furisake mireba
kasuga naru
mikasa no yama ni
ideshi tsuki kamo

8

The Priest Kisen

My mountain hermitage
southeast of Miyako—
such a simple life I lead

on Uji, hill of sadness,
say people down below.

わが庵は
都のたつみ
しかぞ住む
世をうぢ山と
人はいふなり

waga io wa
miyako no tatsumi
shika zo sumu
yo wo ujiyama to
hito wa iu nari

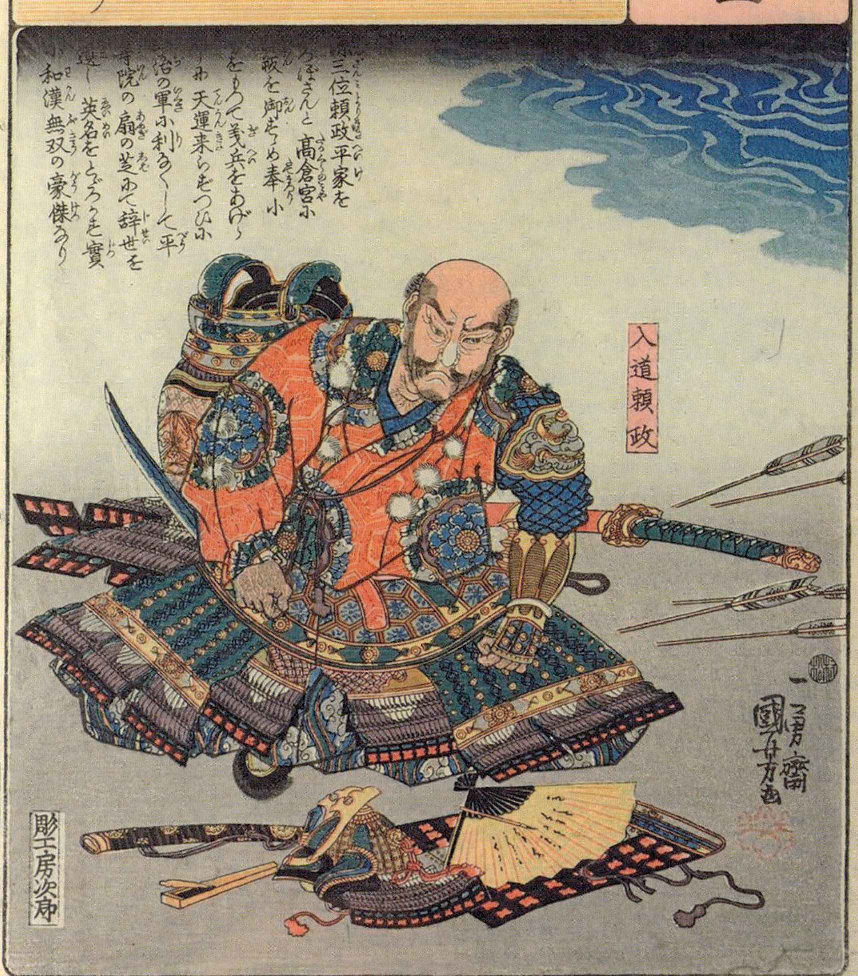

小倉擬百人一首
喜撰法師
わが庵は
みやこのたつみ
しかぞすむ
世をうぢ山と
人はいふなり
入道頼政
一勇齋國芳画
彫工房次郎
八日目伊国芳極

小野小町

花の色は
うつりにけりな
いたづらに
我身よに
ふる
ながめ
せしまに

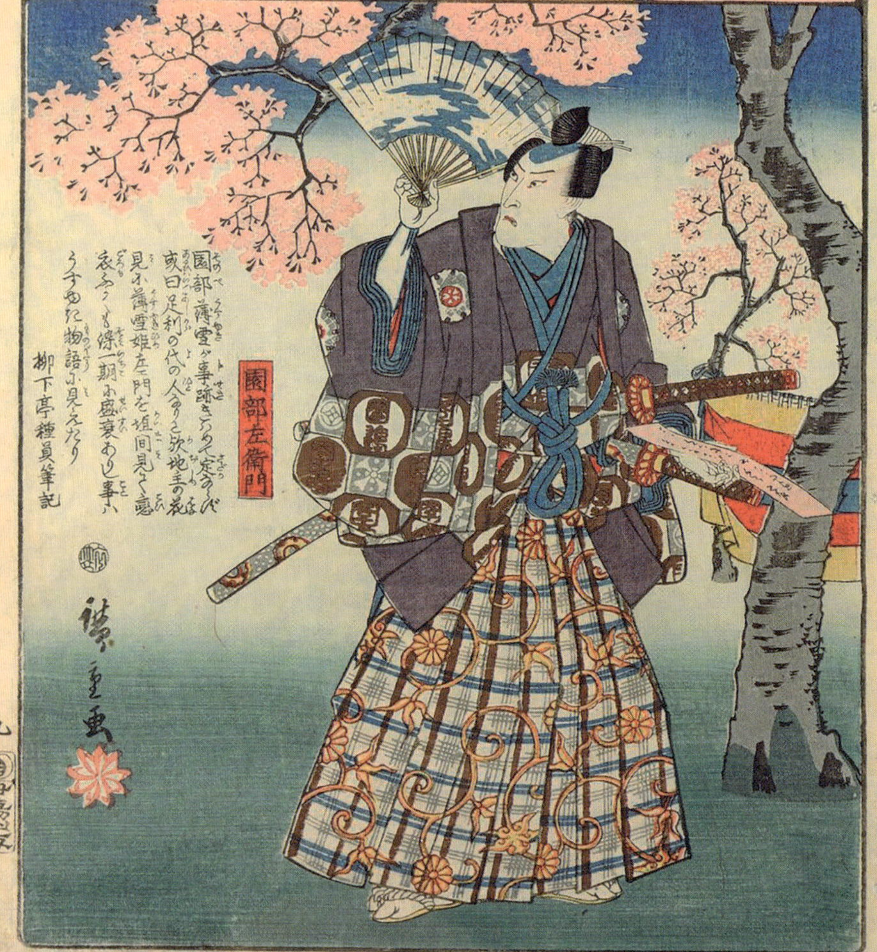

九

9

Ono no Komachi

The color of these petals
wilting in the shower,
useless—

as the time that rains too heavy
on my aging frame.

花
の
色
は
移
り
に
け
り
な
徒
に
わ
が
身
世
に
ふ
る
な
が
め
せ
し
間
に

hana no iro wa
utsuri ni keri na
itazura ni
waga mi yo ni furu
nagame seshi ma ni

10

Semimaru

This is the border for those who leave,
for those who return,
for those who separate,

for those we know and those we don't know—
the hill of meeting.

これやこの
行くも帰るも
別れては
知るも知らぬも
逢坂の関

kore ya kono
yuku mo kaeru mo
wakarete wa
shiru mo shiranu mo
ausaka no seki

40

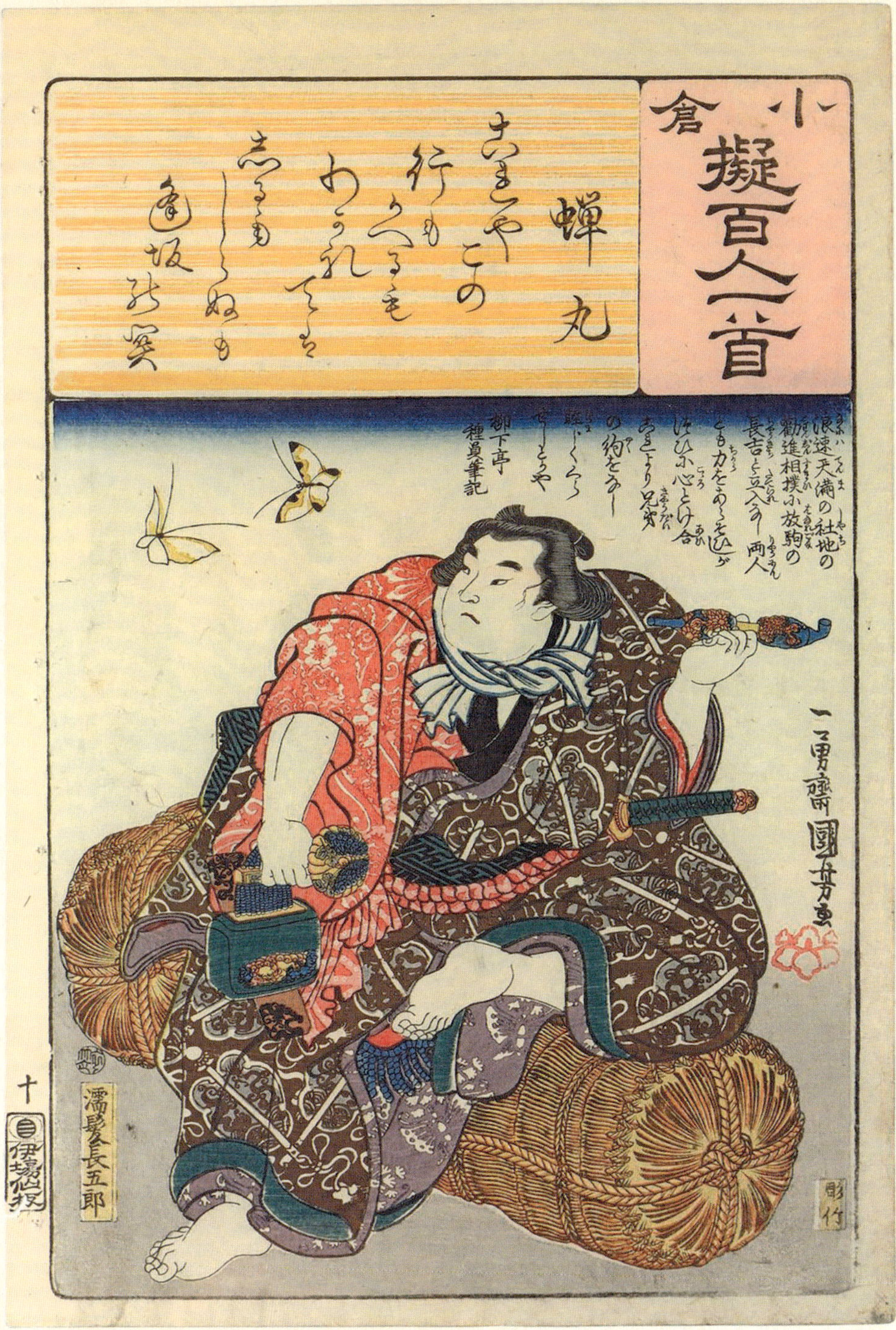

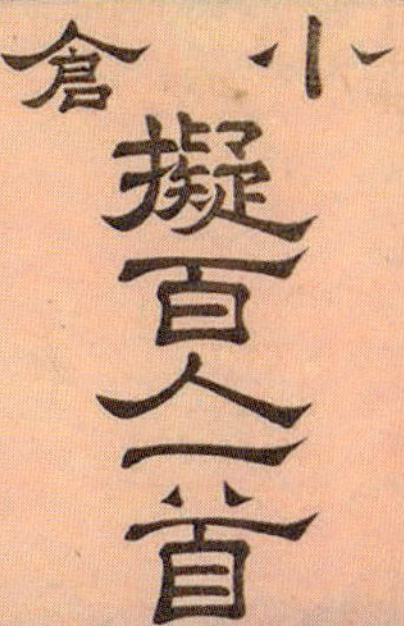

小倉
擬百人一首

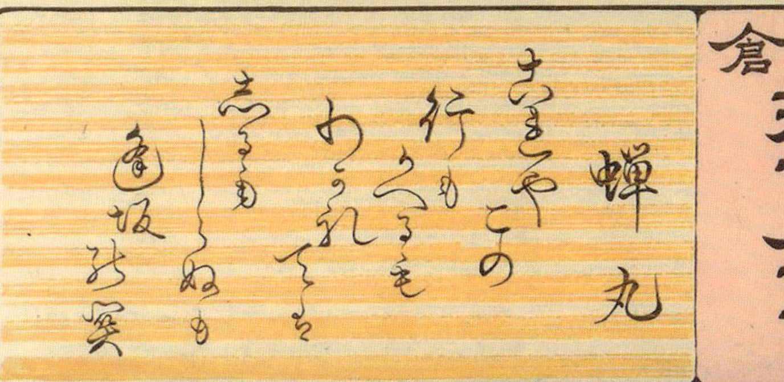

蝉丸
これやこの
行くも
かへるも
わかれては
しるも
しらぬも
逢坂の関

浪速天満の社地の
勧進相撲小放駒の
長吉と云ふの両人
ともに力をあらはさんと
はひふ心とり合
あしこより兄貴
の狗をみ
踞くら／＼
せ一とうや
卿下亭
種員筆記

一勇齋國芳画

濡髪長五郎

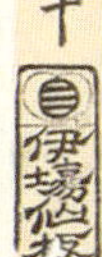

十
伊場仙板

彫竹

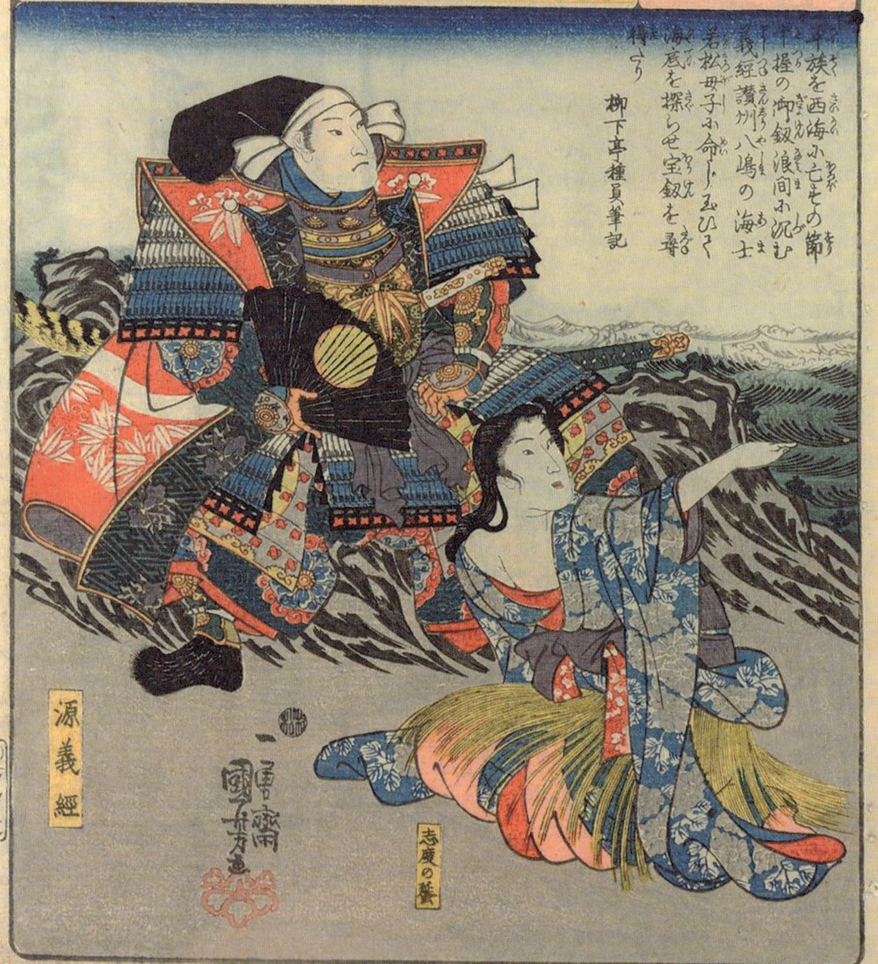
小倉擬百人一首

参議篁

和田の原
八十嶋かけて
こぎ出ぬと
人には告げよ
あまの釣舟

柳下亭種員筆記

源義經

志度の舞鷲

11

Ono no Takamura

Rowing past islands without number
I am pushed across the ocean fields.

Please take my message back,
at least to her—
you tiny fishing boats.

わ た の 原
八 十 島 か け て
漕 ぎ 出 で ぬ と
人 に は 告 げ よ
海 人 の 釣 舟

wata no hara
yasoshima kakete
kogi idenu to
hito ni wa tsugeyo
ama no tsuri bune

The Priest Henjo

Please, windy heavens
close your door and stop
the clouds a moment—

leave to us on earth
these dancing maidens' forms.

天つ風
雲の通ひ路
吹き閉ぢよ
乙女の姿
しばし留めむ

ama tsu kaze
kumo no kayoiji
fuki toji yo
otome no sugata
shibashi todomen

僧正遍昭

あまつ風
雲のかよひ路
ふきとぢよ
乙女すがた
志ばし
とゞめむ

白拍子佛御前

清盛公白拍子祇王を愛し寵愛限りなく
爰に加賀國小佛といへる舞妓あり西條
に來りて入道にまみへ清盛深く其を
寵て祇王が寵は衰へけりとぞ

種員筆記

廣重画

彫工
房次郎

十二
伊場仙板

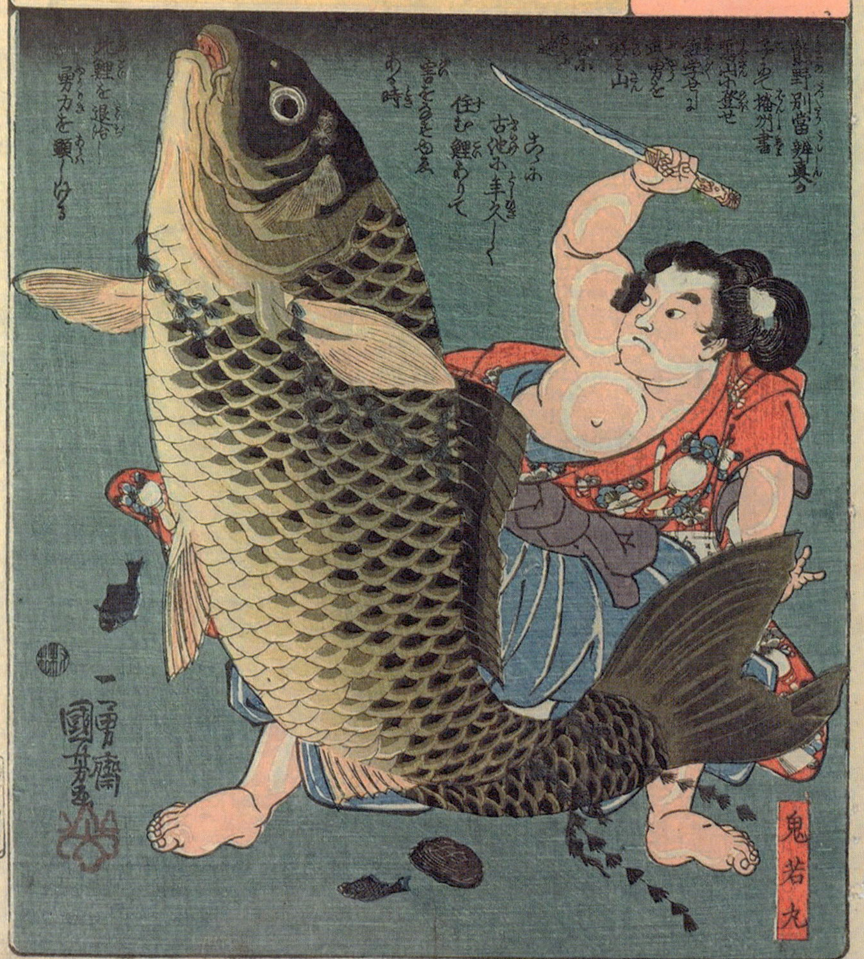

小倉
擬百人一首

陽成院

筑波嶺の
峰より落つる
みなの川
恋ぞつもりて
淵となりぬる

鬼若丸

一勇齋
國芳画

13

Retired Emperor Yozei

The Minano river drops
off Tsukuba's peak
to fearsome depths.

Just so, my heart is plunged
into the abyss of my desire.

筑波嶺の
峰より落つる
みなの川
恋ぞつもりて
淵となりぬる

tsukuba ne no
mine yori otsuru
minano gawa
koi zo tsumorite
fuchi to nari nuru

14
Minamoto no Toru

I stumble through a labyrinth of love
as tangled as the sword-shaped shinobu grasses
in a Michinoku pattern—who led me on?

Impossible to think I wandered here myself
into this realm of chaos and disorder.

陸奥の
しのぶもぢずり
誰故に
乱れそめにし
われならなくに

michinoku no
shinobu mojizuri
tare yue ni
midare some ni shi
ware naranaku ni

河原左大臣

みちのくの
しのぶもぢ摺
たれゆゑに
みだれそめにし
われならなくに

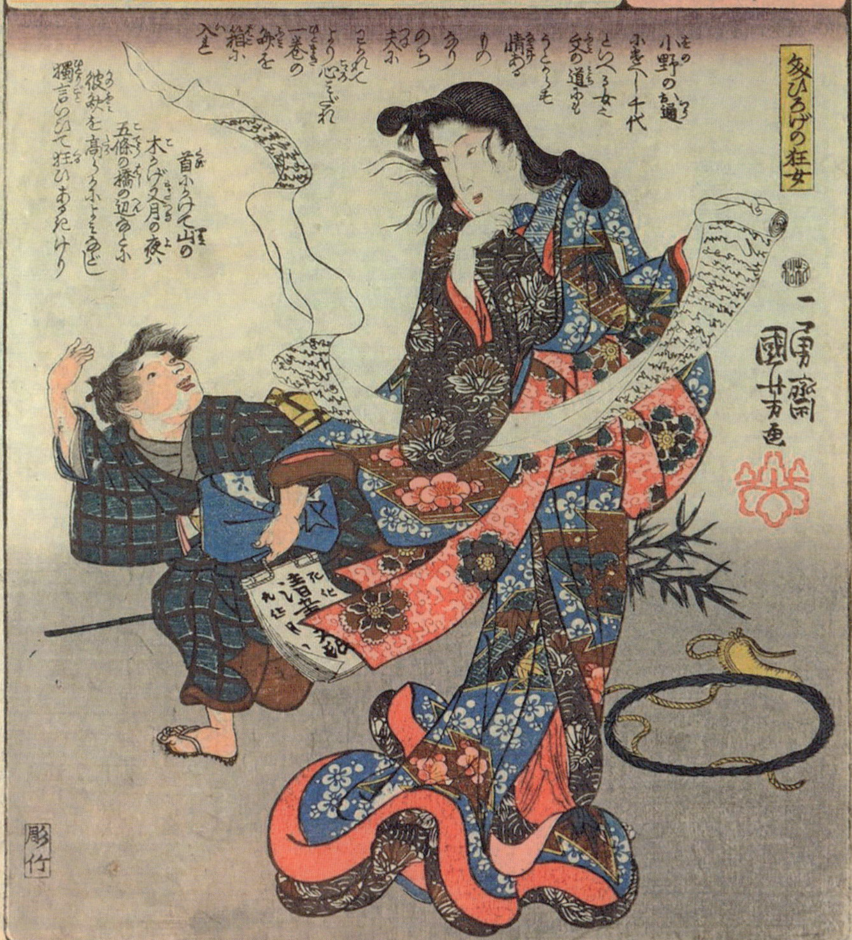

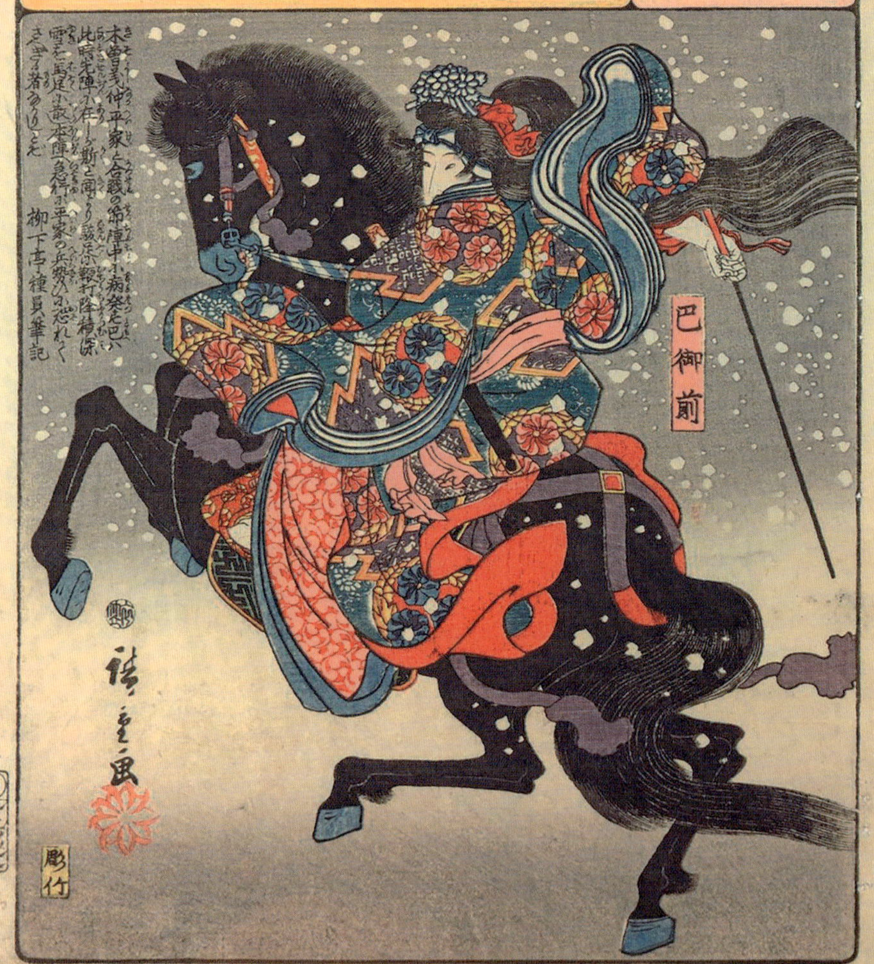

小倉擬百人一首
光孝天皇
君がため
春の野に出でて
若菜つむ
我が衣手に
雪はふりつつ
巴御前

15

Emperor Koko

For you I came outside
into the spring fields,
your tender herbs to gather—

but snowflakes sting my hand
with every leaf I pick.

君がため
春の野に出でて
若菜つむ
わが衣手に
雪は降りつつ

kimi ga tame
haru no no ni idete
wakana tsumu
waga koromode ni
yuki wa furi tsutsu

16

Ariwara no Yukihara

Well then, we must part
but if your voice comes wafting
among the sighs of the Inaba pine

and bends my ear—
back I come in an instant.

立
ち
別
れ
い
な
ば
の
山
の
峰
に
生
ふ
る
ま
つ
と
し
聞
か
ば
今
帰
り
こ
む

tachi wakare
inaba no yama no
mine ni ouru
matsu to shi kikaba
ima kaeri kon

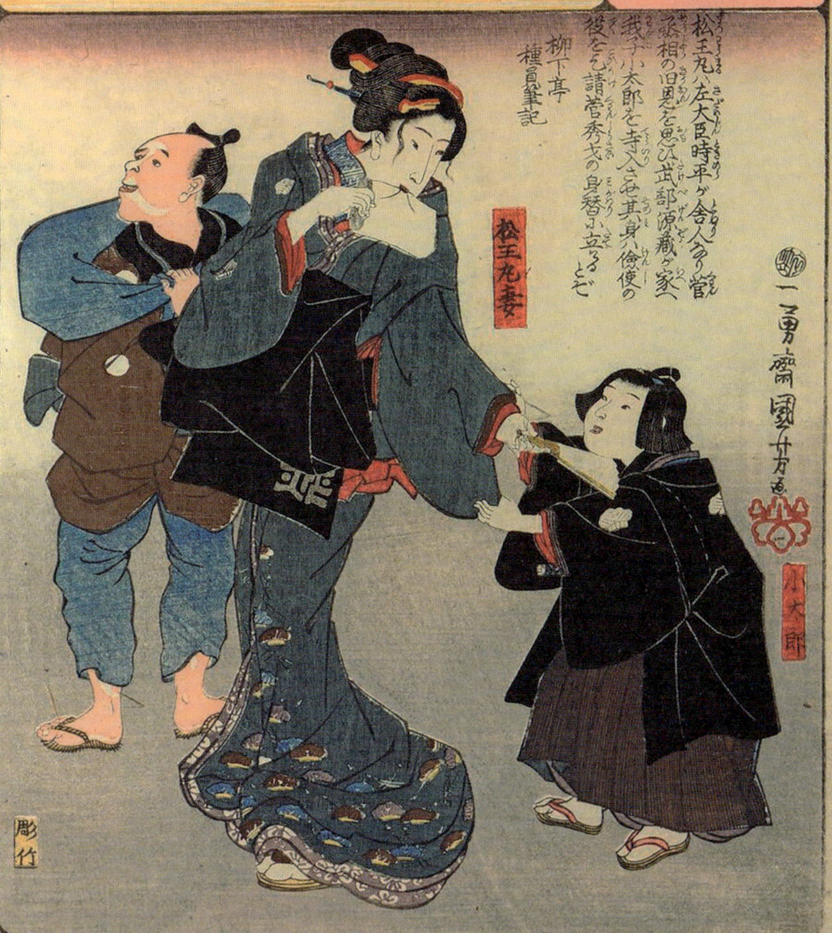

小倉擬百人一首

中納言行平

立ちわかれ
いなばの
山の
みねに
おふる
まつとし
きかば
今かへり
こん

柳下亭
種員筆記

松王丸妻

小太郎

一勇齋國芳画

松王丸ハ左大臣時平ヶ舎人なり菅
丞相の旧恩を思ひ武部源蔵が家へ
我子小太郎を寺入させ其身卒倫使の
役をもて請菅秀才の身替り立るとぞ

十六

彫竹

小倉
擬百人一首

在原業平朝臣

千早振
神代も
きゝず
たつ田川
からくれ
なゐに
水くゞ
るとは

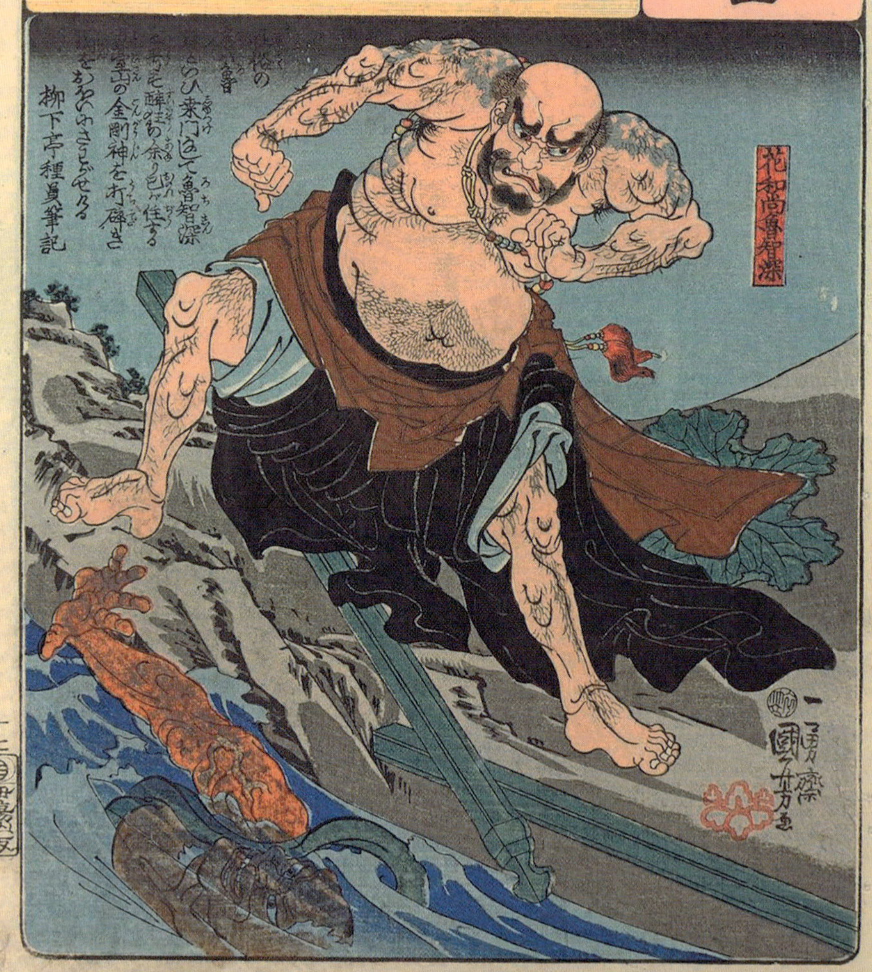

花和尚魯智深

柳下亭種員筆記

17

Ariwara no Narihira

Even when the gods lived here on earth
one never heard of wonders
such as this—

the waters of the Tatsuya flowing
scarlet, dyed bright with fallen maple.

千早ぶる
神代も聞かず
龍田川
から紅に
水くくるとは

chihayaburu
kamiyo mo kikazu
tatsutagawa
kara kurenai ni
mizu kukuru to wa

18

Fujiwara no Toshiyuki

The waves may freely meet
the sand at Sumiyoshi—

why, even in my dreams
must I go to meet my love
in some disguise?

sumi no e no
kishi ni yoru nami
yoru sae ya
yume no kayoi ji
hito me yoku ran

小倉
擬百人一首

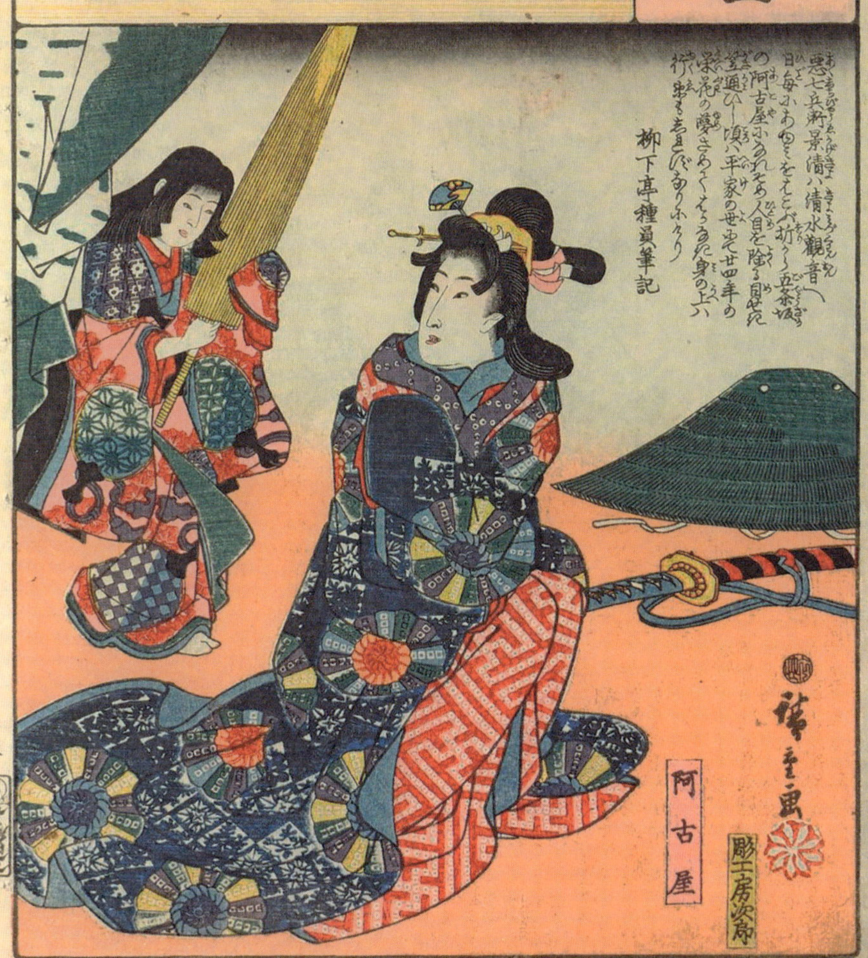
藤原敏行朝臣

住のえの
きしによる
なみよるさへや
夢のかよひぢ
人めよくらん

柳下亭種員筆記

阿古屋

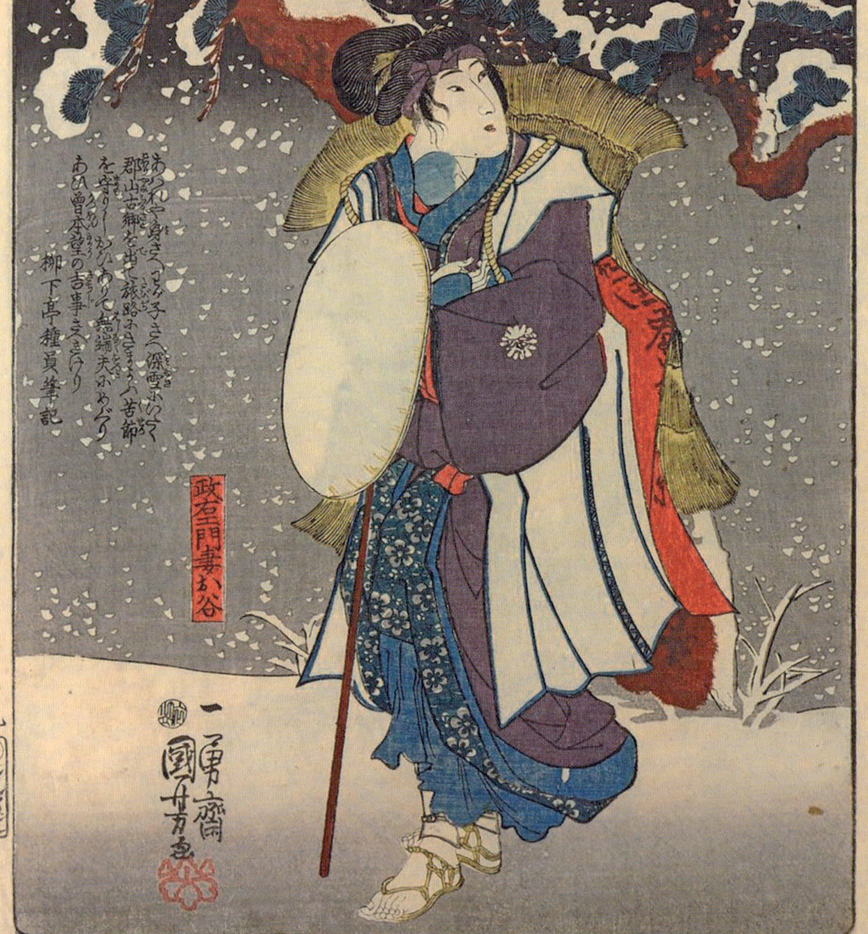
小倉擬百人一首
伊勢
難波がた
みじかき
あしの
ふしの
まも
あひで
このよを
すぐして
よとや
政右門妻お谷
柳下亭種員筆記
一勇斎國芳画
十九

19
Princess Ise

The shortest space
from joint to joint along a reed
plucked over by the shore at Naniwa—

so short a time without you in this world,
even that is asking far too much of me.

難波潟
短かき芦の
ふしの間も
逢はでこの世を
過ぐしてよとや

naniwa gata
mijikaki ashi no
fushi no ma mo
awade kono yo wo
sugushite yo to ya

20

Crown Prince Motoyoshi

So dreary have my days become without you,
it's all the same to me, to live or die—

out past the warning posts at Naniwa,
even to exhaust my very life,
happily I would swim to meet you.

逢はむとぞ思ふ
みをつくしても
難波なる
今はた同じ
わびぬれば

wabi nureba
ima hata onaji
naniwa naru
mi wo tsukushite mo
awan to zo omou

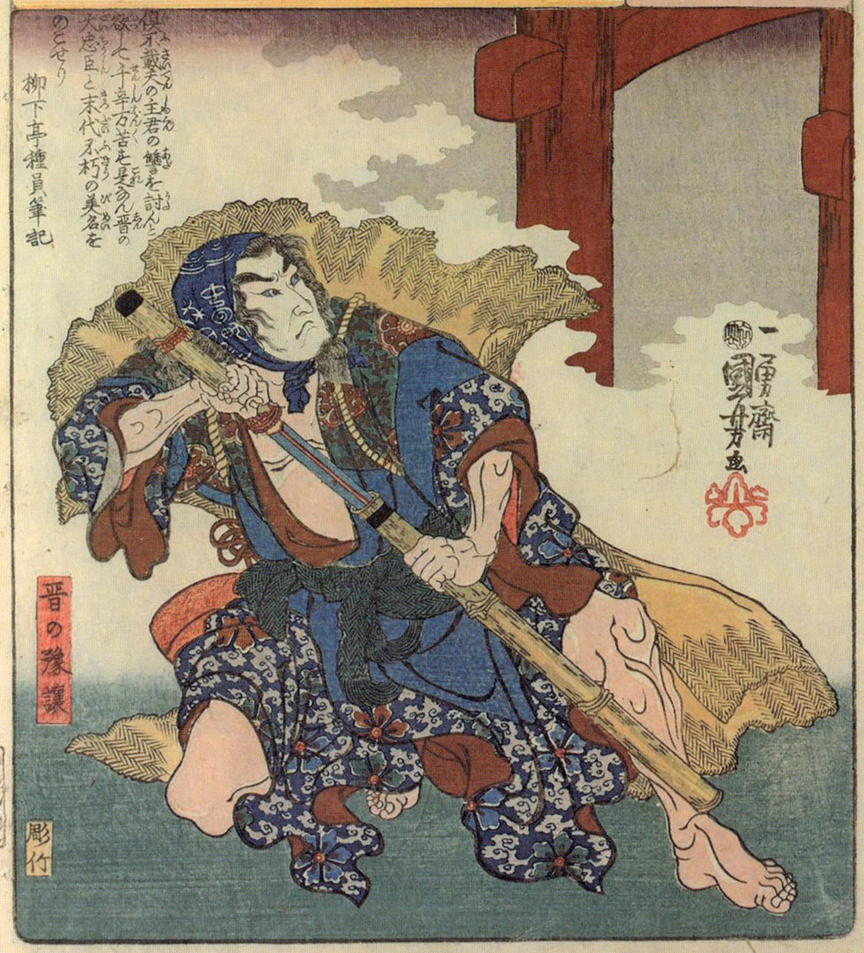

小倉
擬百人一首

元良親王

わびぬれば
今はたおなじ
なにはなる
身を
つくしても
逢はむ
とぞ思ふ

一勇齋
國芳画

晋の豫讓

柳下亭種員筆記

素性法師

今来むと いひしばかりに 長月の 有明の月を 待ち出でつるかな

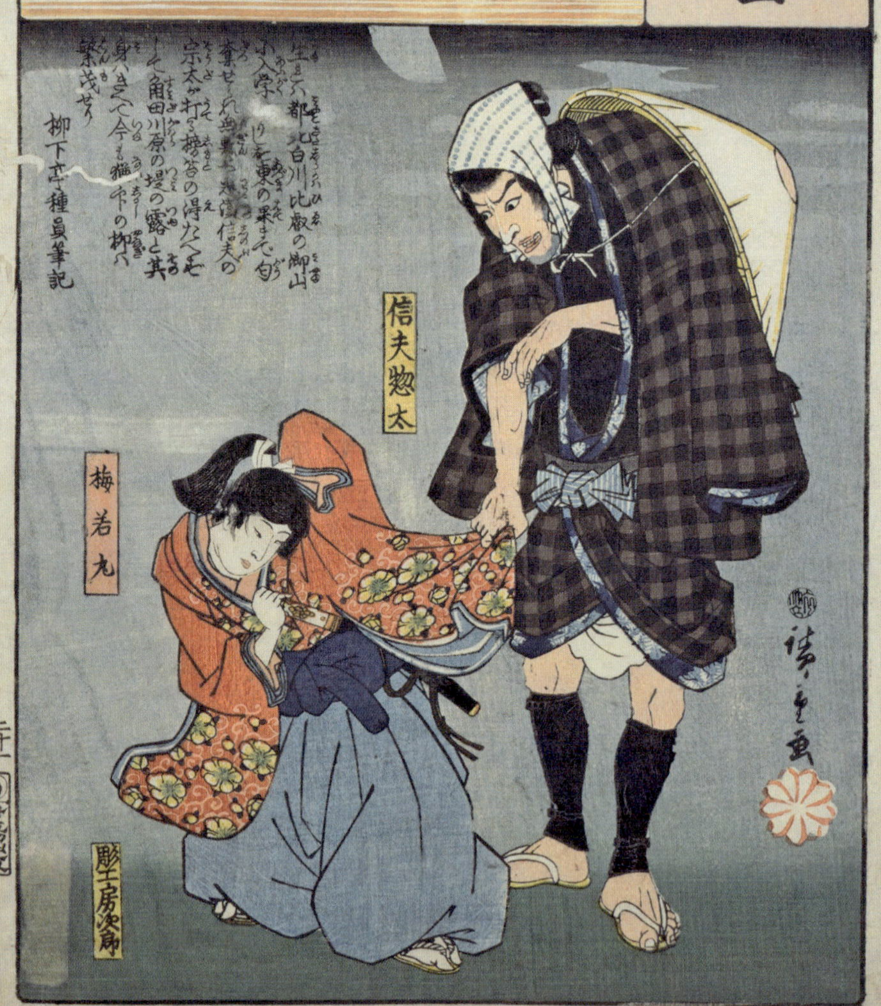

柳下亭種員筆記

廣重画

二十一
伊場仙板
彫工房次郎

21

The Monk Sosei

Believing in your promise
to quickly come,
this long September night I passed—

to find I waited only
for the morning moon.

今来むと
いひしばかりに
長月の
有明けの月を
待ち出でつるかな

ima kon to
iishi bakari ni
nagatsuki no
ariake no tsuki wo
machi idetsuru kana

22

Bunya no Yasuhide

With autumn trees destroyed
and mountain grasses withered
in the wake of your chilling winds—

no wonder then that men say
you leave only devastation.

吹くからに
秋の草木の
しをるれば
むべ山風を
嵐といふらむ

fuku kara ni
aki no kusaki no
shiorureba
mube yama kaze wo
arashi to iuran

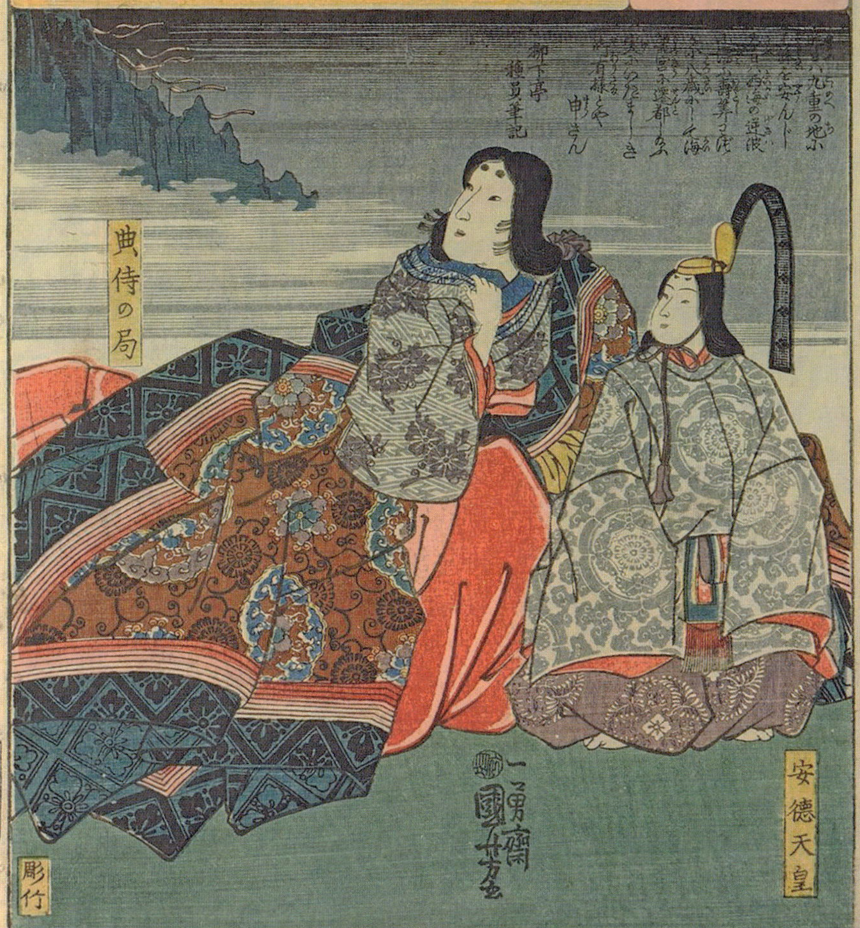

小倉擬百人一首
文屋康秀
吹くからに
秋の草木の
しをるれば
むべ山風を
あらしといふらん
典侍の局
安徳天皇
柳下亭種員筆記
一勇齋國芳
彫竹

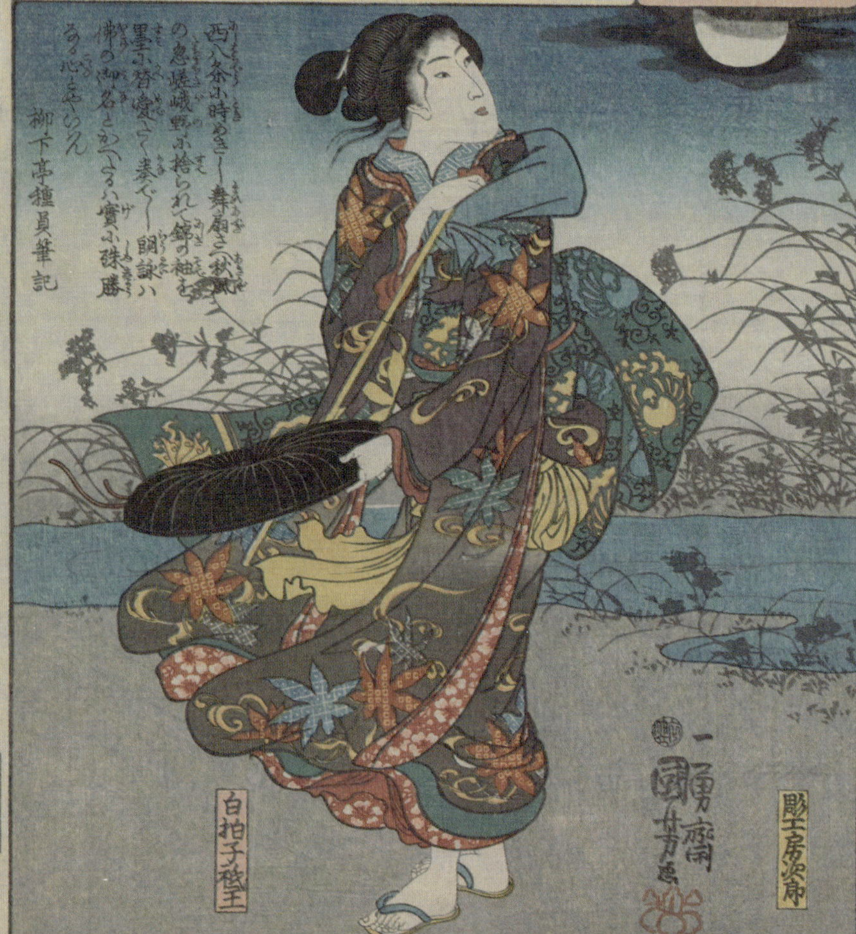

小倉
擬百人一首

大江千里

月みれば
ちぢにものこそ
かなしけれ
わが身ひとつの
秋にはあらねど

白拍子妓王

柳下亭種員筆記

一勇齋
國芳画

彫工房次郎

23

Oe no Chisato

A thousand thoughts that trouble me
dissolving into sadness
as I gaze upon the moon—

but not to me alone
does autumn finally come.

月見れば
千々にものこそ
悲しけれ
わが身ひとつの
秋にはあらねど

tsuki mireba
chiji ni mono koso
kanashi kere
waga mi hitotsu no
aki ni wa aranedo

24

Sugawara no Michizane

This visit I could not offer
proper brightly colored prayers—

please mercifully accept instead this
rich brocade of maple leaves
that gathered on Mount Tamuke.

神のまにまに
紅葉の錦
手向山
幣も取り敢へず
このたびは

kono tabi wa
nusa mo toriaezu
tamukeyama
momiji no nishiki
kami no mani mani

小倉擬百人一首
菅家
此たびは
ぬさも
とりあへぞ
手向山
もみぢ乃
にしき
神の
まにまに
髙尾
廣重画

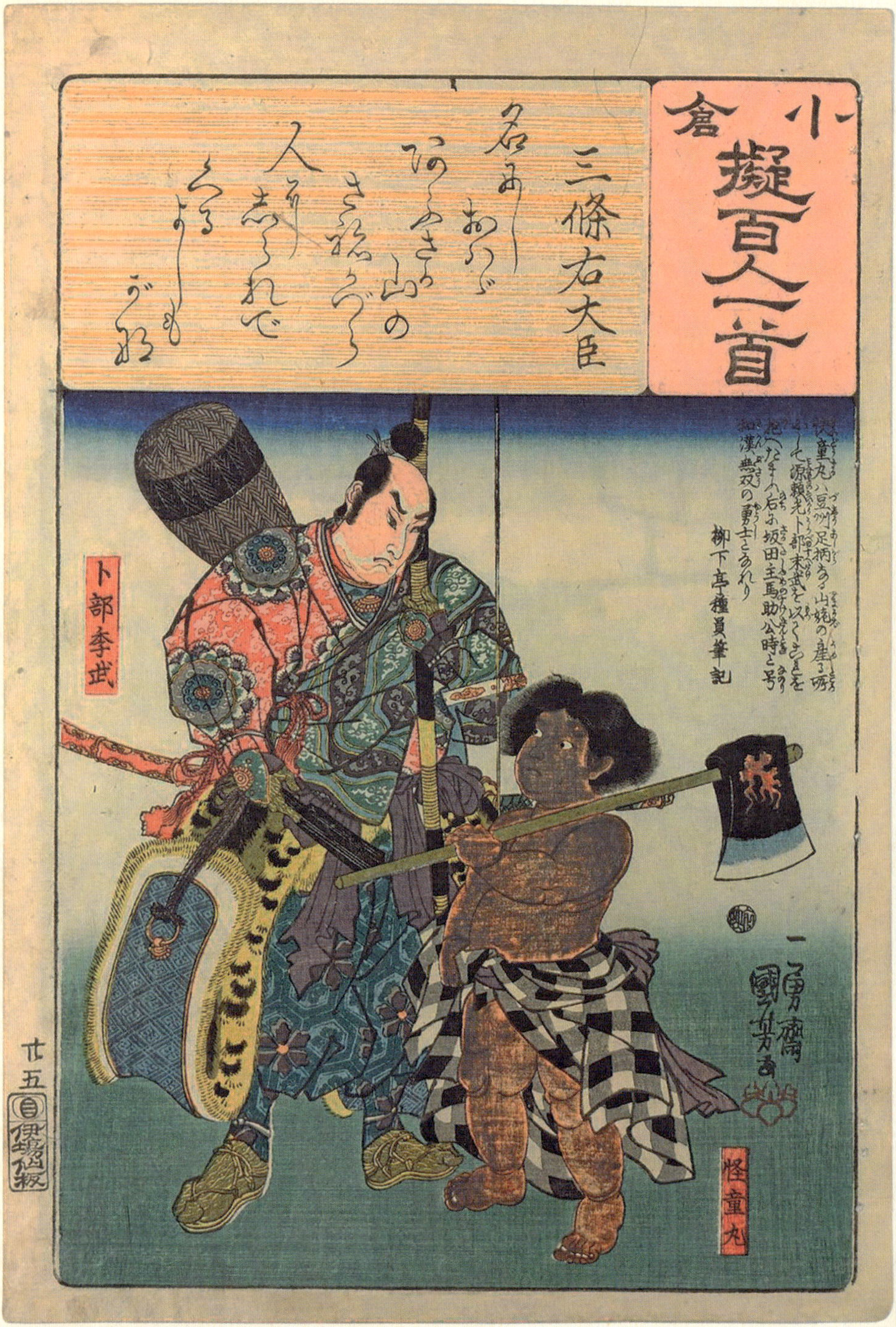

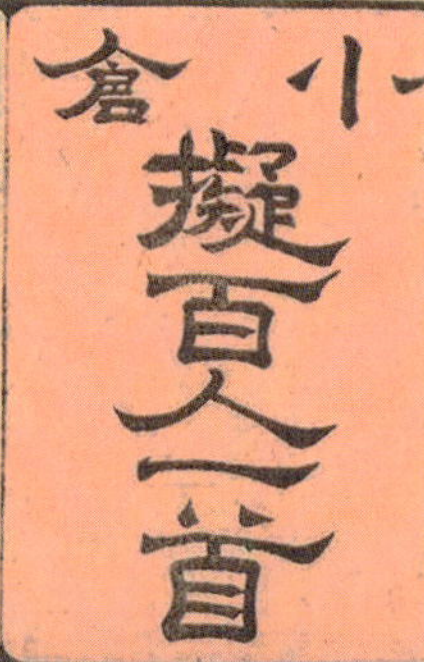

小倉
擬百人一首
三條右大臣
名にしおはゞ
あふさか
あふさか山の
さねかづら
人にしられで
くるよしもがな
卜部季武
怪童丸
怪童丸ハ豆州足柄なる山姥の産る所
にして源頼光卜部末武をしたがへしを
たすけの右ふ坂田主馬助公時と号
し漢和無双の勇士とあれり
柳下亭種員筆記
一勇斎國芳画

25

The Minister Sadakata

Is "trysting mountain" worthy of its name?
Why then can't I draw you here,
as men pull vines from off these hills,

to make a secret visit, where even the tendrils
whisper—come recline with me?

名にし負はば
逢坂山の
さねかづら
人に知られで
くるよしもがな

na ni shi owaba
ausakayama no
sanekazura
hito ni shirarede
kuru yoshi mo gana

26

Prince Teishin

If you have a heart,
you maple leaves of Ogura,
prolong your stay upon its peak.

Just wait,
the emperor is coming!

小倉山
峰のもみじ葉
心あらば
今ひとたびの
みゆき待たなむ

ogurayama
mine no momijiba
kokoro araba
ima hitotabi no
miyuki matanan

小倉擬百人一首

貞信公
小倉山
みねのもみぢ葉
こゝろあらば
今ひとたびの
みゆきまたなん

東祇園の片辺に一人の賤の女あり、天然の美貌白川院垣間見たまひしく、懇望の余り入て女御小備さまふ依て、祇園女御と称ゑ平相國清盛公を女性の産所あり
柳下亭種員筆記

祇園女御

朝櫻楼國芳画

廿六
伊場仙板
彫竹

中納言兼輔

みかの原
わきて流るる
いづみ川
いつ見きとてか
恋しかるらん

狐葛の葉

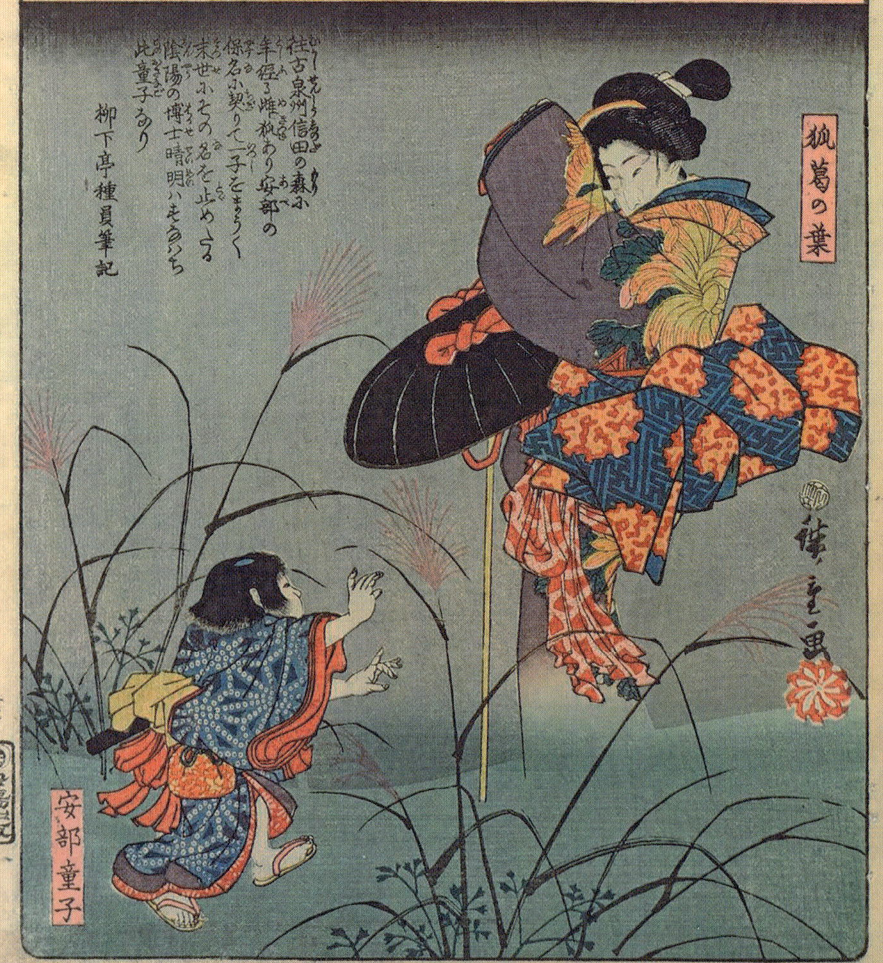

いにしへ往古泉州信田の藪に
牝狐住みて雄狐と契りて一子を
まうけ其の名を小契りて一子をまうく
末世ふその名を止めける
陰陽の博士晴明ハもとより
此童子なり

柳下亭種員筆記

安部童子

27

Kanesuke

Bubbling up from Mika's plain,
spring waters flow together and create
Izumi's rushing river.

Is it so long ago we met?
Must I wait so long until we meet again—
my passions boiling over?

みかの原
わきて流るる
泉川
いつ見きとてか
恋しかるらむ

mika no hara
wakite nagaruru
izumigawa
itsu mi kitote ka
koishi karuran

28

Minamoto no Muneyuki

These mountain huts and hamlets
are lonelier by far
when winter comes around.

Just as the grass has withered,
friends too have vanished—so it seems.

山里は
冬ぞ寂しさ
まさりける
人目も草も
かれぬと思へば

yamazato wa
fuyu zo sabishisa
masari keru
hitome mo kusa mo
karenu to omoeba

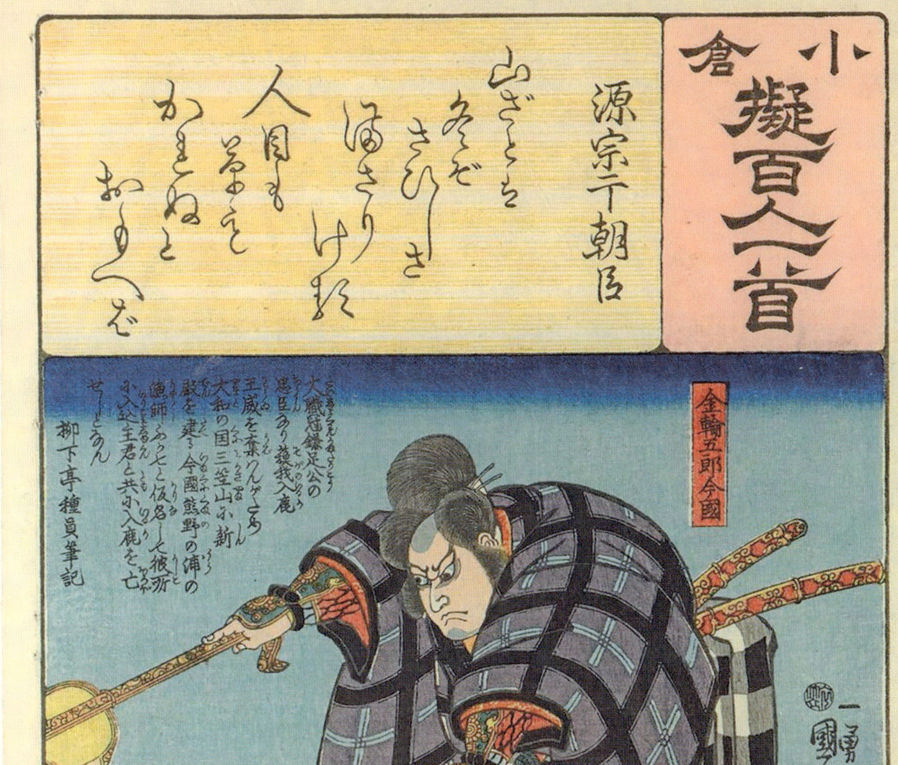

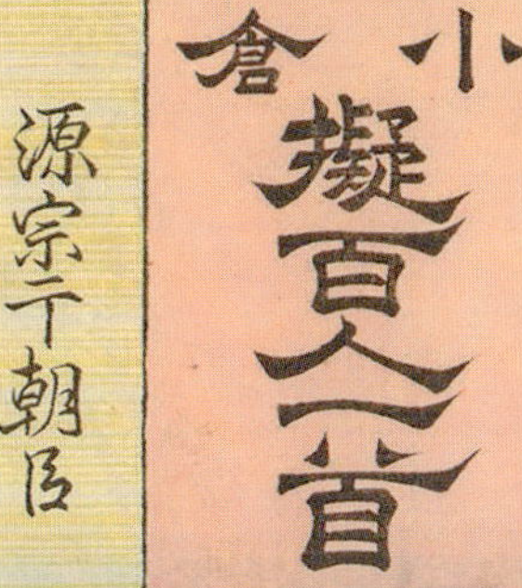

小倉擬百人一首

源宗于朝臣

山ざとは
ふゆぞ
さびしさ
まさりける
人目も草も
かれぬと
おもへば

金輪五郎今國

一勇齋
國芳画

彫工 房次郎

柳下亭種員筆記

廿八
伊場仙板

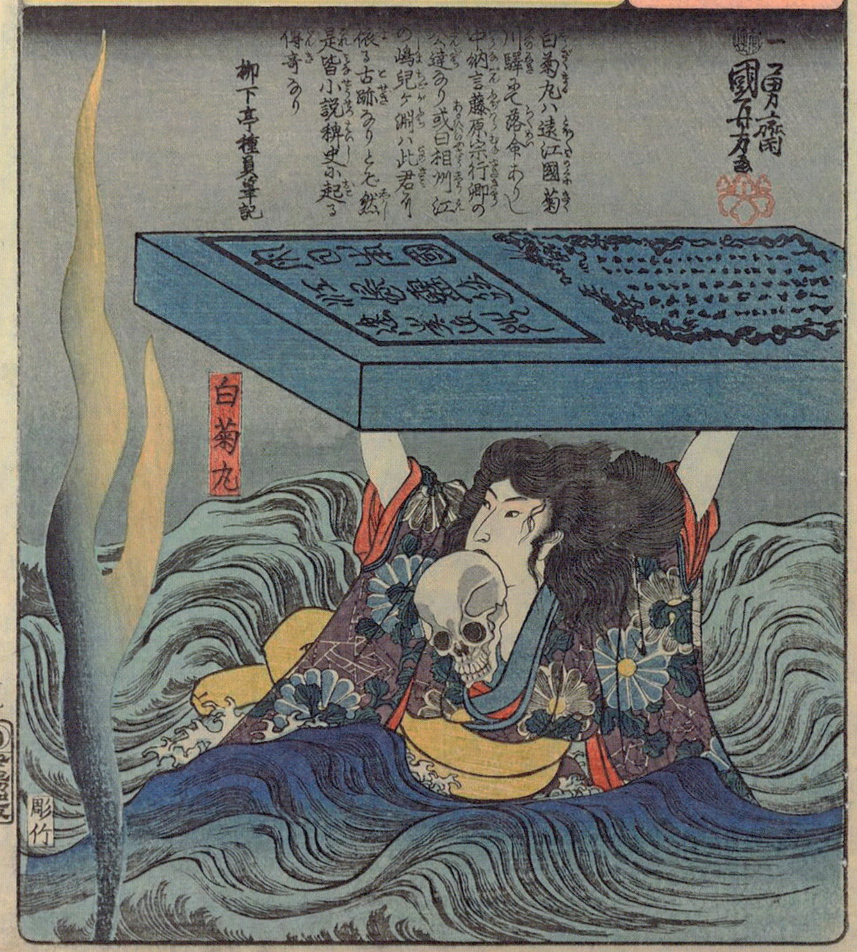

小倉擬百人一首
凡河内躬恒
こゝろあてに
をらばやをらん
初霜の
おきまどはせる
志ら菊の花
一勇斎國芳画
白菊丸
柳下亭種員筆記
彫竹

29

Oshikochi no Mitsune

My heart must guide me
to make the choice I need to make—

and find the white chrysanthemum
among the rest, all painted
with autumn's early frost.

心あてに
折らばや折らむ
初霜の
置きまどはせる
白菊の花

kokoro ate ni
oraba ya oran
hatsushimo no
oki madowaseru
shiragiku no hana

30

Mibu no Tadamine

In the pale dawn
your coldness as we parted
froze my heart—

nothing now so chills me
as morning's early light.

有
明
の
つ
れ
な
く
見
え
し
別
れ
よ
り
暁
ば
か
り
憂
き
も
の
は
な
し

ariake no
tsurenaku mieshi
wakare yori
akatsuki bakari
uki mono wa nashi

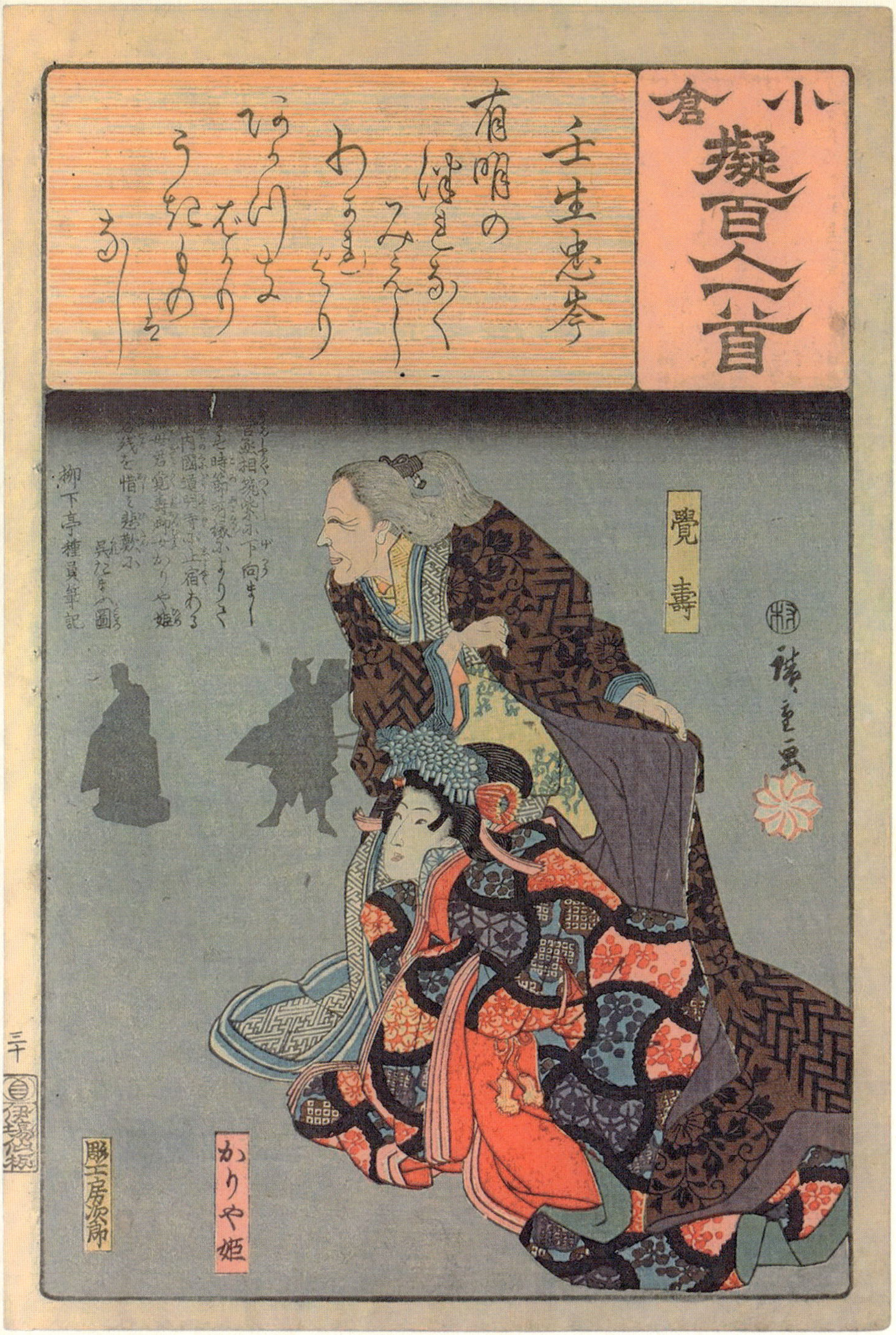

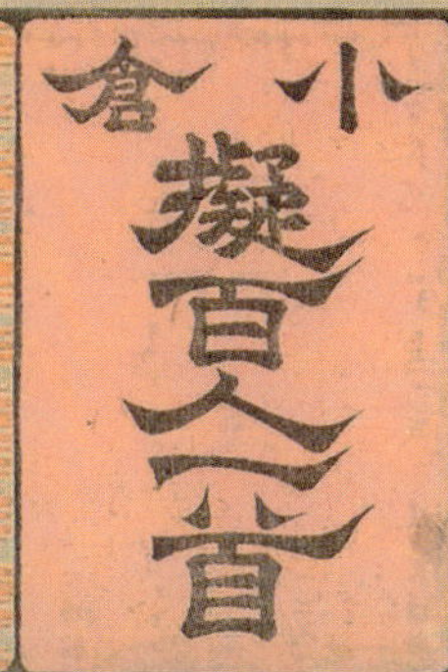
小倉擬百人一首

壬生忠岑

有明の
はじまりく
みえし
わかれ
より
ひつりよ
ばかり
うきもの
は
なし

覺壽

廣重画

かりや姫

彫工房次郎

柳下亭種員筆記

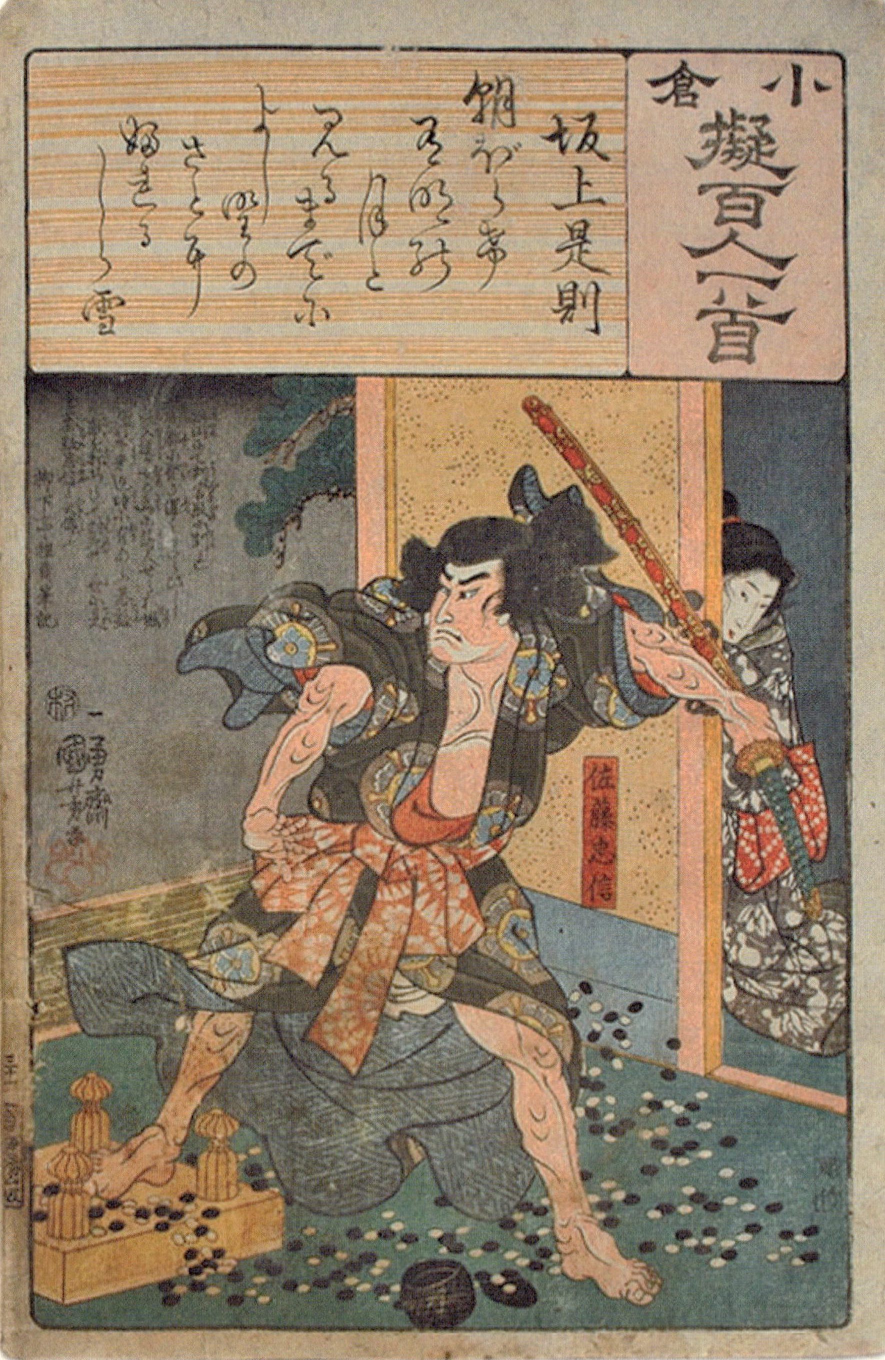
小倉擬百人一首
坂上是則
朝ぼらけ
有明の月と
見るまでに
よしのゝ里に
ふれる
しら雪
佐藤忠信
一勇斎國芳画

31

Sakanoue no Korenori

The waning early moon
had bathed this scene in pale winter light—
or so I thought, until I could discern

Yoshino village bedded down
in fresh white fallen snow.

朝ぼらけ
有明けの月と
見るまでに
吉野の里に
降れる白雪

asaborake
ariake no tsuki to
miru made ni
yoshino no sato ni
fureru shirayuki

32

Harumichi no Tsuraki

A barrier
the cold winds made
to stop this mountain stream—

bright maple leaves so thickly packed
its waters cannot flow.

山川に
風のかけたる
しがらみは
流れもあへぬ
紅葉なりけり

yama kawa ni
kaze no kaketaru
shigarami wa
nagare mo aenu
momiji nari keri

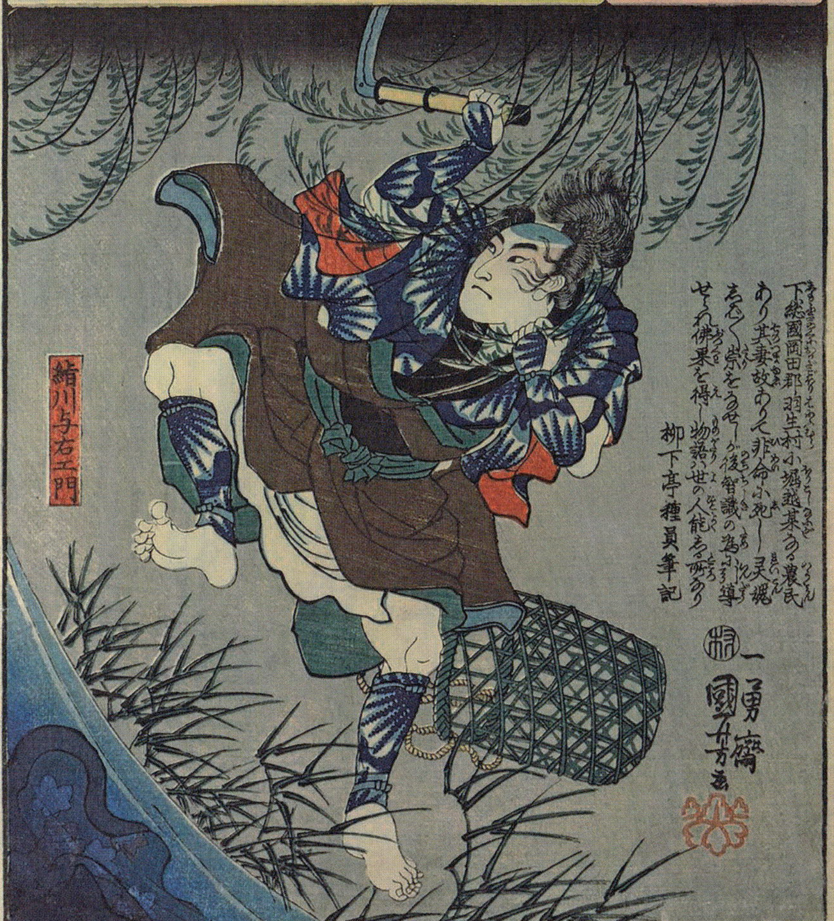

小倉
擬百人一首

春道列樹

山河に
風のかけたる
しがらみは
ながれもあへぬ
もみぢなりけり

絹川与右エ門

一勇齋
國芳画

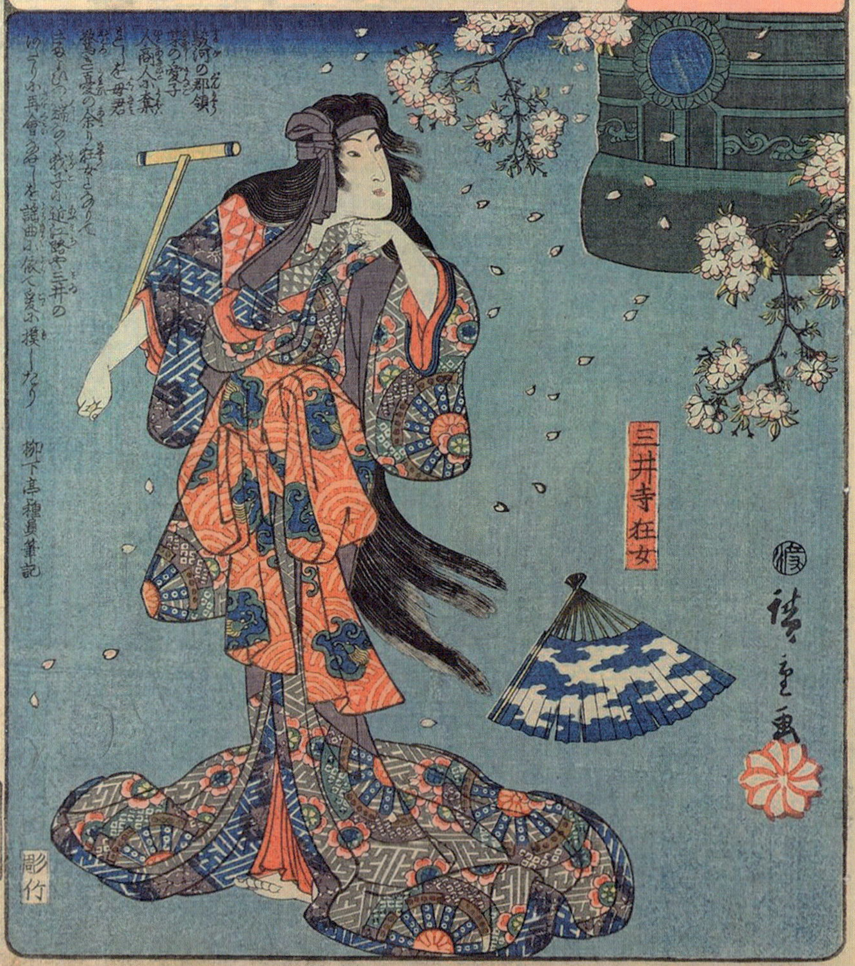
小倉
擬百人一首

紀友則

久かたの
光のどけき
春の日に
しづ心なく
花のちるらん

三井寺狂女

廣重画

柳下亭種員筆記

三十三

33

Ki no Tomonori

A new spring day it seems
as sunlight plays upon the grass,
my heart both calm and restful—

until I spy the cherry blossoms
rushing to destruction.

久方の
光のどけき
春の日に
しづ心なく
花の散るらむ

hisakata no
hikari nodokeki
haru no hi ni
shizu gokoro naku
hana no chiruran

87

34

Fujiwara no Okikaze

Has not one of all
my long-time friends stayed on?

These pines of Takasago
as ancient as myself—
if only they'd converse with me!

誰をかも
知る人にせむ
高砂の
松も昔の
友ならなくに

tare wo ka mo
shiru hito ni sen
takasago no
matsu mo mukashi no
tomo nara naku ni

88

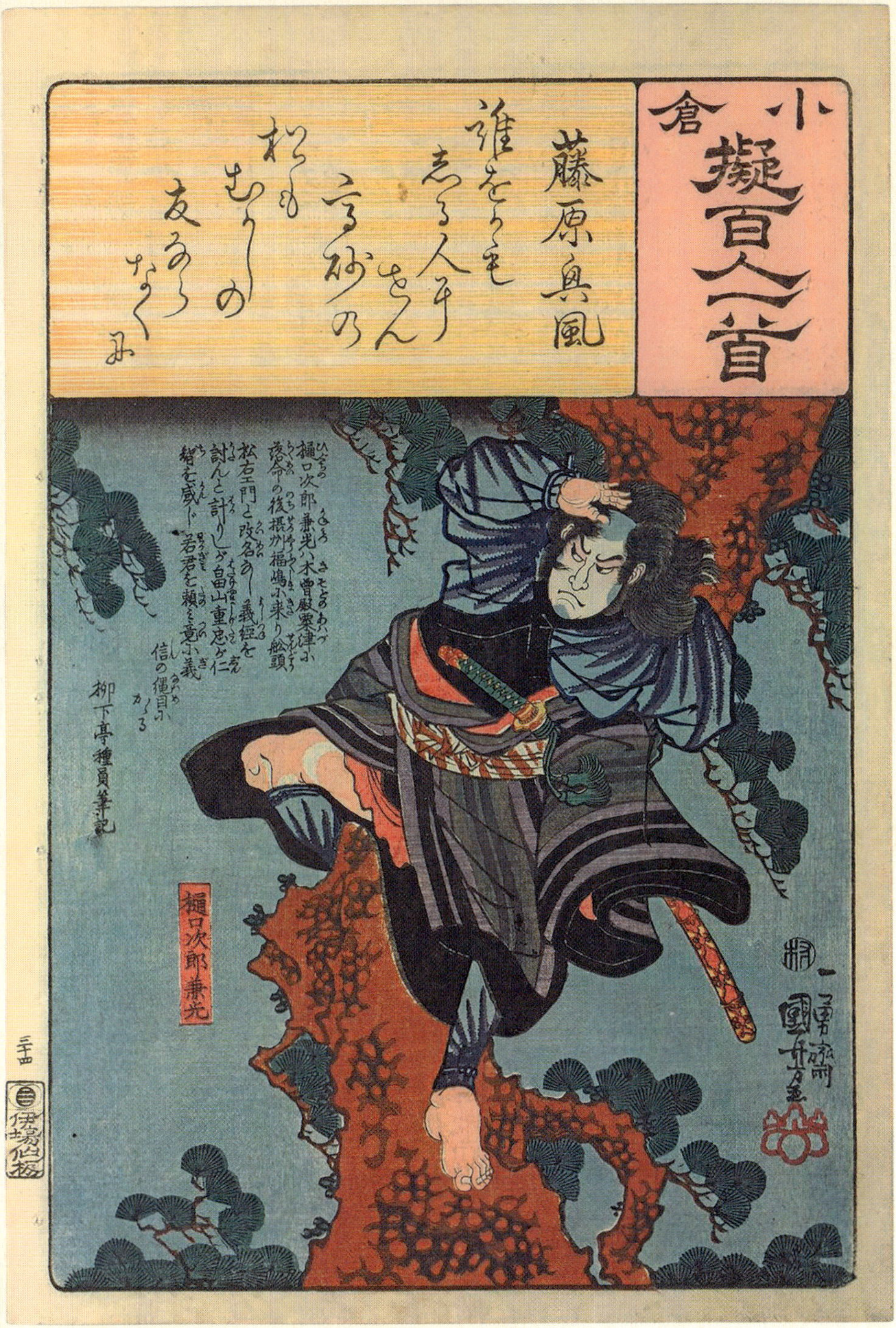

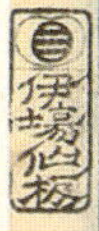
小倉擬百人一首
藤原眞風
誰をかも
しる人せん
たかさごの
松も
むかしの
友なら
なくみ
樋口次郎兼光
柳下亭種員筆記
一勇斎国芳画

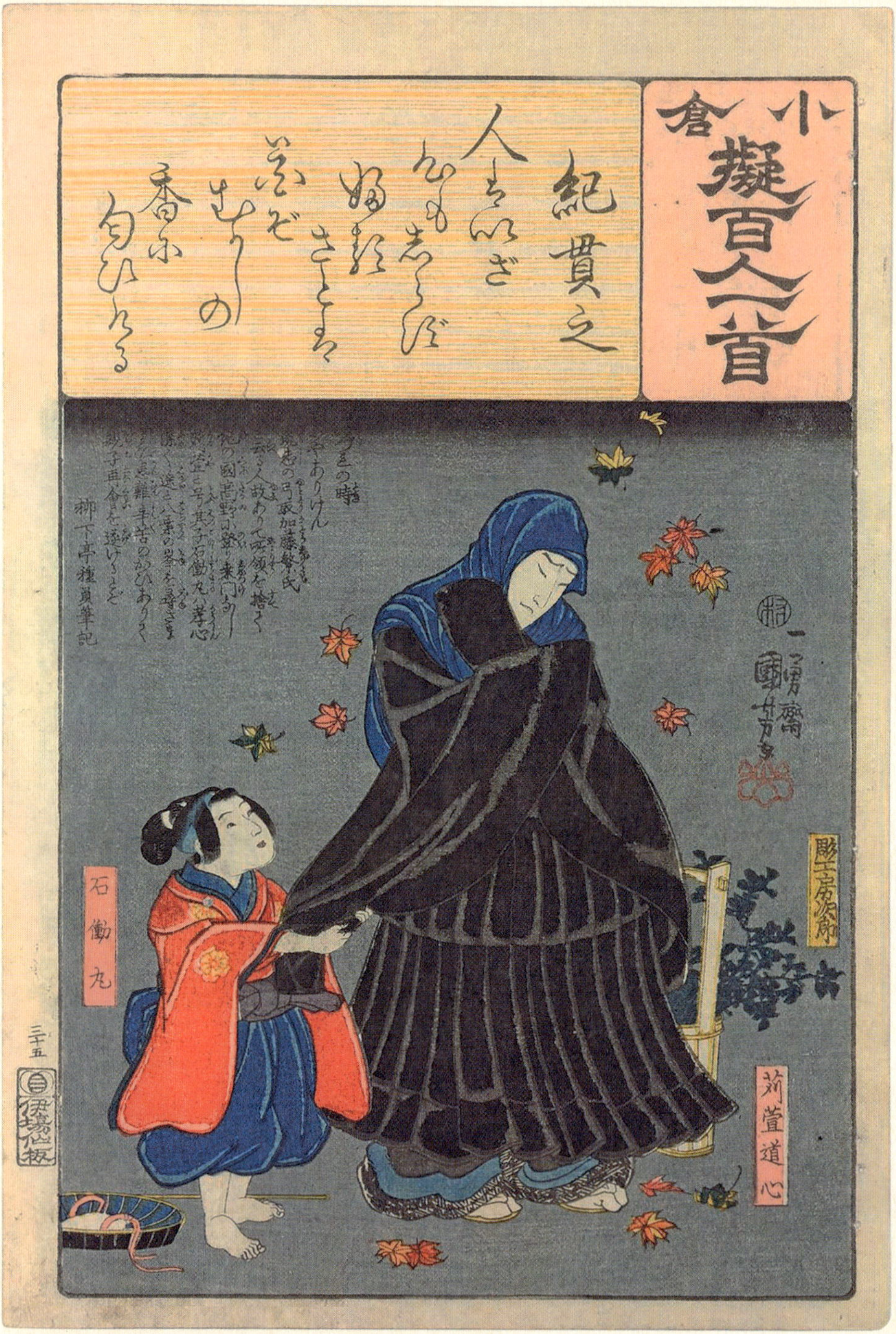

紀貫之

人はいさ
心もしらず
ふるさとは
花ぞむかしの
香に匂ひける

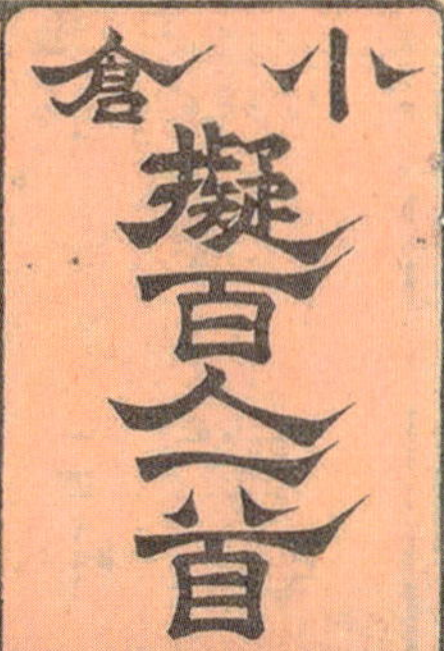

35

Ki no Tsurayuki

People's ways and human hearts
I'll never understand—

only the plum trees
in my father's garden
remain faithful in their fragrance.

人はいさ
心も知らず
ふるさとは
花ぞ昔の
香に匂ひける

hito wa isa
kokoro mo shirazu
furusato wa
hana zo mukashi no
ka ni nioi keru

36

Kiyowara no Fukayabu

This summer night
so short that it grew light
while I still thought it evening—

where, blanketed in clouds tonight,
sleeps the morning moon?

夏の夜は
まだ宵ながら
明けぬるを
雲のいづくに
月宿るらむ

natsu no yo wa
mada yoi nagara
akenuru wo
kumo no izuku ni
tsuki yadoruran

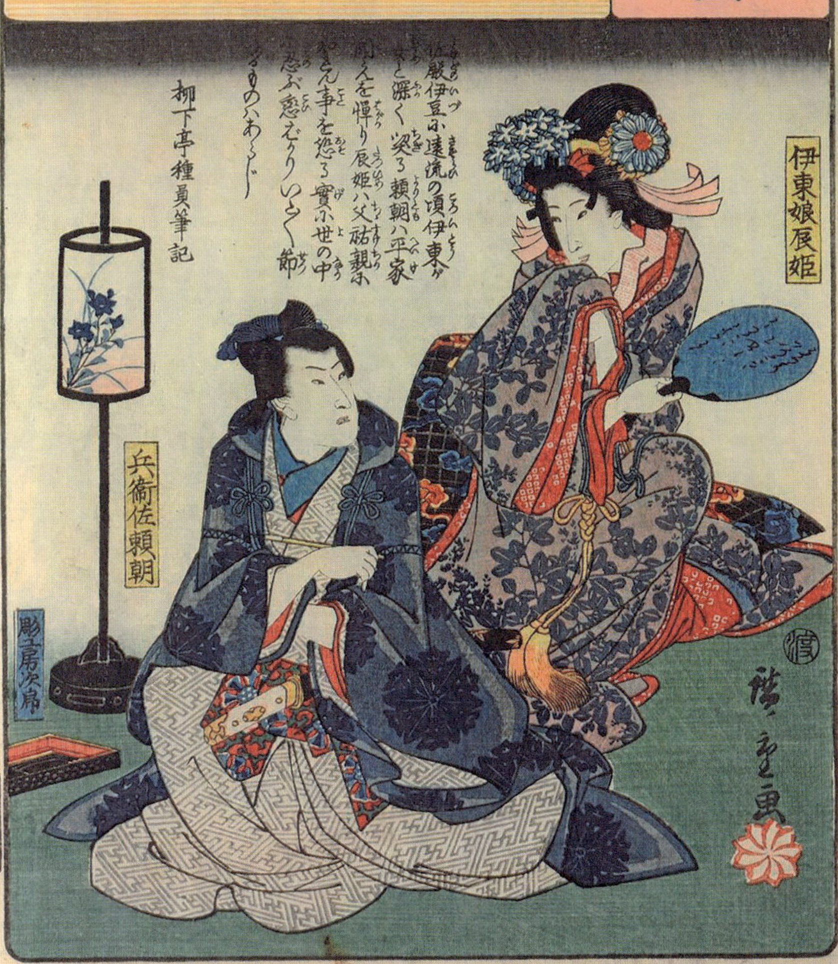
小倉擬百人一首
清原深養父
夏の夜は まだ宵ながら 明けぬるを 雲のいづこに 月やどるらむ
伊東娘辰姫
兵衛佐頼朝
柳下亭種員筆記
彫工房次郎
三十六
広重画

文屋朝康

白露に
風の吹きしく
秋の野は
つらぬきとめぬ
玉ぞちりける

あらあらし
近衛院の宇治姫小玉藻といへる美女あり
元是人倫のものにあらされ三國伝来の妖怪より
安居院康頼か祈りにあはれ三浦上總両輔
夕武勇の為に退治せられて那須野の
住四と偽ふける

柳下亭種員筆記

朝櫻楼
國芳画

37

Bunya no Asayasu

As pearls come unstrung
and scattered, roll about the floor—

so dewdrops flitting in the breeze
dance across this autumn field.

白露に
風の吹きしく
秋の野は
つらぬきとめぬ
玉ぞ散りける

shiratsuyu ni
kaze no fukishiku
aki no no wa
tsuranuki tomenu
tama zo chiri keru

38

Lady Ukon

Go ahead, forget me,
I'll survive—

but will the gods
forget the vow you made
and let you off so easily?

忘らるる
身をば思はず
誓ひてし
人の命の
惜しくもあるかな

wasuraruru
mi wo ba omowazu
chikaite shi
hito no inochi no
oshiku mo aru kana

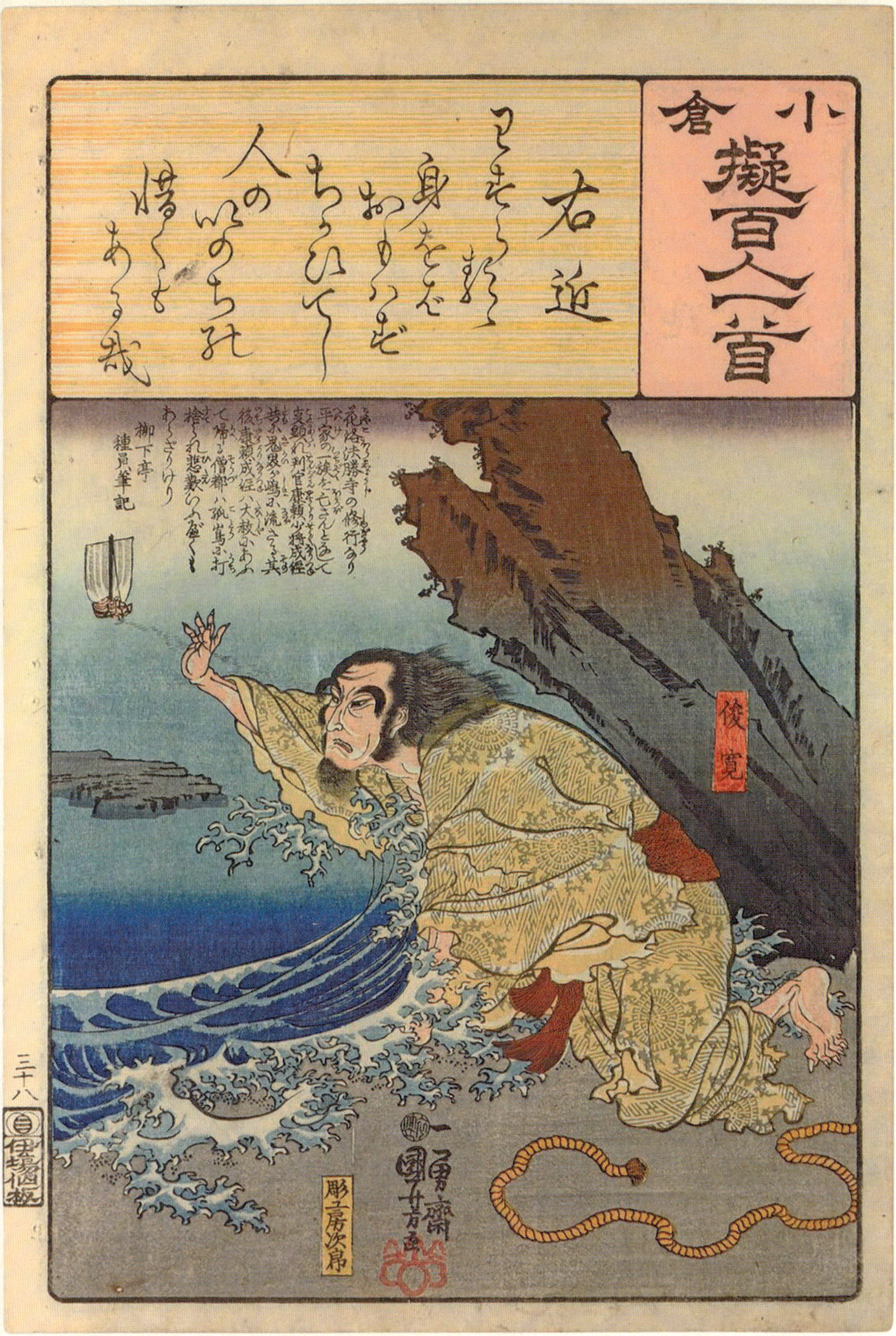

右近

忘らるる
身をばおもはず
ちかひてし
人のいのちの
惜しくも
あるかな

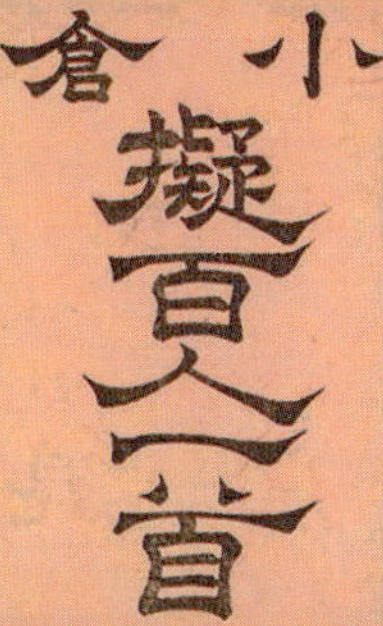

花洛法勝寺の修行より
平家の一族を亡さんとて
叛れ刑官康頼小将成経
と共に
俊寛鬼が島に流さる其
後康頼成経は大赦にあひ
て帰る僧都は孤嶋に打
捨てられ悲歎のあまり
あくがれけり

柳下亭
種員筆記

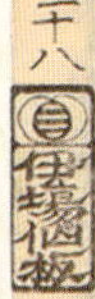

小倉擬百人一首

参議等

ひさきふの
をの
志のはら
忍ふれど
あまりて
なとか
人の
恋しき

柳下亭種員筆記

洛北岩倉の里を住れ
宗玄といふ釈門あり大
友の息女折琴姫ヶ艶る
姿ありしが破戒無慙の有
様なりしが其兄道助ヶ為不

宗玄

彫竹

39

Minamoto no Hitoshi

Like a small bamboo thicket
concealed by waving grass—

my desperate hidden feelings
may burst out any minute,
no matter how I try.

浅茅生の
小野の篠原
忍ぶれど
あまりてなどか
人の恋しき

asajiu no
ono no shinohara
shinoburedo
amarite nado ka
hito no koishiki

40

Taira no Kanemori

Though desperate to hide
the color of this passion,
it spreads across my face—

until my friends, concerned, ask
who or what's possessed you?

忍ぶれど
色に出でにけり
わが恋は
ものや思ふと
人の問ふまで

shinoburedo
iro ni ide ni keri
waga koi wa
mono ya omou to
hito no tou made

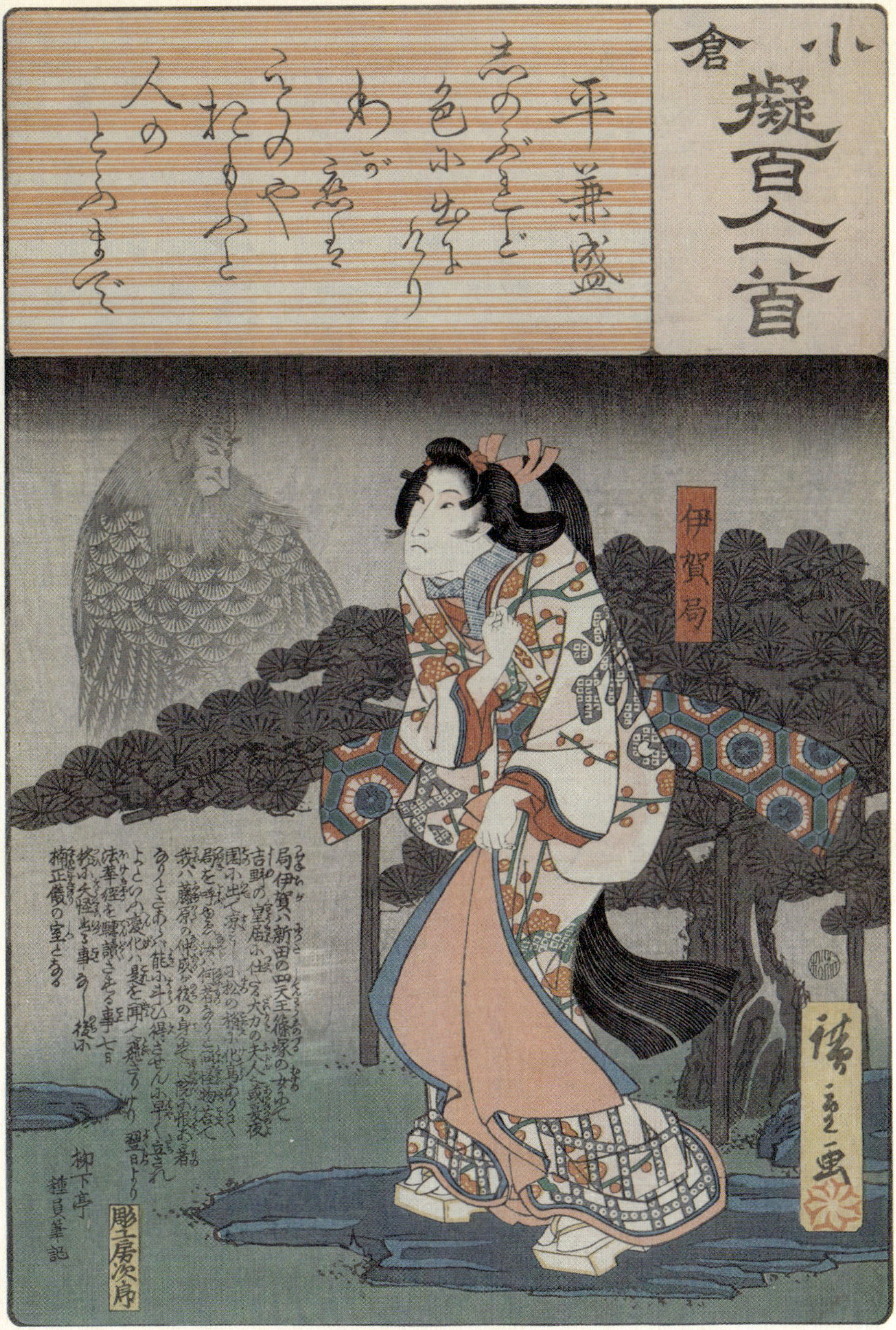

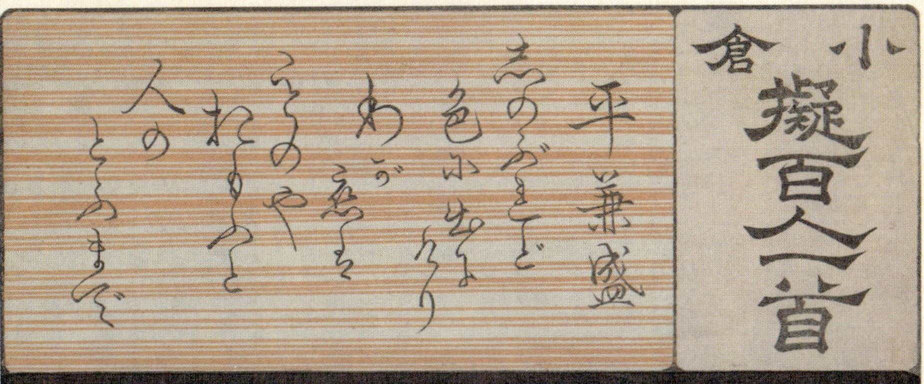

小倉
擬百人一首

平兼盛

しのぶれど
色小出でにけり
わがこひは
ものや思ふと
われものと
人の
とふまで

伊賀局

局伊賀ハ新田の四天王篠塚の女にして
吉野の皇居小供
園小出つ京
日松の旅立
家八藤原の佛師運慶の身をせ
よとの命令婦の佛殿と提の身をせ
れよりこそ能小斗ひ得せん小早く京され
火急宮経を聴詠させる事七日
渡し妖怪当る斬り一擬
十房次房 彫工房次房

柳下亭
種員筆記

廣重
一立齋
画

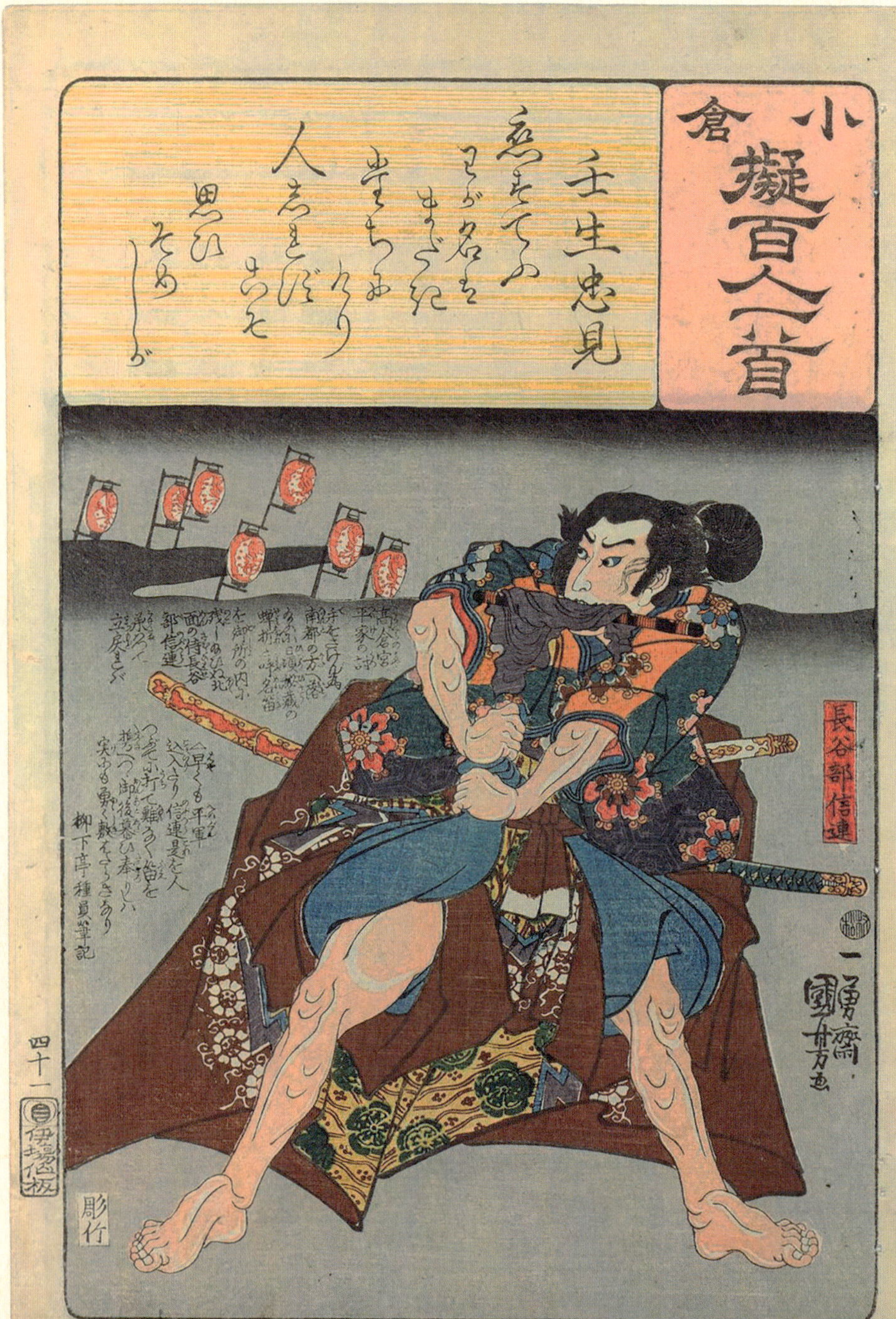

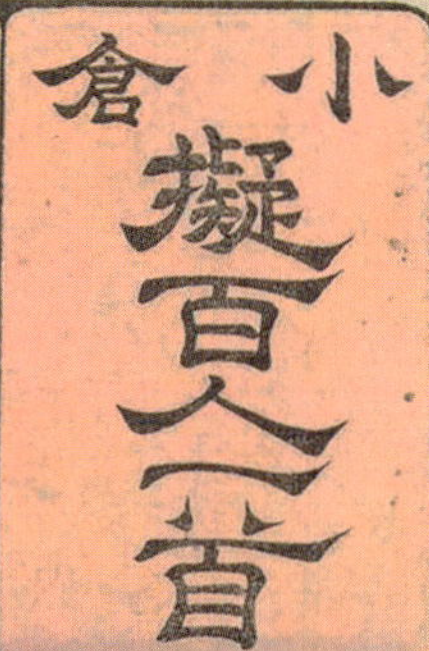
小倉擬百人一首

壬生忠見

恋すてふ
わが名はまだき
立ちにけり
人しれずこそ
思ひそめしか

長谷部信連

一勇齋國芳画

彫竹

41

Mibu no Tadami

This rumor of my love adorns
the lips of every fool—

oh what disgrace
to think I thought my secret safely hid.
Was it the color of my face?

恋すてふ
わが名はまだき
立ちにけり
人知れずこそ
思ひそめしか

koisu cho
waga na wa madaki
tachi ni keri
hito shirezu koso
omoi someshi ka

42

Kiyowara no Motosuke

But we promised!
Face to face and through our tears
to love beyond all time.

Yet in the end it seems
the waves—they did wash over Matsuyama.

契りきな
かたみに袖を
しぼりつつ
末の松山
浪越さじとは

chigiriki na
katami ni sode wo
shibori tsutsu
sue no matsuyama
nami kosaji to wa

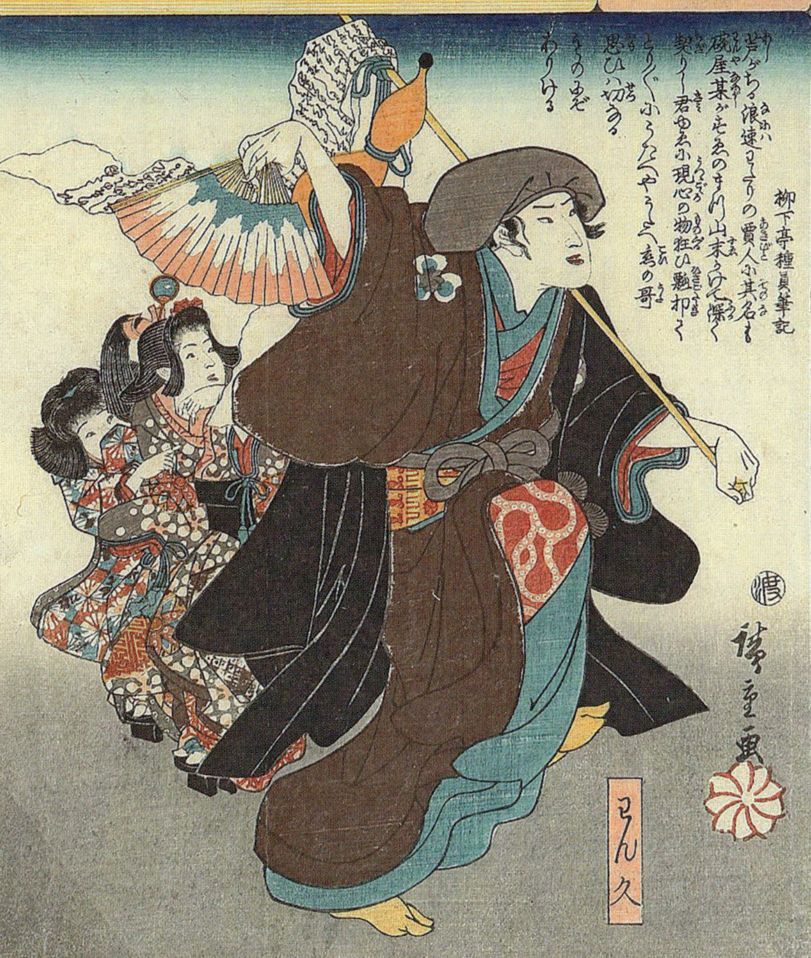

小倉擬百人一首

清原元輔

契りきな
かたみに袖を
しぼりつつ
末の松山
なみこさじとは

柳下亭種員誌
当やぐちゑ浪速ゝ巳り
碗屋某がせぞのすけ巳末ふ巳深く
契りて君ゑ巳現心の物狂ひ艶抑く
とりぐふらなやうゝよ之の哥
思ひ切る
うの其ぞ
わりける

廣重画

弓ん久

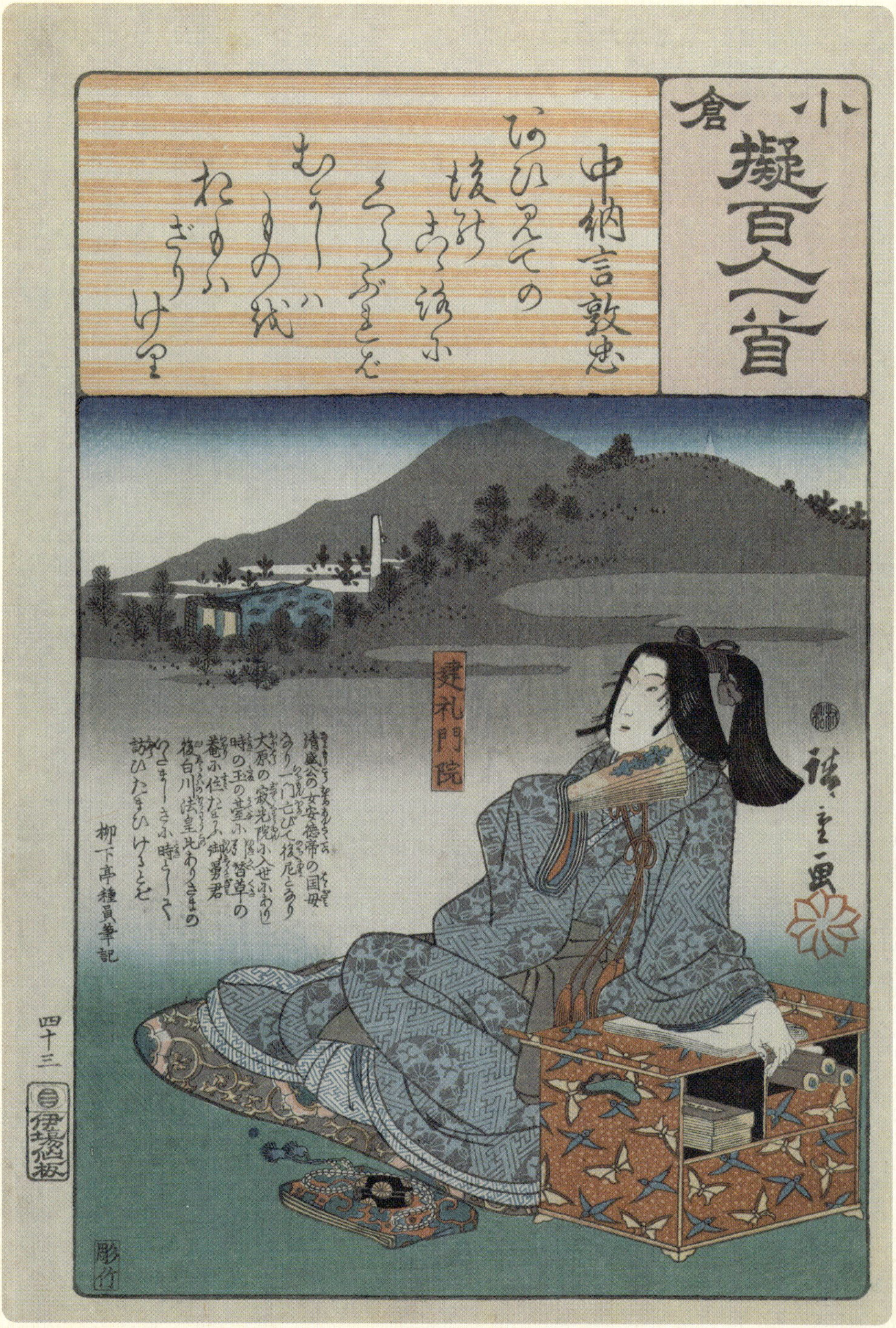

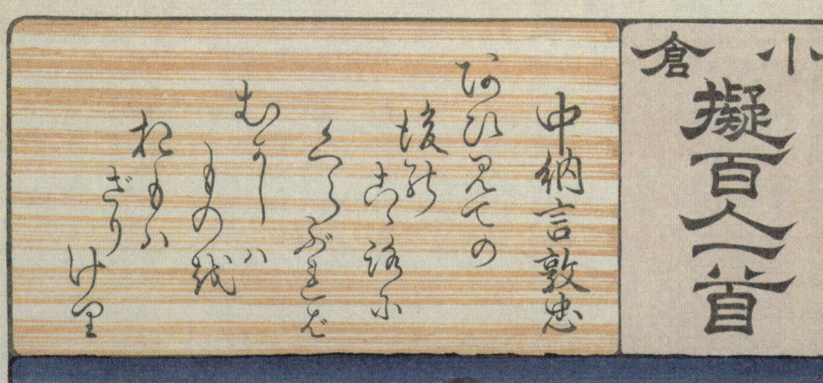
小倉擬百人一首
中納言敦忠
あひみての のちの
こゝろに くらぶれば
むかしは ものを
おもひ ざりけり
建礼門院
清盛公の女安徳帝の国母
なり 一門亡びて後尼となり
大原の寂光院に入世ふあり
時の玉の台に皆草の
巻小住なふ御男君
後白川法皇光ありさまの
つましさふ時らしく
訪ひたまひけりと
柳下亭種員謹記
廣重画

43
Atsutaka

My wanting her
before I tried to spend
a night with her was nothing
compared to after—

the craze that drives me now!

逢ひ見ての
後の心に
くらぶれば
昔はものを
思はざりけり

ai mite no
nochi no kokoro ni
kurabureba
mukashi wa mono wo
omowazari keri

44

Chunagon Asatada

If men and women never tried
to spend the night together,
you'd never see them
heaping blame upon themselves—

or one another.

逢ふことの
絶えてしなくば
中々に
人をも身をも
恨みざらまし

au koto no
taete shi nakuba
nakanaka ni
hito wo mo mi wo mo
urami zaramashi

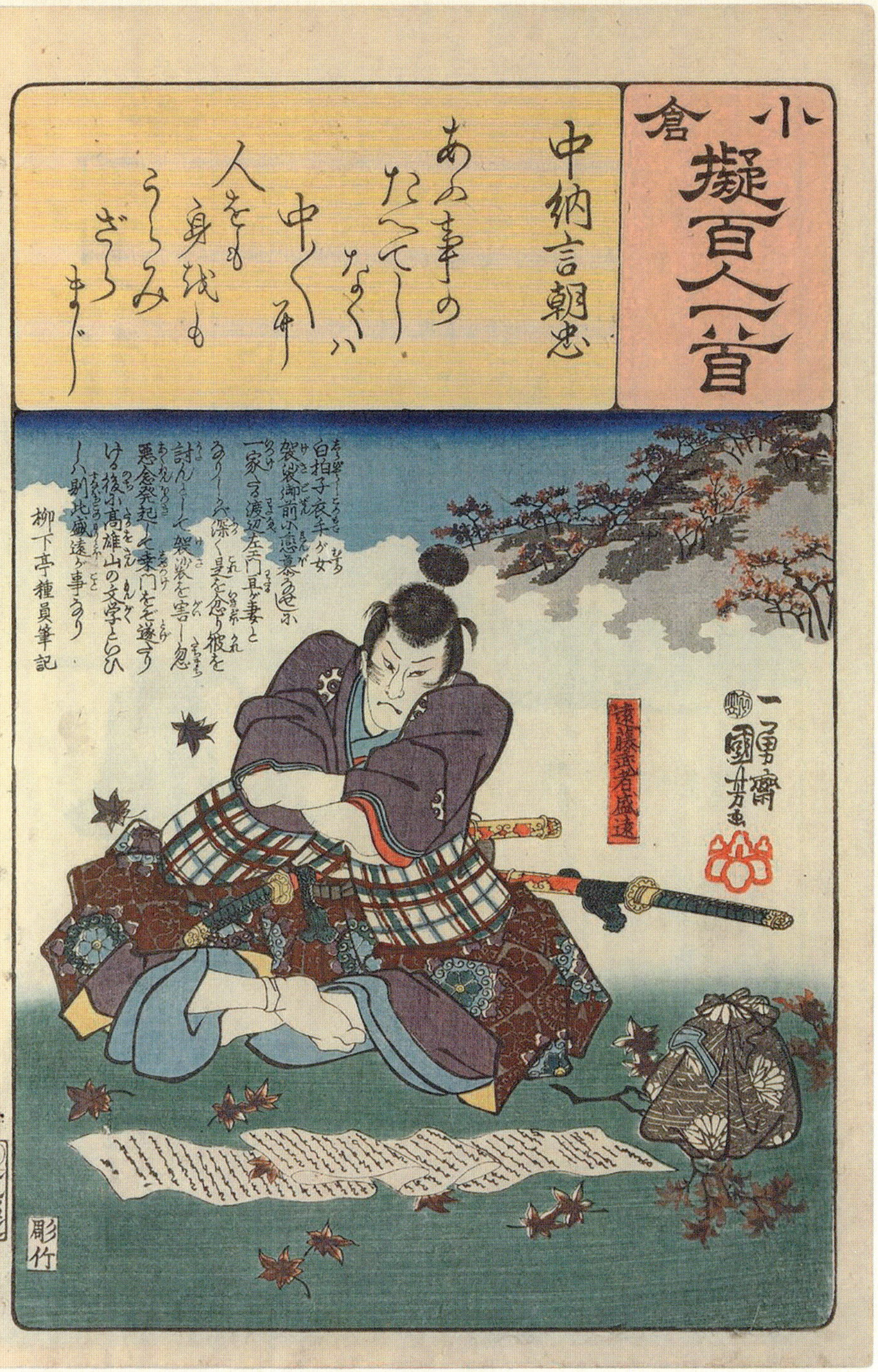

小倉
擬百人一首

中納言朝忠

あふ事の
たへてし
なくは
中／＼に
人をも
身をも
うらみ
ざら
まし

一勇齋國芳画

遠藤武者盛遠

柳下亭種員筆記

四十四

彫竹

伊場仙板

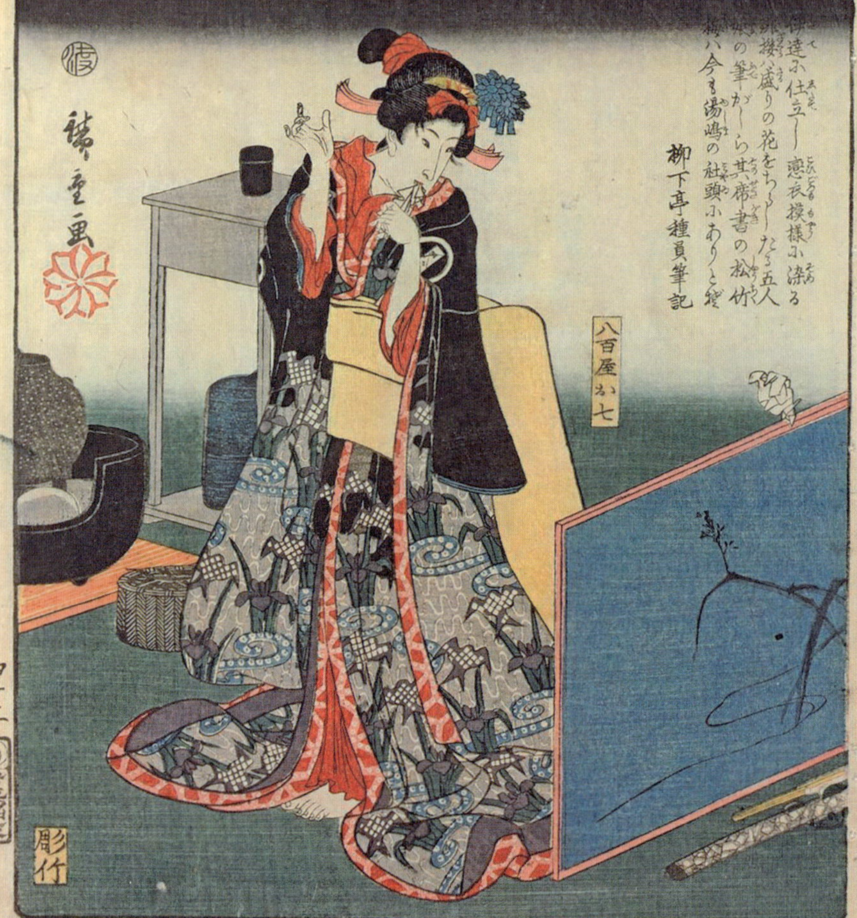
小倉擬百人一首
謙徳公
あはれとも
いふべき人は
おもほえで
身のいたづらに
なりぬべきかな
う郎
八百屋お七
廣重画
柳下亭種員筆記
四十五
伊場仙板
彫竹

45

Prince Kentoku

She above all I would have thought
might breathe me words of compassion
but alas—

my life now seems so empty,
I will surely not survive.

哀れとも
いふべき人は
思ほえで
身のいたづらに
なりぬべきかな

aware to mo
iu beki hito wa
omooede
mi no itazura ni
narinu beki kana

46

Sone Yoshitada

The Yura Channel boatman
with a broken rudder
cannot point his ship—

in just this way, I'm spun about
by torrents of desire.

由
良
の
戸
を
渡
る
船
人
楫
を
絶
え
行
く
方
も
知
ら
ぬ
恋
の
道
か
な

yura no to wo
wataru funabito
kaji wo tae
yukue mo shiranu
koi no michi kana

小倉擬百人一首

曽祢好忠

ゆらのとを
わたる舟人
かぢをたえ
ゆくへも志らぬ
恋のみちかな

浅ぢふの 旅立ふ日の善悪もあらそて
園部が端をおひ鳥の巣込ん
契りをと恋の大和路うて人行
木津の渡りの舟よりも
みぐさ心もいとてつり行に
　　　　　　柳下亭種貞筆記

薄雪姫

廣重画

渡し守

四十六
伊場仙板

小倉
擬百人一首

惠慶法師

八重むぐら
しげれる宿の
さびしきに
人こそ見えね
秋は來にけり

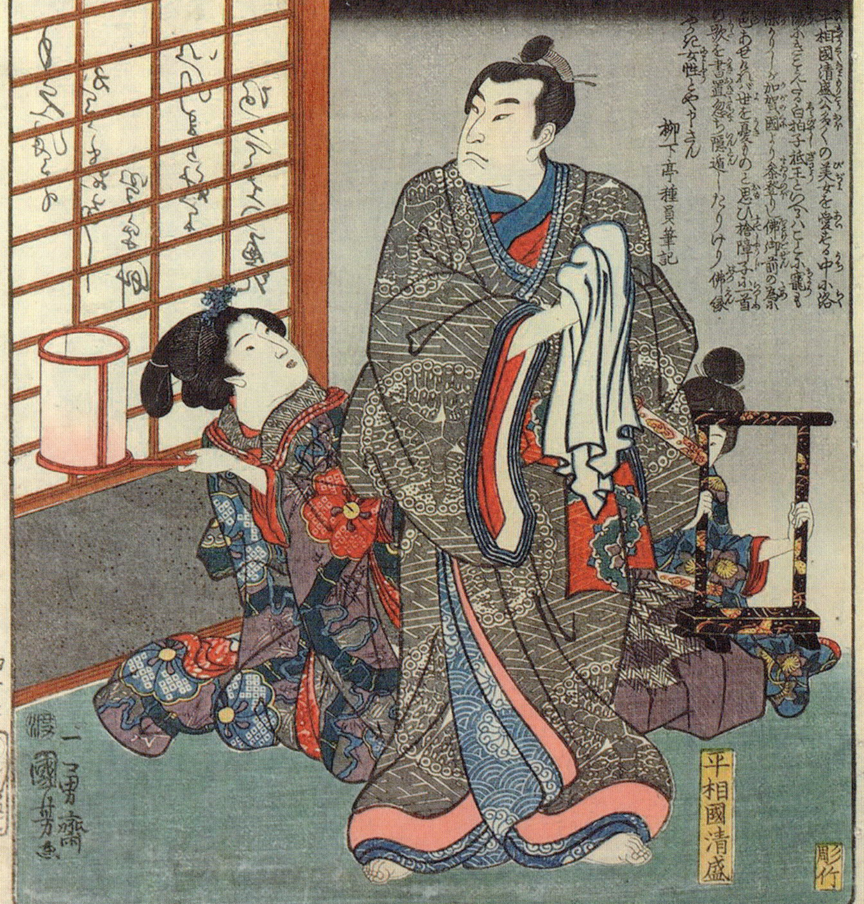

平相國清盛公ハ多くの美女を愛せる中小路
の方さこそ白拍子祇王とやいひけん寵愛
他にことなりしか佛御前の参りしより
寵さめて今はうとみ給ふそれにつけても
人のうき世を思ひ檜垣本の小路
の歌を書置忍びて隱れ遁れたりけり佛縁
より死しても女性とやらん
　　柳下亭種員筆記

平相國清盛

四十七

一勇齋
國芳画

47

The Priest Ekei

This weathered weed-grown
wasted hermitage,
its loneliness—

no one has come to call
but autumn's chill.

八重むぐら
しげれる宿の
さびしきに
人こそ見えね
秋は来にけり

yaemugura
shigereru yado no
sabishiki ni
hito koso miene
aki wa ki ni keri

48

Minamoto no Shigeyuki

Whipped by the wind, these frenzied waves
fling themselves upon the rocks,
only to be dashed so uselessly to spray.

As uselessly, I break myself upon the rock
of your implacable rebuff.

風をいたみ
岩うつ浪の
おのれのみ
くだけてものを
おもふ頃かな

kaze wo itami
iwa utsu nami no
onore nomi
kudakete mono wo
omou koro kana

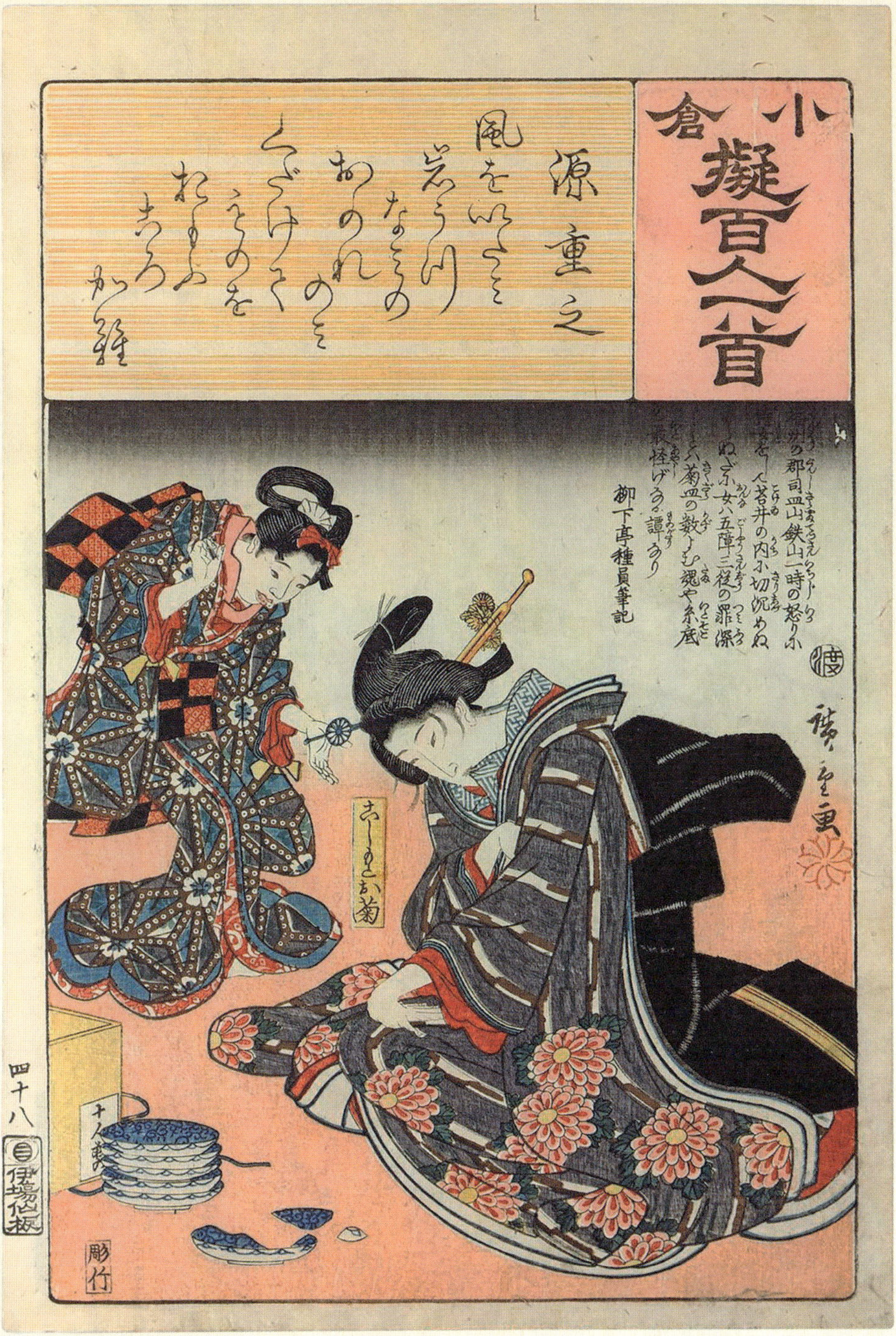

小倉擬百人一首

源重之

風をいたみ
いはうつなみの
おのれのみ
くだけて物を
おもふころ
かな

柳下亭種員筆記

播州の郡司皿山鉄山一時の怒りふ
とりらせ女若井の内小切沈めね
ねざぶ女八五陪三従の罪源
六菊皿の数たる魂や糸底
を残怪げする譚なり

ひろしげ

四十八

十人妻

おきくあ菊

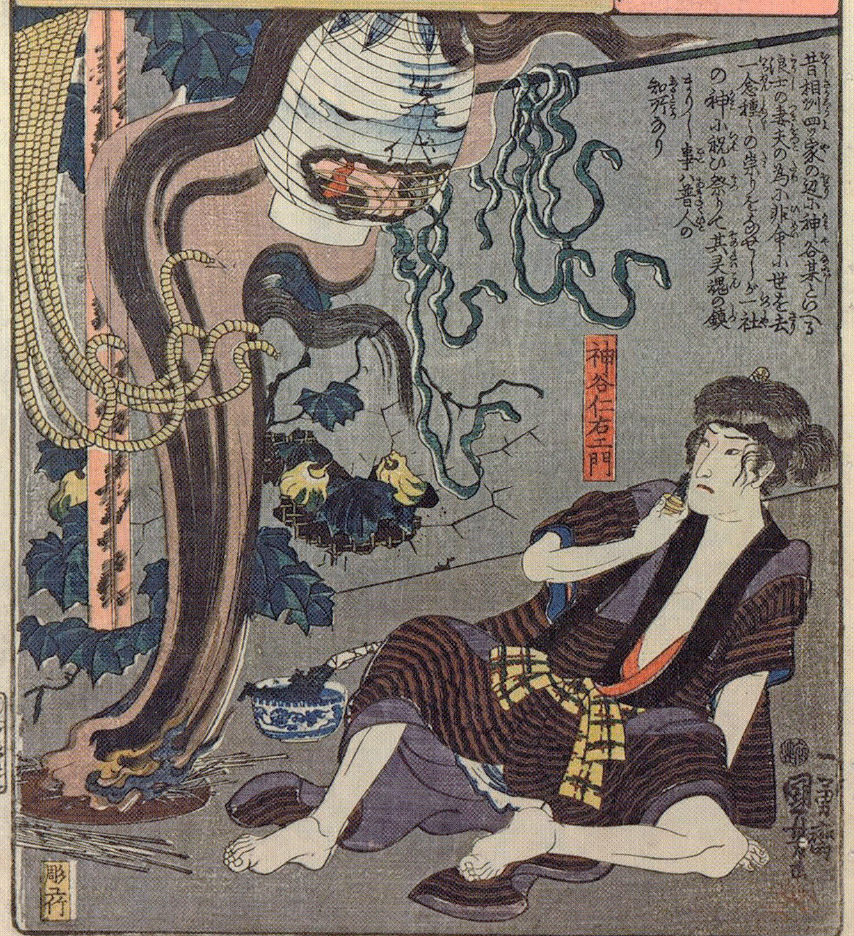

小倉擬百人一首
大中臣能宣朝臣
みかきもり
衞士のたく火の
よるはもえて
ひるはきえつゝ
ものをこそおもへ
神谷仁右エ門

49

Yoshinobu

Just like the fire lit by footmen
who guard the palace walls,

all night a raging furnace
but dissipated, cool by day.
I ponder why—but that just drives me to distraction.

御垣守
衛士の焚く火の
夜は燃え
昼は消えつつ
ものをこそ思へ

mikakimori
eji no taku hi no
yoru wa moe
hiru wa kie tsutsu
mono wo koso omoe

50

Fujiwara no Yoshitaka

A dreary life
I would have thrown away
for just this one encounter—

but now we've been together,
I want it long
I want it very very long.

君がため
惜しからざりし
命さへ
長くもがなと
思ひけるかな

kimi ga tame
oshi kara zari shi
inochi sae
nagaku mo gana to
omoi keru kana

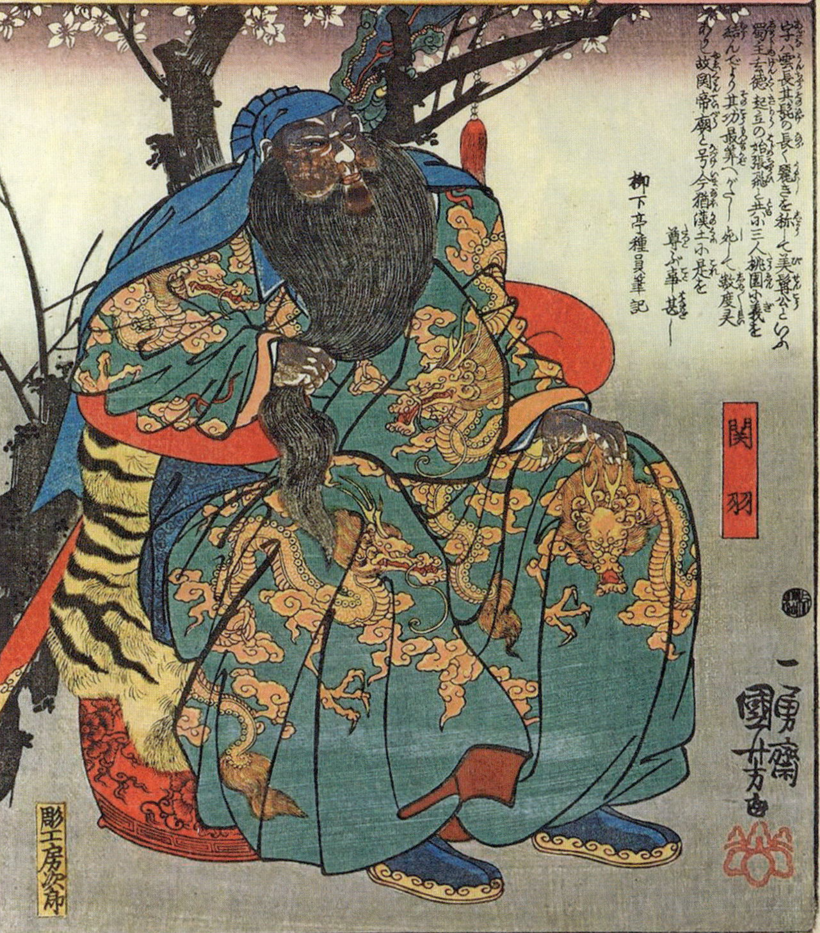

小倉擬百人一首

藤原義孝

君がため
をしから
ざりし
いのちさへ
ながくもがな
と思ひ
けるかな

関羽

一勇齋
國芳画

柳下亭種員筆記

五十

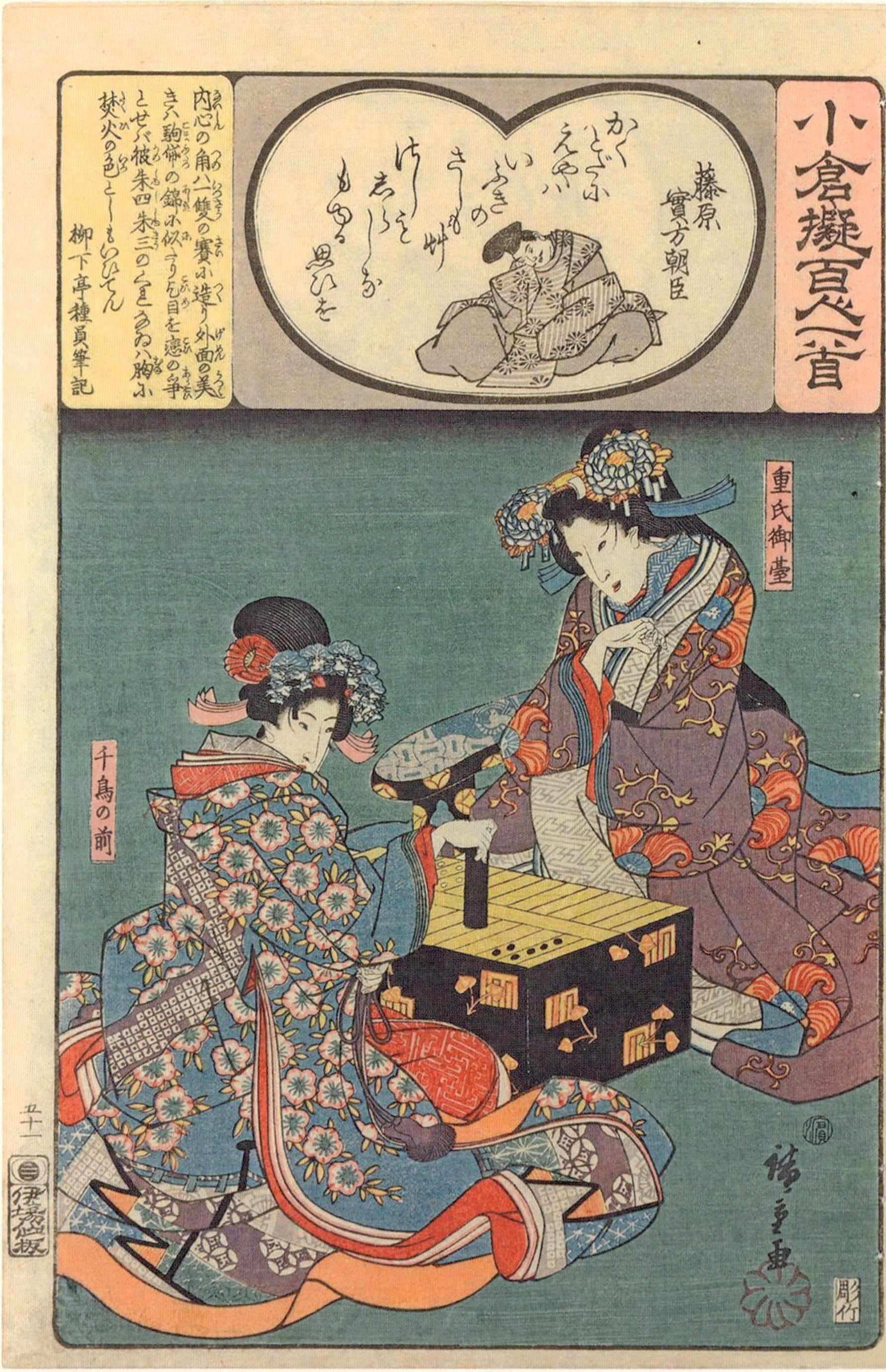

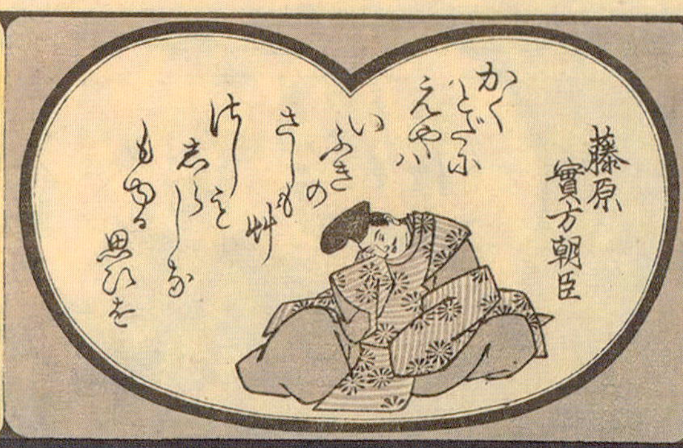

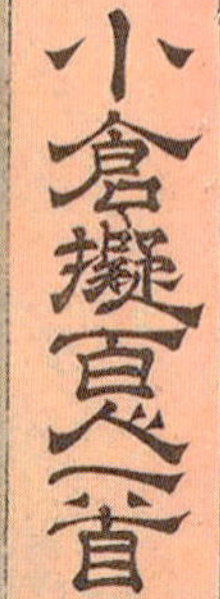

内心の角八雙の實を造り外面の美
き八駒齢の錦に似より○目を恋の争
とせば被朱四朱三の○を○る八胸ふ
焚火の色と○もいひてん

柳下亭種員筆記

重氏御堂

千鳥の前

五十一

伊場仙板

廣重画

彫竹

Fujiwara no Sanetaka

I long to cry out, tell you
of the searing pain I feel, like a pyre lit
from moxa grass that penetrates my soul—

yet I simply will not speak of it
so you can never know.

かくとだに
えやはいぶきの
さしも草
さしも知らじな
燃ゆる思ひを

kaku to dani
eyawa ibuki no
sashimogusa
sashimo shiraji na
moyuru omoi wo

Fujiwara no Michinobu

This sun-drenched morning
fades again to secret darkness,
that is sure—

yet still, I hate the crack of dawn
that forces us apart.

明けぬれば
暮るるものとは
知りながら
なほ恨めしき
朝ぼらけかな

akenureba
kururu mono to wa
shiri nagara
nao urameshiki
asaborake kana

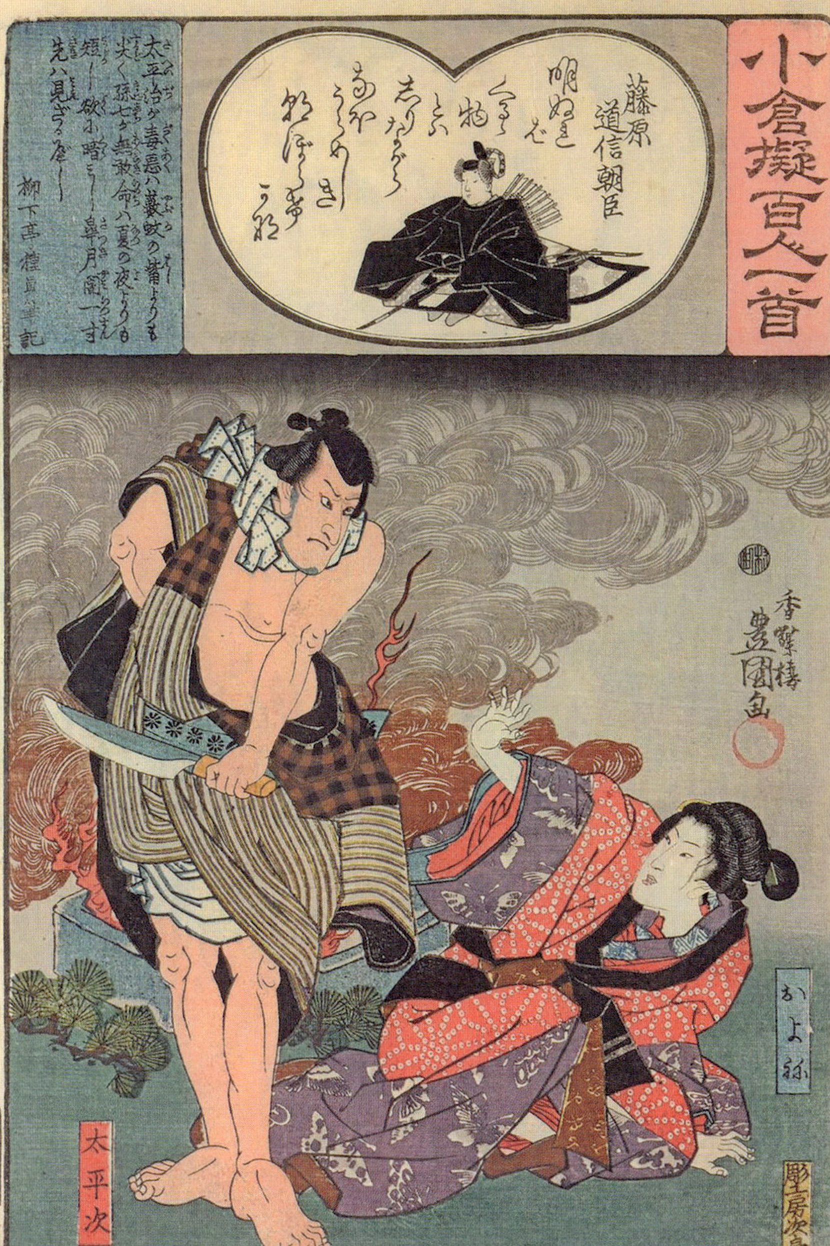

小倉擬百人一首
藤原道信朝臣
明けぬれば
くるるものとは
しりながら
なほうらめしき
朝ぼらけ哉
香蝶楼
豊国画
およし
太平次
五十二

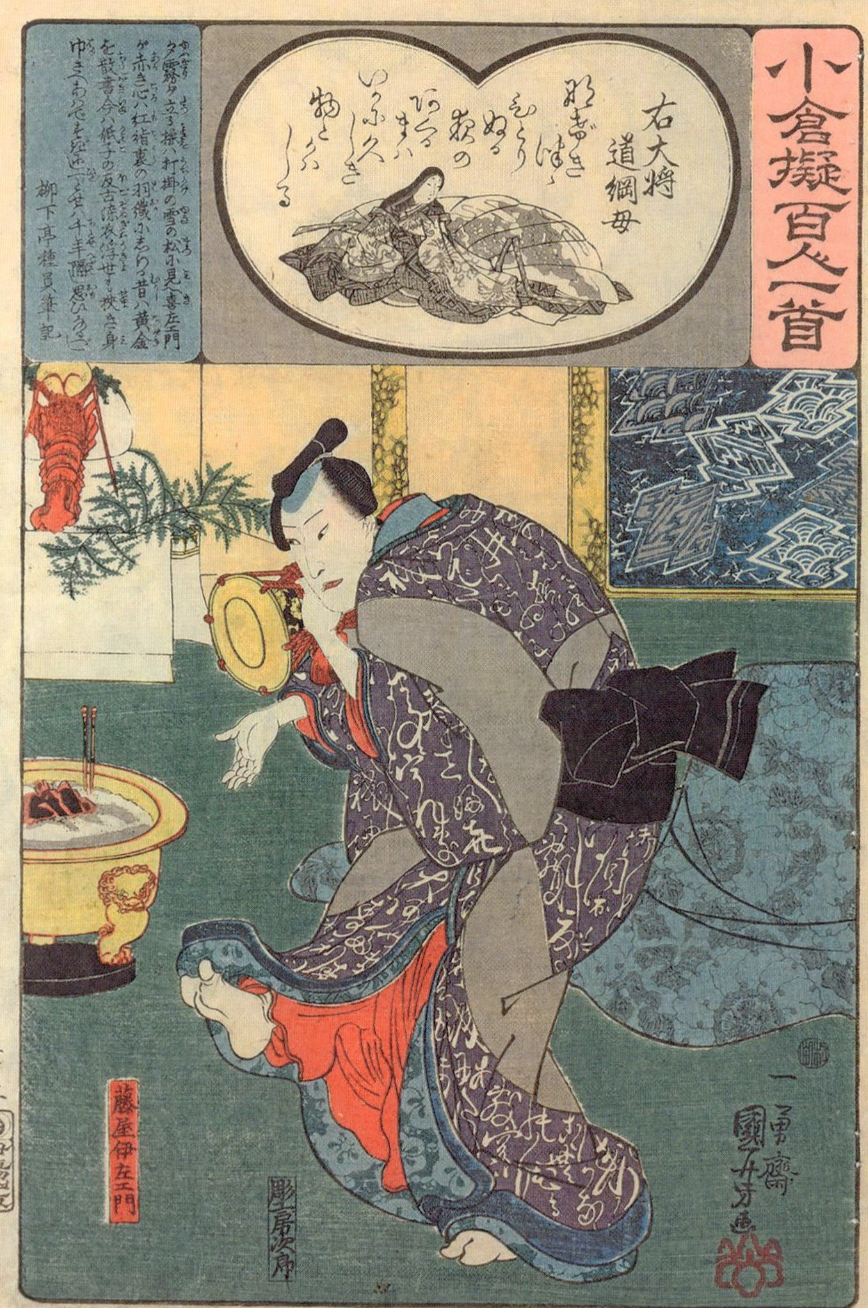

小倉擬百人一首

右大将
道綱母

なげきつつ
ひとりぬる夜の
あくるまは
いかにひさしき
ものとかはしる

五十三

藤屋伊左エ門

彫房次郎

一勇齋
國芳画

伊場仙板

53

The Mother of Michitsuna

Weeping in sorrow night after night,
condemned to wait alone
for the dawn that never comes.

What could you possibly know
about eternities like this?

嘆きつつ
ひとり寝る夜の
明くる間は
いかに久しき
ものとかは知る

nageki tsutsu
hitori nuru yo no
akuru ma wa
ikani hisashiki
mono to ka wa shiru

54

The Mother of Korechika

Vowing never to forget me
is very brave indeed—

but rather would I live just this one night
and rest securely in your mind.

忘れじの
行末までは
難ければ
今日を限りの
命ともがな

wasureji no
yukusue made wa
katakereba
kyo wo kagiri no
inochi to mo gana

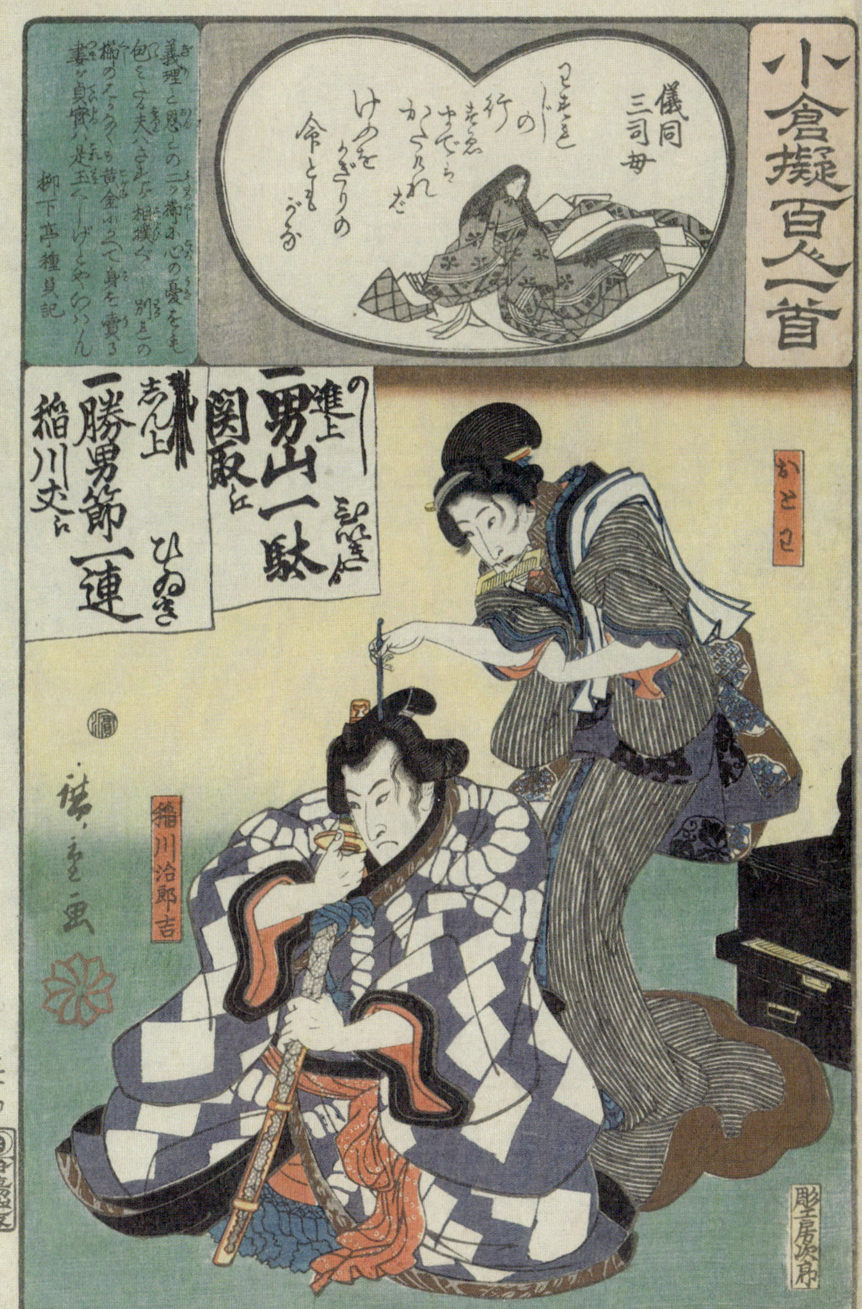

小倉擬百人一首
儀同三司母
わすれじの
行く末までは
かたければ
けふをかぎりの
命ともがな
さりながら義理と恩との二つ櫛の愛をかけ
包を丈夫へ出し相撲る　別上の
稲のみやくゞる黄金ぶつて身を賣る
妻ヶ奥實ハ是玉一げとやふぶん
柳下亭種員記
進上
男山一駄
関取に
志ん上
ひぬき
一勝男節一連
稲川丈に
稲川治郎吉
五十四
ひろしげ画
伊場仙板
彫工房次郎
おとの

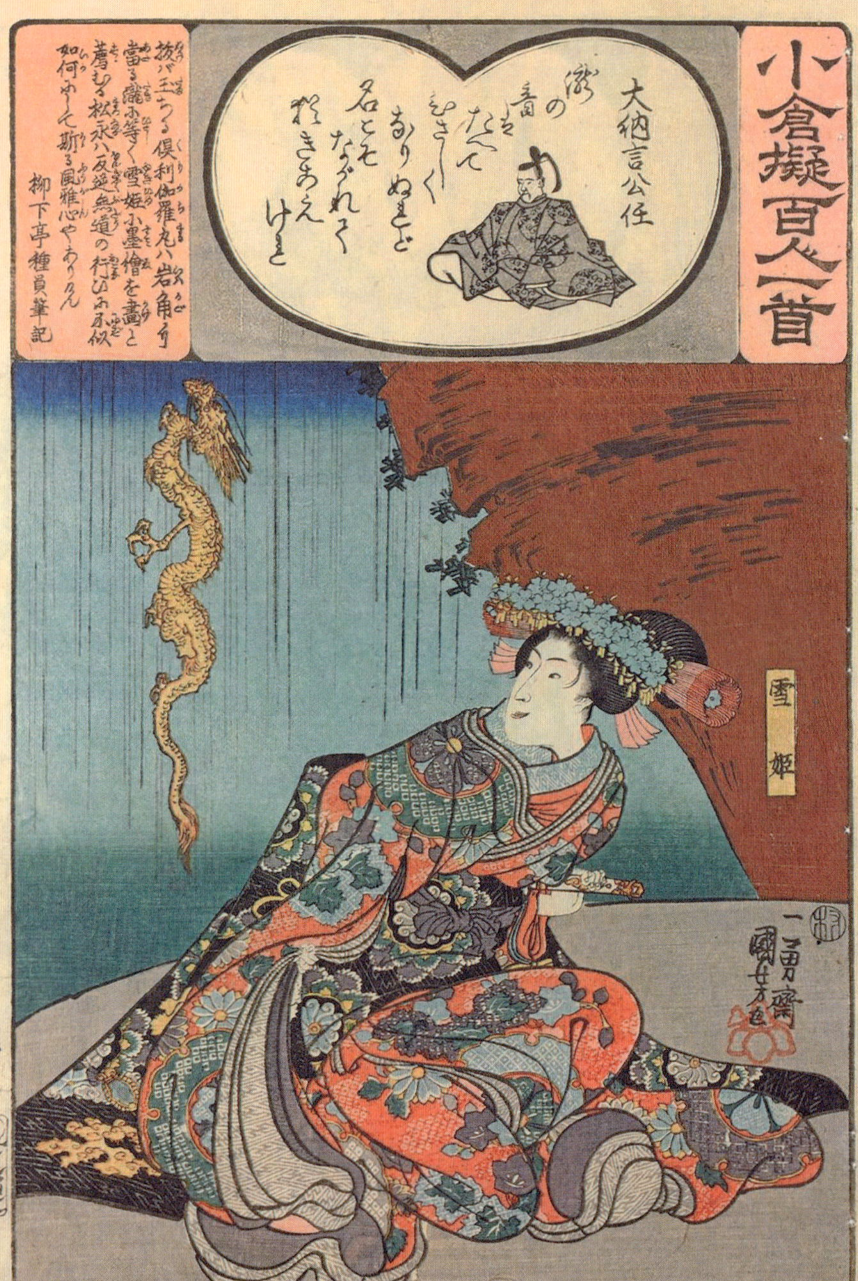

小倉擬百人一首

大納言公任
滝の音は
たえて
ひさしく
なりぬれど
名こそ
ながれて
なほきこえ
けれ

抜ば玉ちる 俱利伽羅丸八巌角り
當る瀧ふ等ぐ雪姫小墨僧を畫と
蕾むる松永八反逆無道の行ひみ似
如何みつて斯る風雅心やありん
　　　柳下亭種員筆記

雪姫

一勇齋
國芳画

五十五

55

Dainagon Kinto

For years and years
the splashing of this waterfall
has not been heard—

yet all around the world
men still speak of it with awe.

瀧の音は
絶えて久しく
なりぬれど
名こそ流れて
なほ聞こえけれ

taki no oto wa
taete hisashiku
narinuredo
na koso nagarete
nao kikoe kere

56

Lady Izumi Shikibu

Though to a better world
I may indeed be passing,
some memories I wish to take along—

just one more time, I beg you,
come to me tonight.

あらざらむ
この世の外の
思ひ出に
今ひとたびの
逢ふこともがな

arazaran
kono yo no hoka no
omoide ni
ima hitotabi no
au koto mo gana

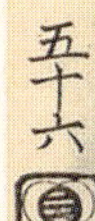
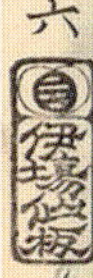

小倉擬百人一首

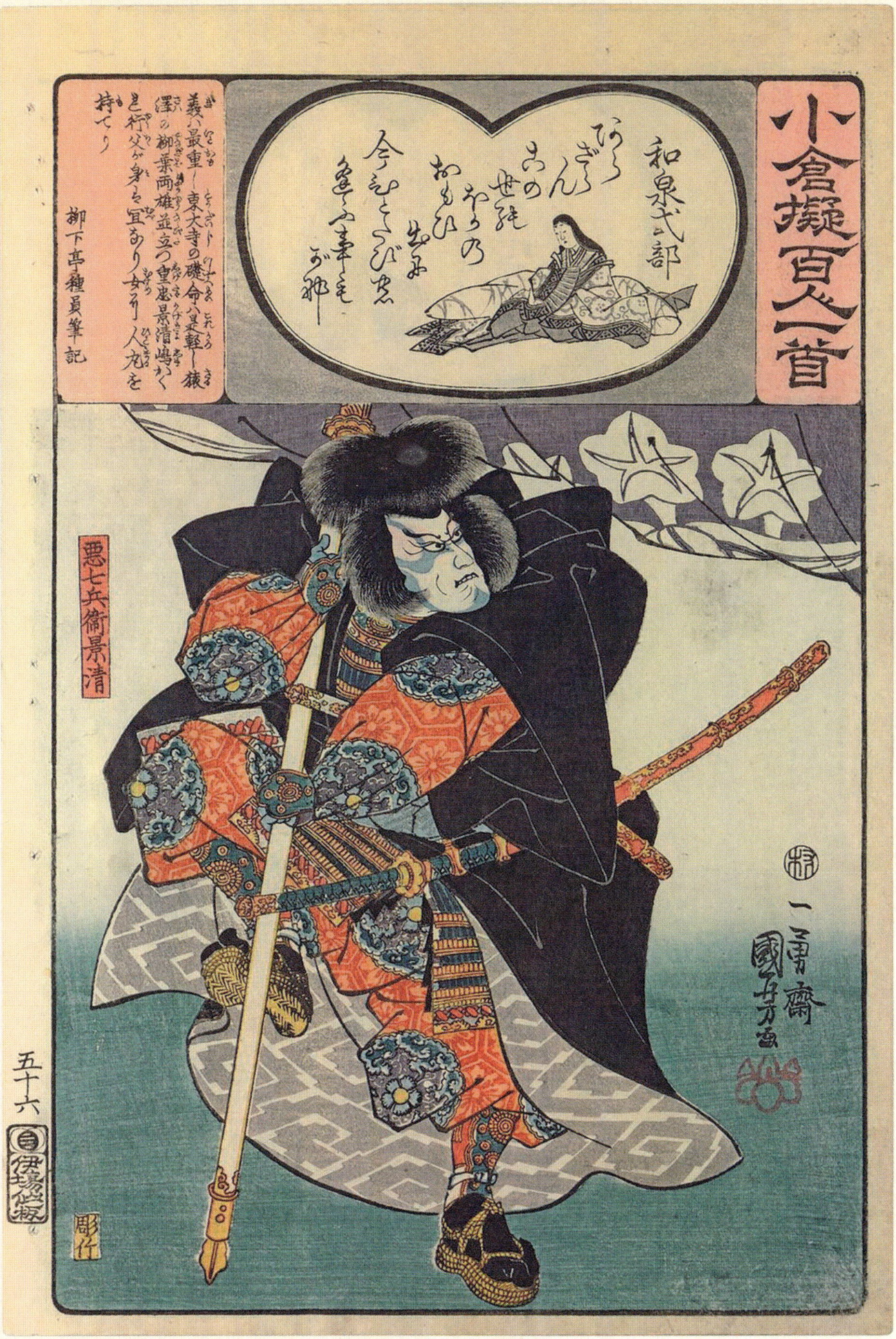

和泉式部

あらざらむ
この世のほかの
おもひ出に
今ひとたびの
逢ふこともがな

義ハ最重ㇳ東大寺の礎命ハ是ㇳ軽ㇳ猿
澤の柳葉両雄並立つ重忠景清嶋ㇵく
是行父が身ㇳ宜ありㇳ女ㇳ人丸を
持てり

柳下亭種員筆記

悪七兵衛景清

一勇齋
國芳画

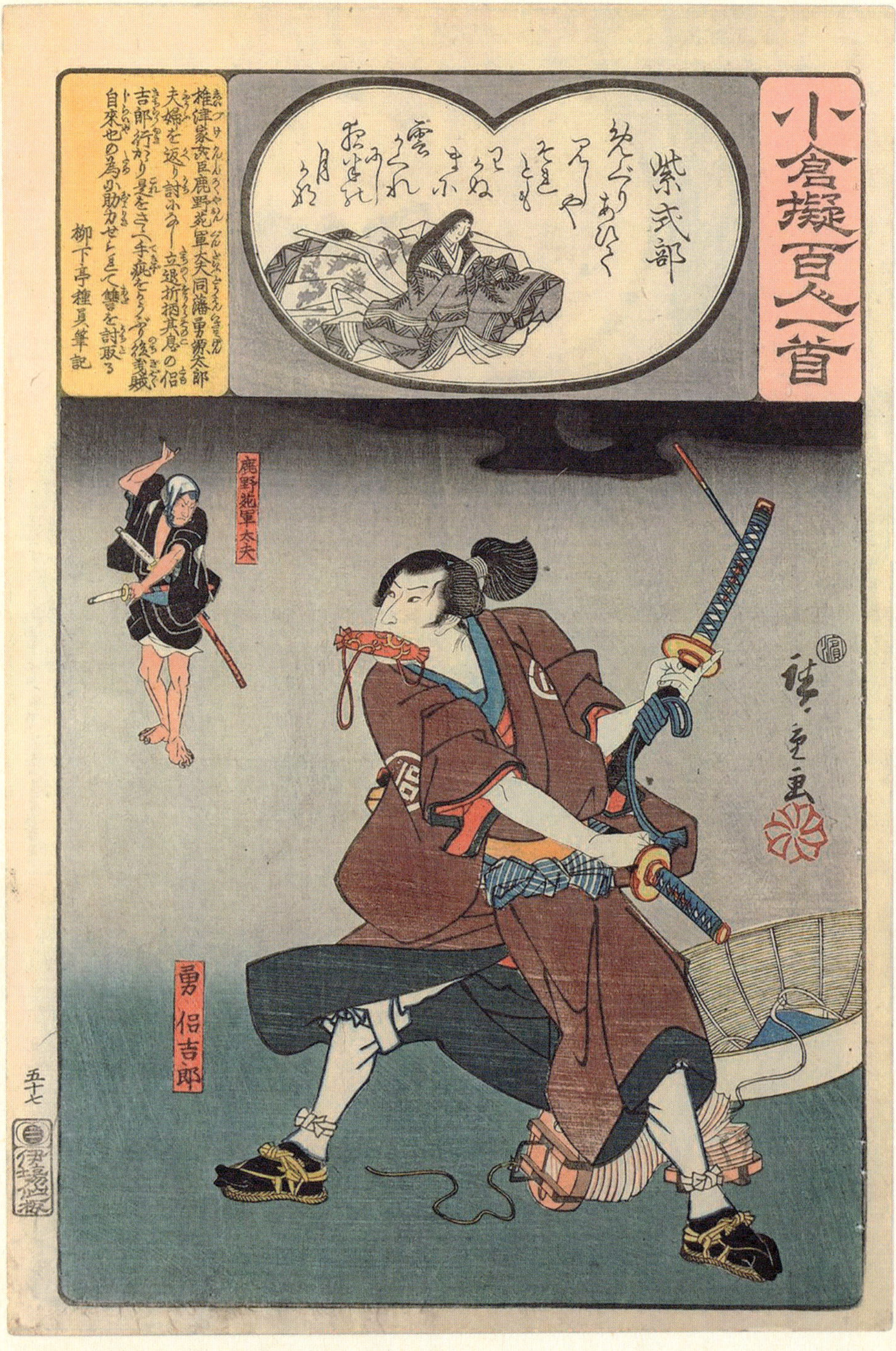

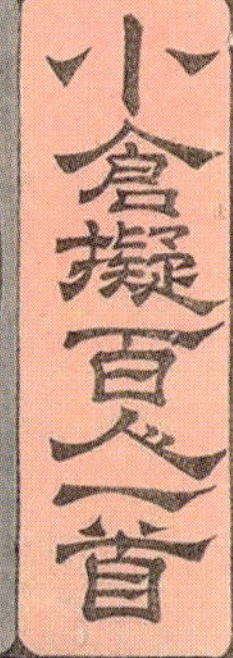

小倉擬百人一首

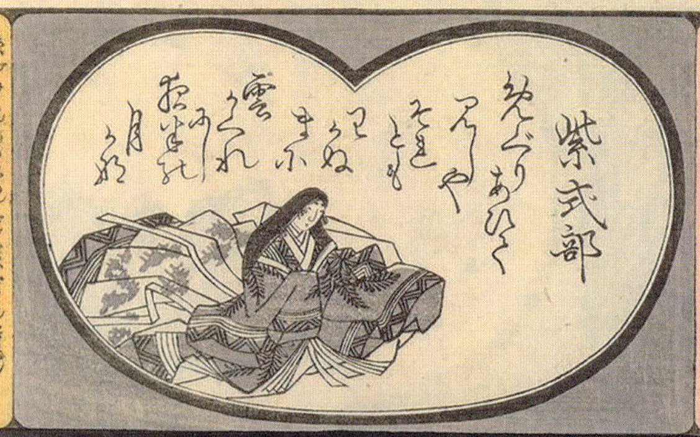

紫式部
めぐりあひて
見しやそれとも
わかぬまに
雲がくれにし
夜半の月かな

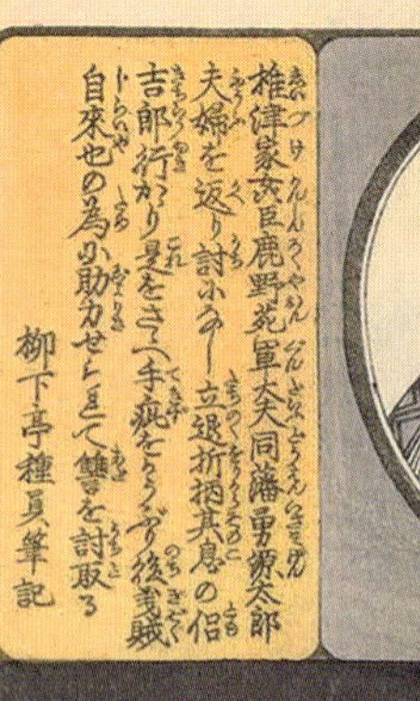

椎津豪次臣鹿野苑軍太夫同藩勇僕源太郎
夫婦を返り討ふ〲立退折捕其息の侶
吉郎行かゝり是をさへ手疵をゝゝがて後義賊
自來也の為か助力せしとて讐を討取る
柳下亭種員筆記

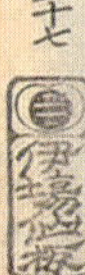

鹿野苑軍太夫
勇侶吉郎
廣重画

57

Lady Murasaki Shikibu

Once we were so close
that friend and I—
a glimpse I saw? A memory?

Amid the gathering darkness,
a moon obscured by clouds.

廻り逢ひて
見しやそれとも
わかぬ間に
雲隠れにし
夜半の月影げ

meguri aite
mishi ya sore to mo
wakanu ma ni
kumogakure ni shi
yowa no tsuki kage

58

Lady Kataiko

The wind from Mount Arima
blows hard across the Ina Plain,
bamboo stalks trembling in its wake;

just so—how can I, a stalk so shaken,
ever be expected to forget you?

有馬山
猪名の笹原
風吹けば
いでそよ人を
忘れやはする

arimayama
ina no sasawara
kaze fukeba
ide soyo hito wo
wasure ya wa suru

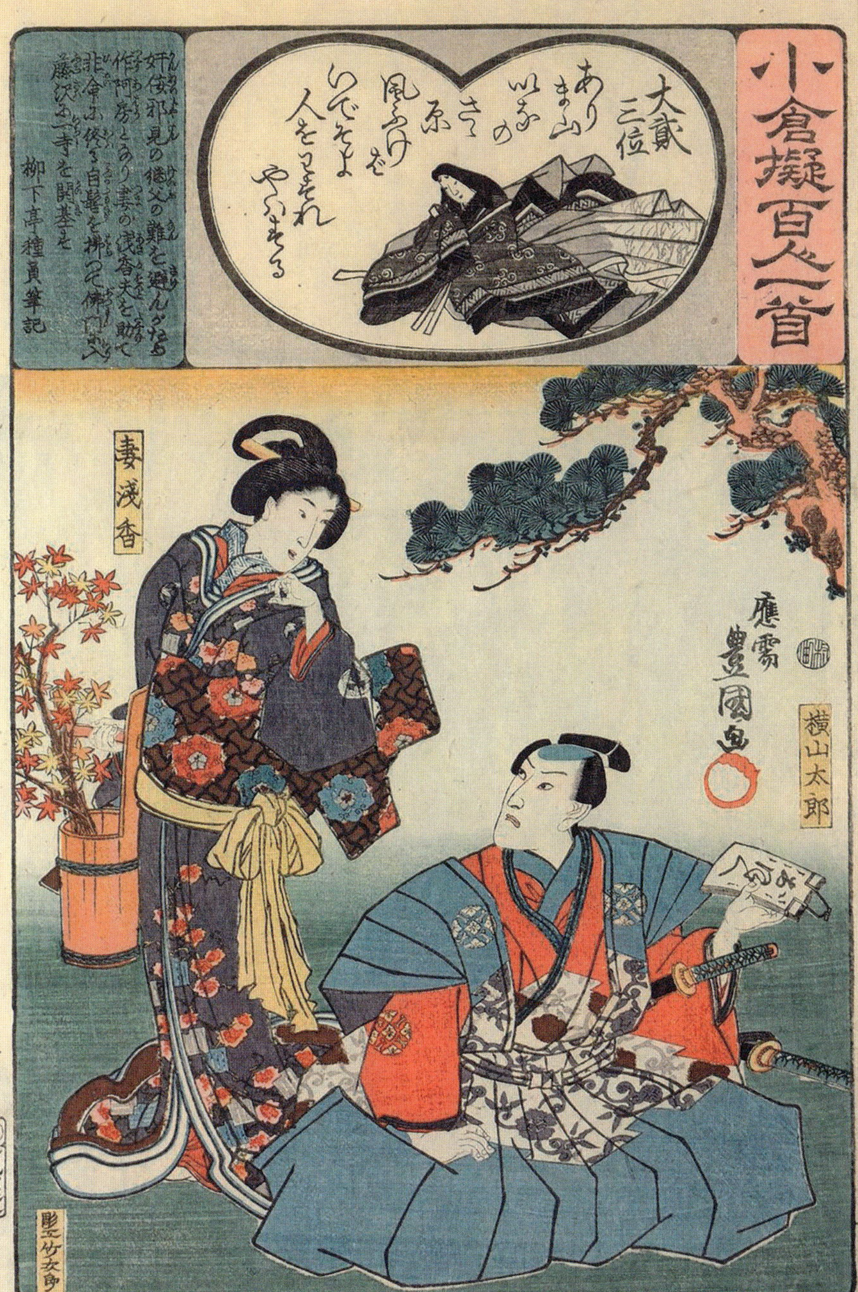

小倉擬百人一首
大貳三位
ありま山
ゐなのさゝ原
風ふけば
いでそよ
人をわすれ
やはする
柳下亭種員筆記
妻浅香
横山太郎
應需 豊國画
五十八
彫竹次郎

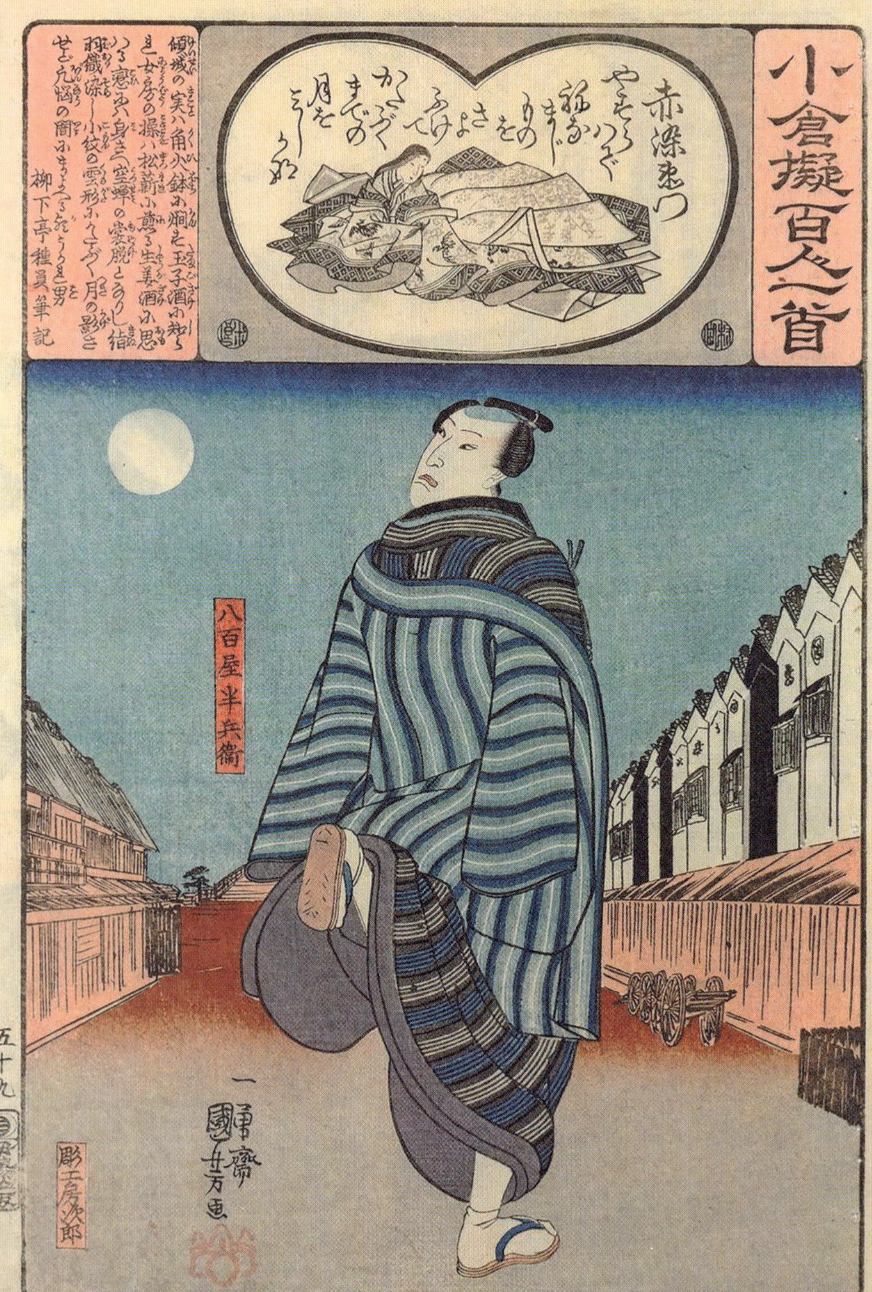

小倉擬百人一首
八百屋半兵衛
一勇齋國芳画
彫工房次郎
五十九

59

Lady Akazome Emon

No, I wasn't waiting,
I merely thought it nice
instead of sleeping

to sit here all night long
and glimpse the morning moon.

やすらはで
寝なましものを
小夜更けて
傾くまでの
月を見しかな

yasurawade
nenamashi mono wo
sayo fukete
katabuku made no
tsuki wo mishi kana

60

Lady-in-Waiting Koshikibu

The road my mother's taken
passing Ikuno, and even Oe Mountain—

so far, her letter cannot come
nor can I go to see her
at the foot of Heaven's Bridge.

大江山
いく野の道の
遠ければ
まだふみも見ず
天の橋立

oeyama
ikuno no michi no
to kereba
mada fumi mo mizu
ama no hashidate

140

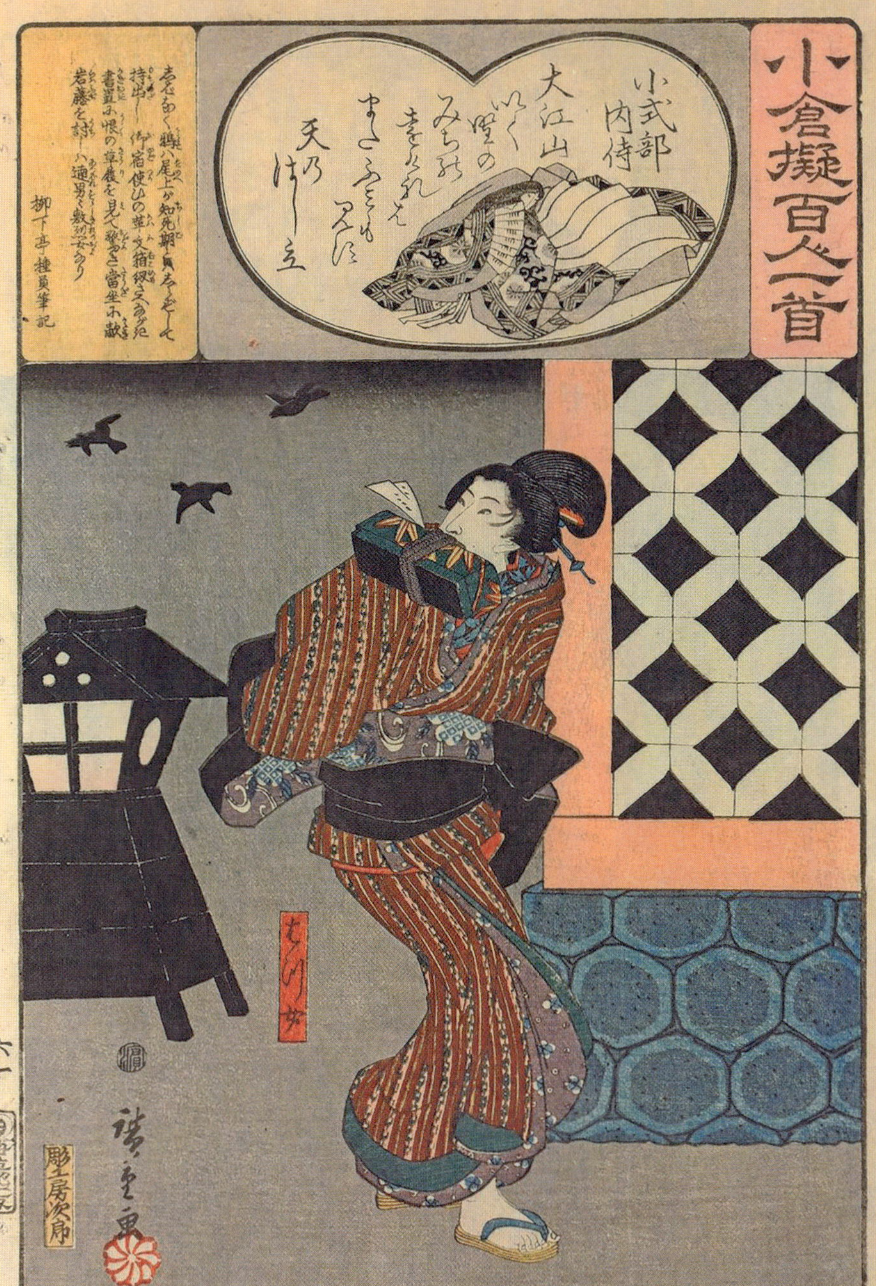

小倉擬百人一首

小式部内侍

大江山
いく野の
里の
みちの
まだふみも
みず
天の橋立

志を立て鵜八尾上が知免朝に頁志をゝて
持出し　御宿使ひの華文箱級さへうつた
書置子恨の草庵を見て驚きと當坐不敢
岩藤を討し八通男ゝ敷切安のり
柳下亭種員筆記

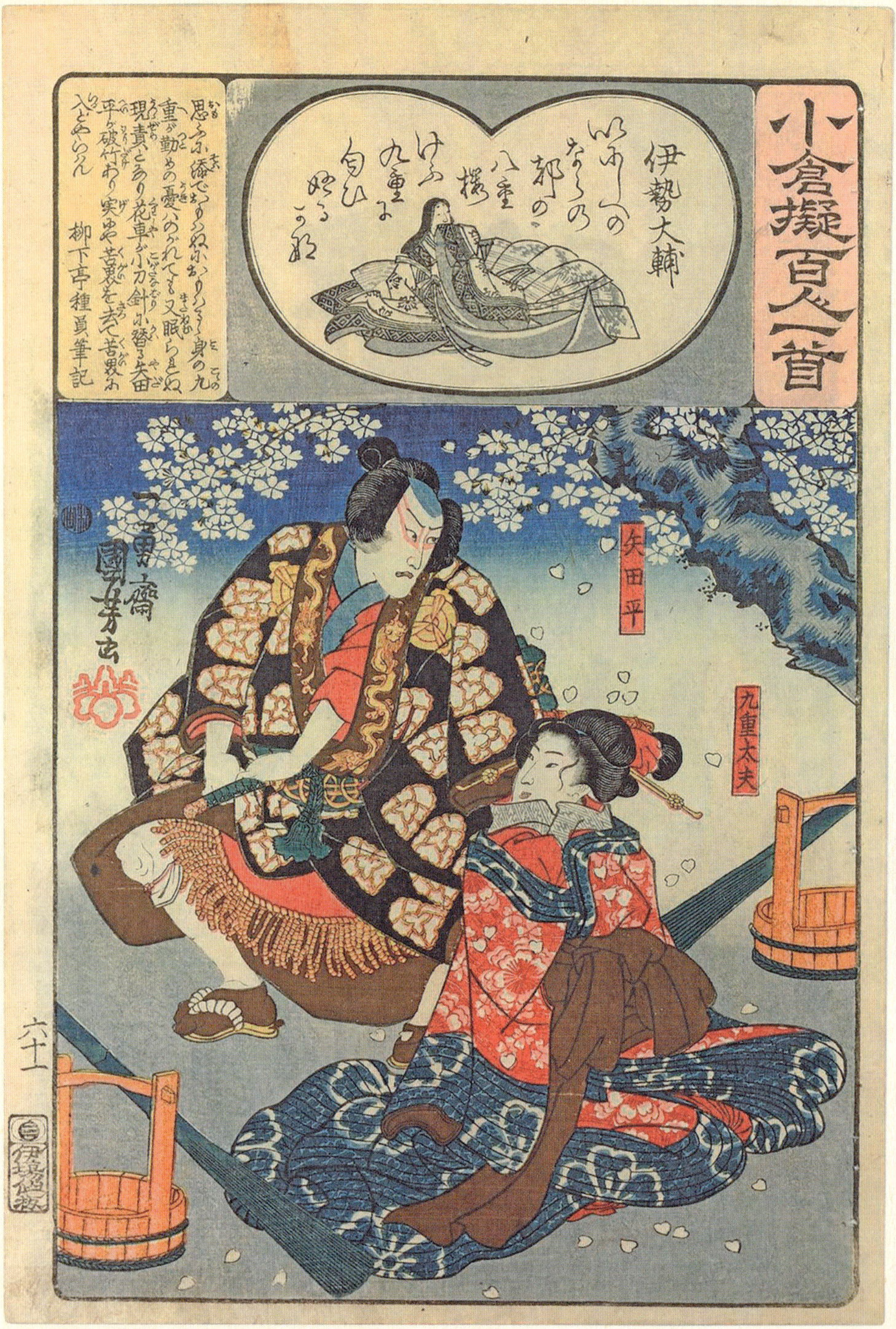

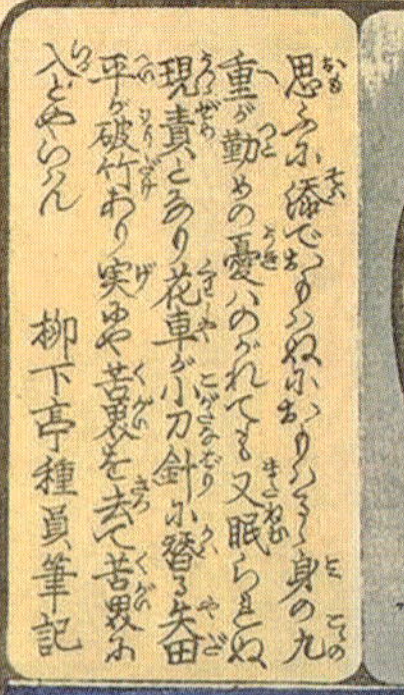
思ふ余情でおつのねふおりくつ身の九
重が勤めの愛ハのぶれても又眠らもぬ
現責とるり花車が小刀針小替る矢田
平ヶ破竹あり実ゆや苦敷を老て苦敷ゆ
入どやらん
　柳下亭種員筆記

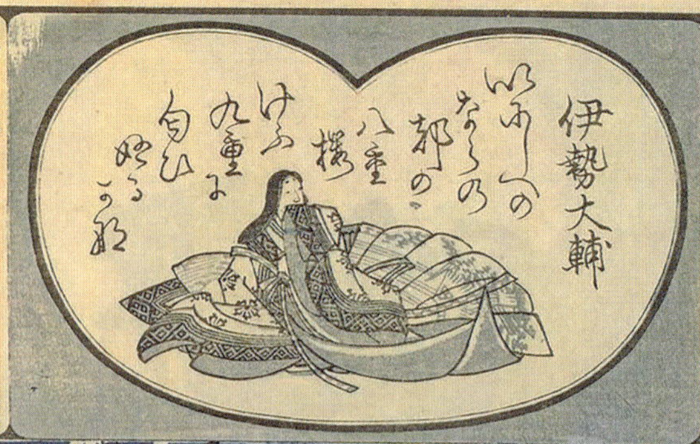
伊勢大輔
いにしへの
奈良の都の
八重桜
けふ九重に
匂ひぬるかな

矢田平
九重太夫
一勇齋
國芳画

六十一

61

Lady Ise no Osuke

Out of yesterday, our ancient capital of Nara
has brought these eightfold cherries
to us today—with what delight we smell

their fragrance as it permeates throughout
the ninefold courts of Heaven's realm.

古の
奈良の都の
八重桜
今日九重に
匂ひぬるかな

inishie no
nara no miyako no
yaezakura
kyo kokonoe ni
nioi nuru kana

<h1 style="text-align:center">62</h1>

Lady Sei Shonagon

Deep in the night, pretense of a rooster's crow
might fool an enemy, or even just a friend—

but do not dare to think
mere imitation of a cock
will open up the gate that's tightly shut.

夜をこめて
鳥の空音は
はかるとも
世に逢坂の
関はゆるさじ

yo wo komete
tori no sorane wa
hakaru tomo
yo ni ausaka no
seki wa yurusaji

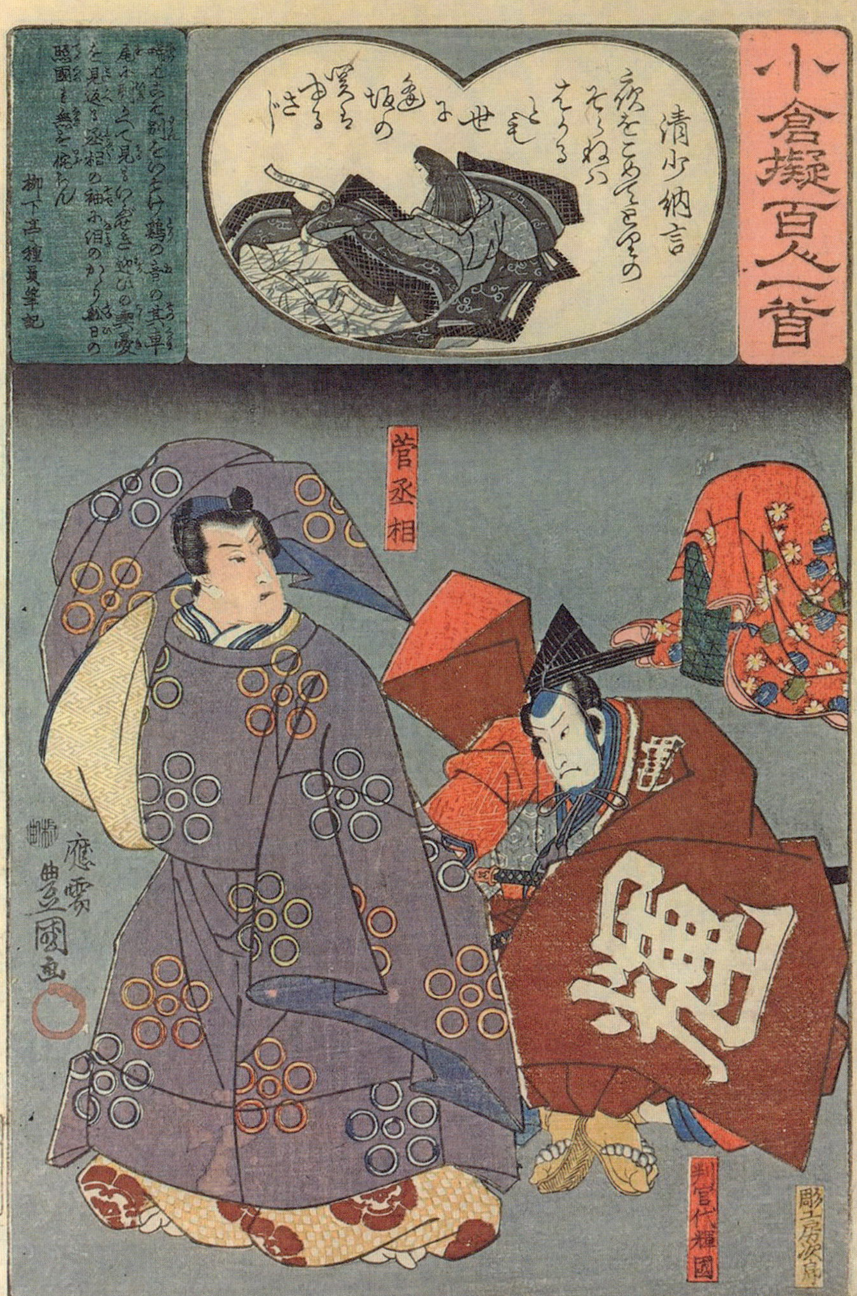
小倉擬百人一首
清少納言
夜をこめて鳥のそらねは
はかるとも
よに逢坂の
関はゆるさし
菅丞相
判官代輝國
應需
豊國画
六十二
彫工房次郎

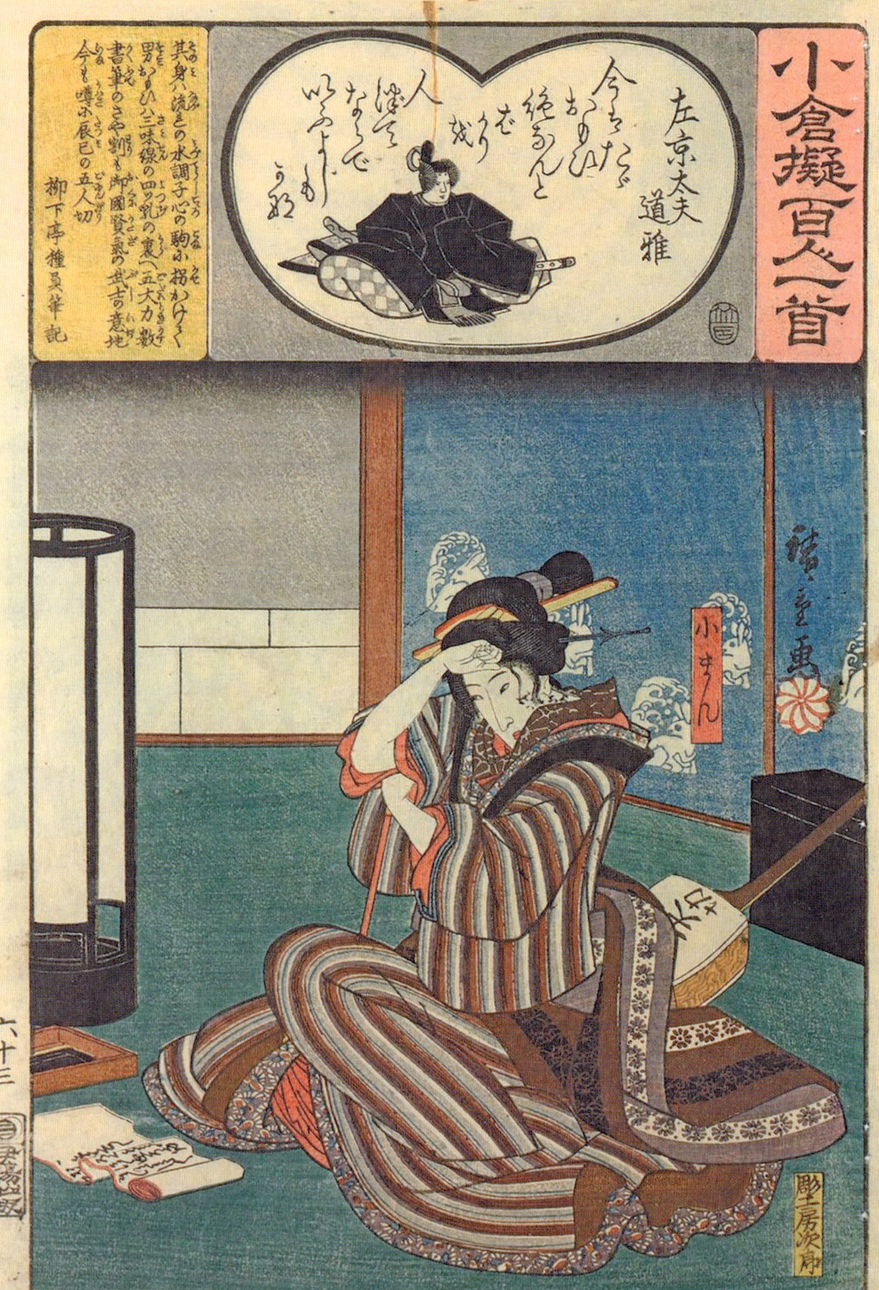
小倉擬百人一首
左京太夫
道雅
今はただ
おもひ
絶えなむと
ばかりを
人
づてならで
いふよし
もがな
其身は流との水調子心の駒ふ拐かけく
男ふひ三味線の四ツ乳の裏（一五大力数
書華のさや鞘も御國賢氣の武士の意地
今も噂ふ辰巳の五人切
柳下亭種員華記
小まん
廣重画
六十三

63

Sakyo Dayu Michimasu

To visit you again is risking death.
We must give up—in time our passions will subside.

I only wish to speak these thoughts to you myself,
and not that you should hear them
from the tawdry lips of others.

今はただ
思ひ絶えなむ
とばかりを
人づてならで
言ふよしもがな

ima wa tada
omoi taenan
to bakari wo
hitozute nara de
iu yoshi mo gana

64

Fujiwara no Sadayori

The morning fog rolls off
the Uji River to reveal
here and there

the softly bobbing
poles of peasant fishers.

朝ぼらけ
宇治の川霧
絶えだえに
あらはれ渡る
瀬々の網代木

asaborake
uji no kawagiri
taedae ni
araware wataru
zeze no ajirogi

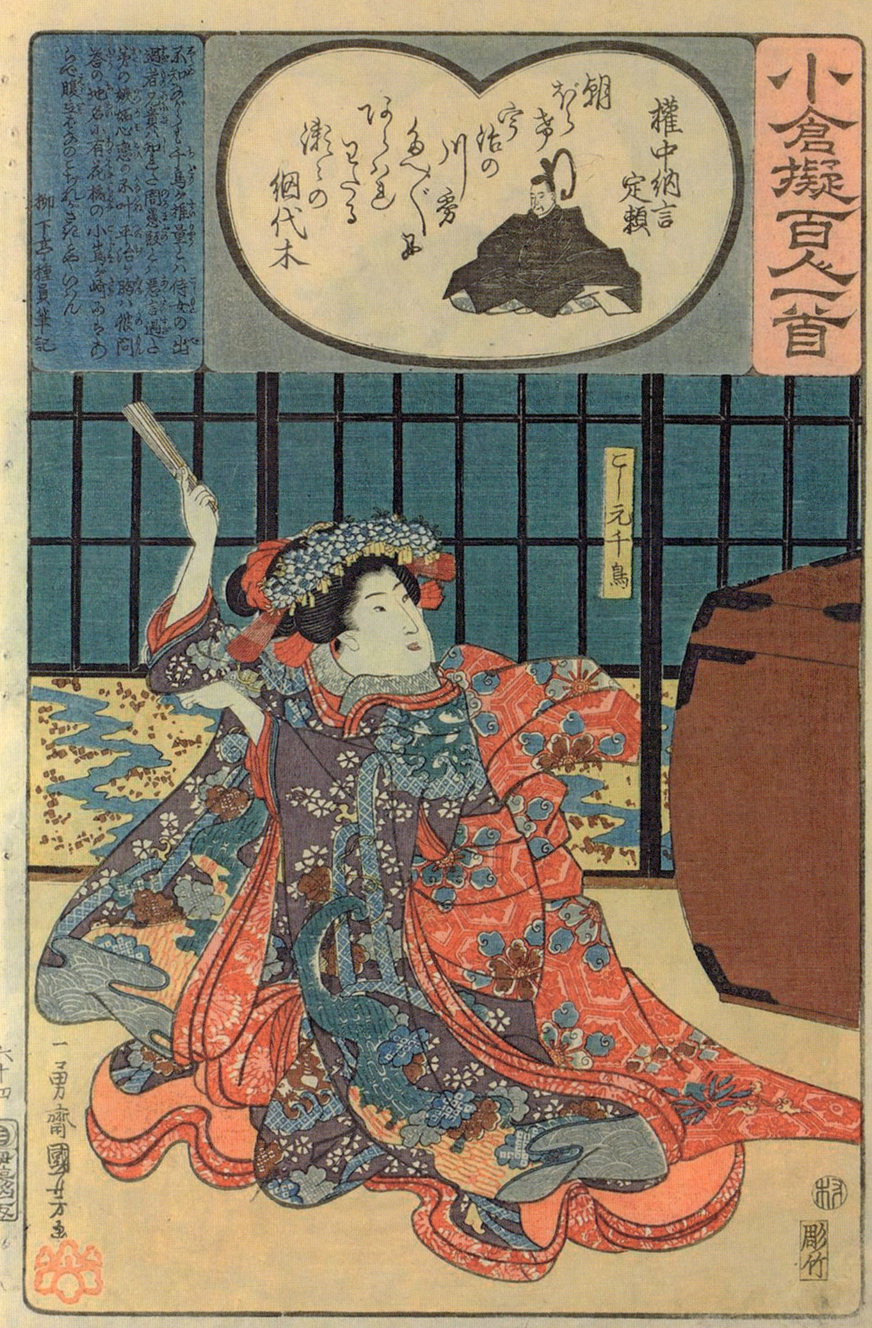
小倉擬百人一首
權中納言定頼
朝ぼらけ
宇治の川霧
たえだえに
あらはれわたる
瀬々の網代木
へ一元千鳥
柳下亭種員筆記
六十四
伊場仙板
一勇齋國芳画
彫竹

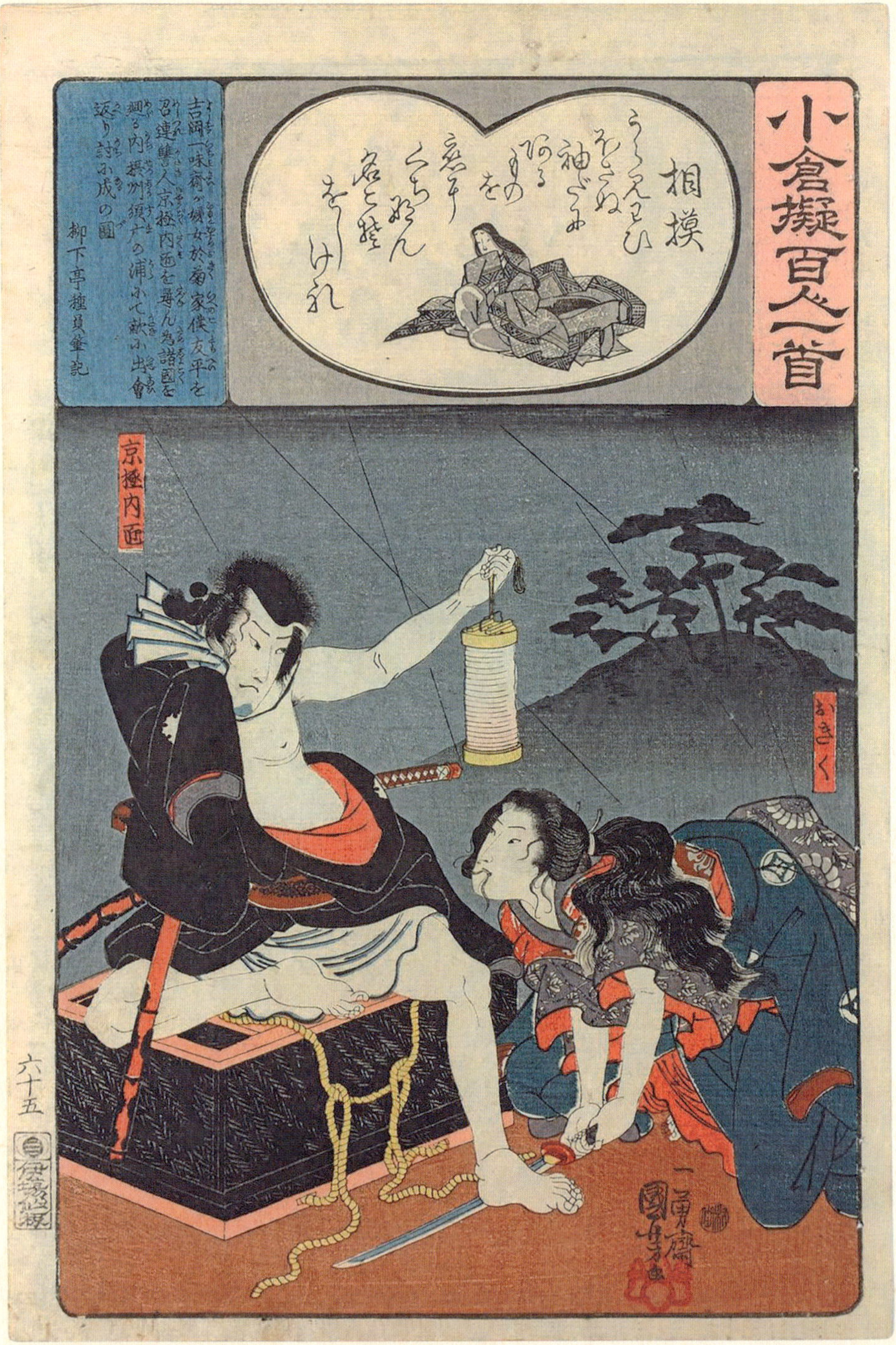

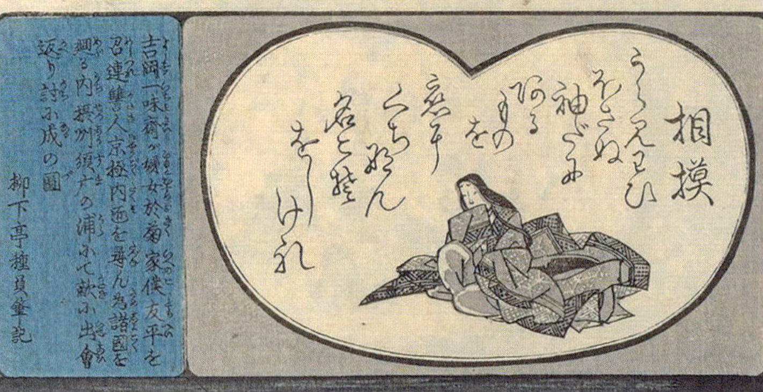
小倉擬百人一首
相模
うらみわび
ほさぬ袖だに
あるものを
恋にくちなん
名こそ惜し
けれ
京極内匠
おきく
六十五
一勇斎
国芳画
柳下亭種員誌

65

Lady Sagami

In bitter loneliness, my sleeves so wet
I think they'll never dry.
It's not for loss of love I suffer so,

but every fool upon
the street is laughing at my folly.

恨み侘び
ほさぬ袖だに
あるものを
恋に朽ちなむ
名こそ惜しけれ

urami wabi
hosanu sode da ni
aru mono wo
koi ni kuchinan
na koso oshi kere

66

Former Archbishop Gyoson

Surprised to find you, mountain cherry!
We should have pity on each other—
our lives are short

and well you know, for both of us,
no other friends are left.

諸共に
哀れと思へ
山桜
花より外に
知る人もなし

morotomo ni
aware to omoe
yamazakura
hana yori hoka ni
shiru hito mo nashi

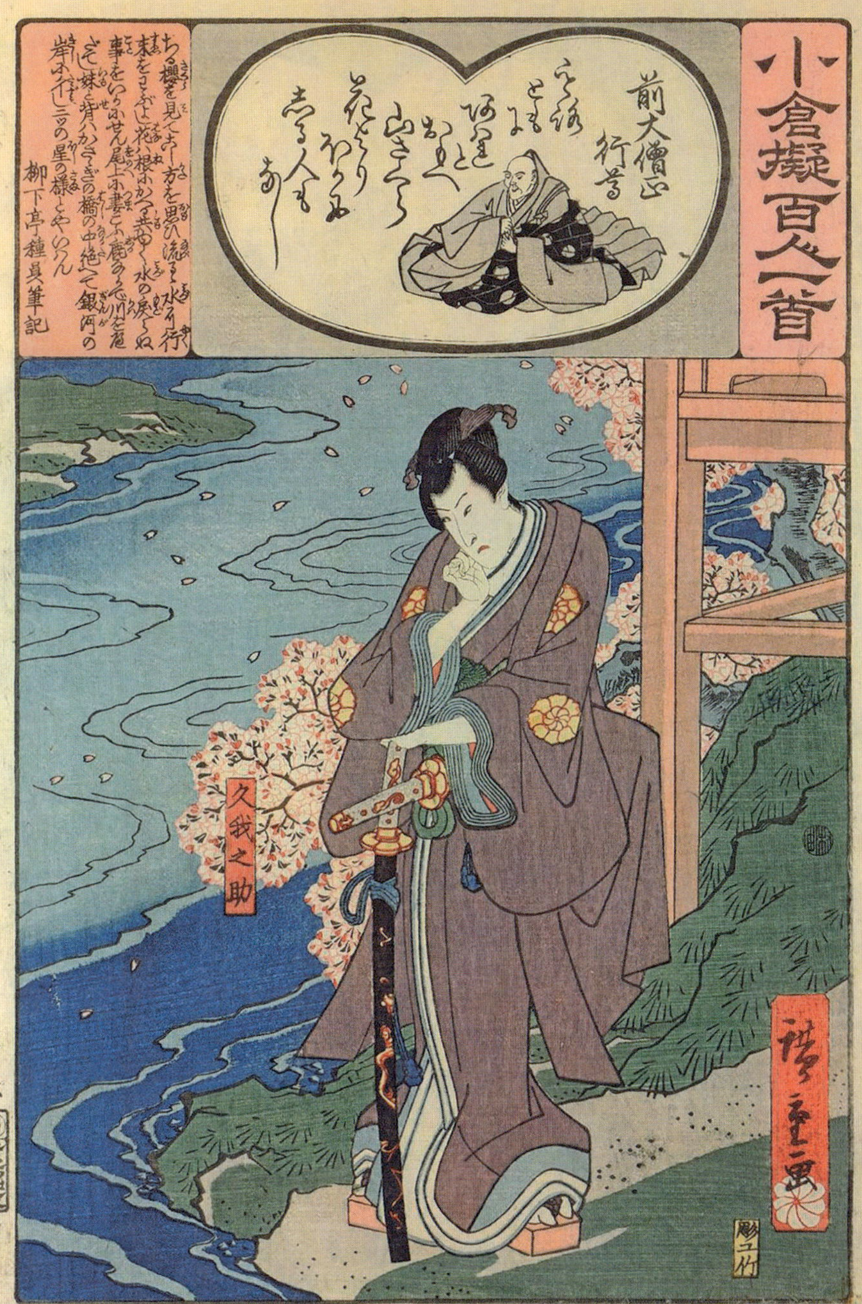
小倉擬百人一首
前大僧正行尊
もろともに
あはれと思へ
山さくら
花よりほかに
しる人もなし
久我之助
廣重画

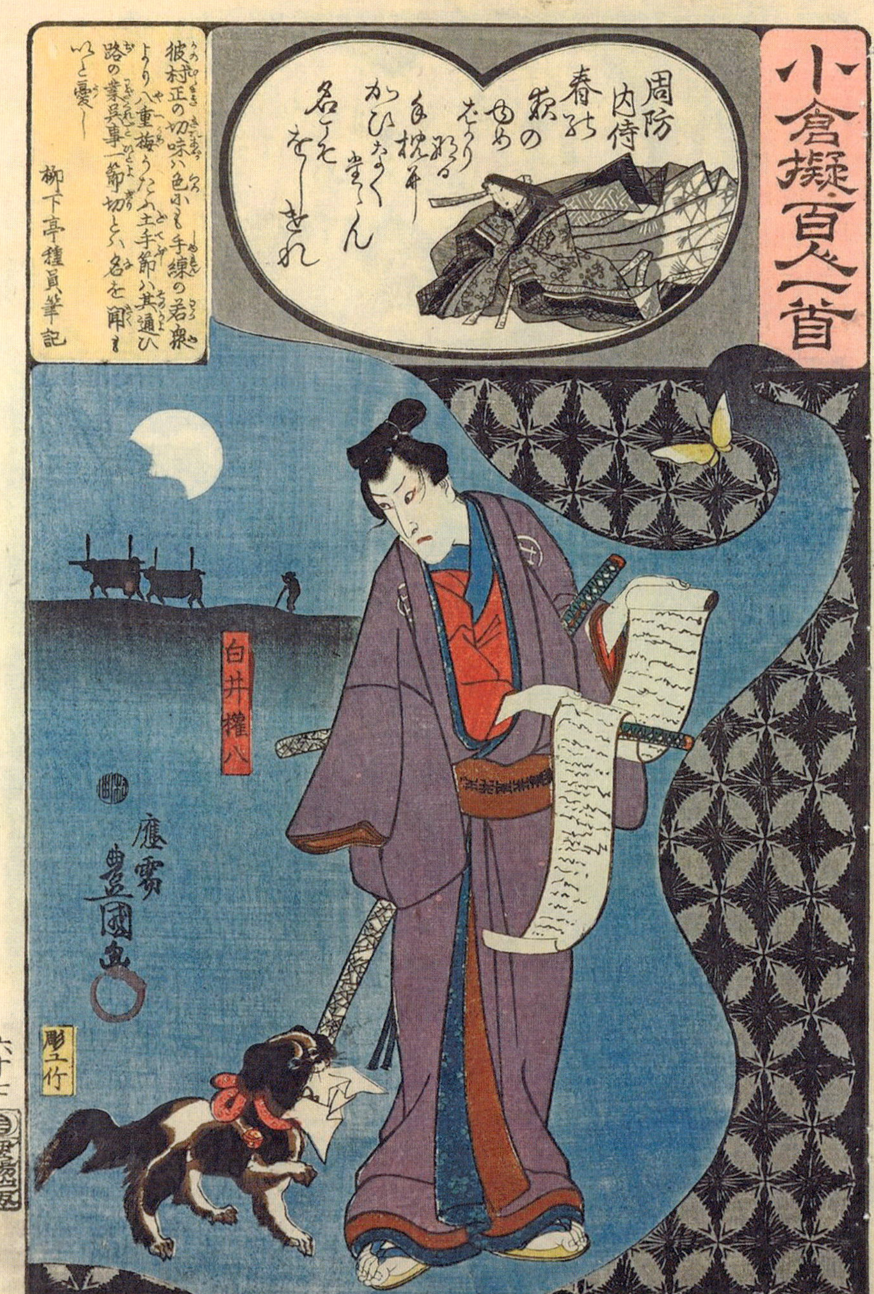

小倉擬百人一首

周防内侍
春の夜の
夢ばかりなる
手枕に
かひなく立たん
名こそを
しけれ

彼村正の切味は色々も手練の若衆
よりハ八重梅うたふ主手節ハ其通ひ
路の業呉事一節切とふ名を聞き
いとゞ愛し

柳下亭種員筆記

白井権八

応需
豊国画

彫工竹

六十七

67

Lady-in-Waiting Suwo

This fine spring night
invites me, as if it were a dream—

but if I so much as lay my head
upon your arm,
what rumors then would fly!

haru no yo no
yume bakari naru
tamakura ni
kainaku tatan
na koso oshi kere

68

Emperor Sanjo

I'm done with this treacherous
and fickle world—
if I must stay on longer,

the peaceful moon I see tonight
will only haunt my memories.

心
に
も
あ
ら
で
う
き
世
に
な
が
ら
へ
ば
恋
し
か
る
べ
き
夜
半
の
月
か
な

kokoro ni mo
arade ukiyo ni
nagaraeba
koishikaru beki
yowa no tsuki kana

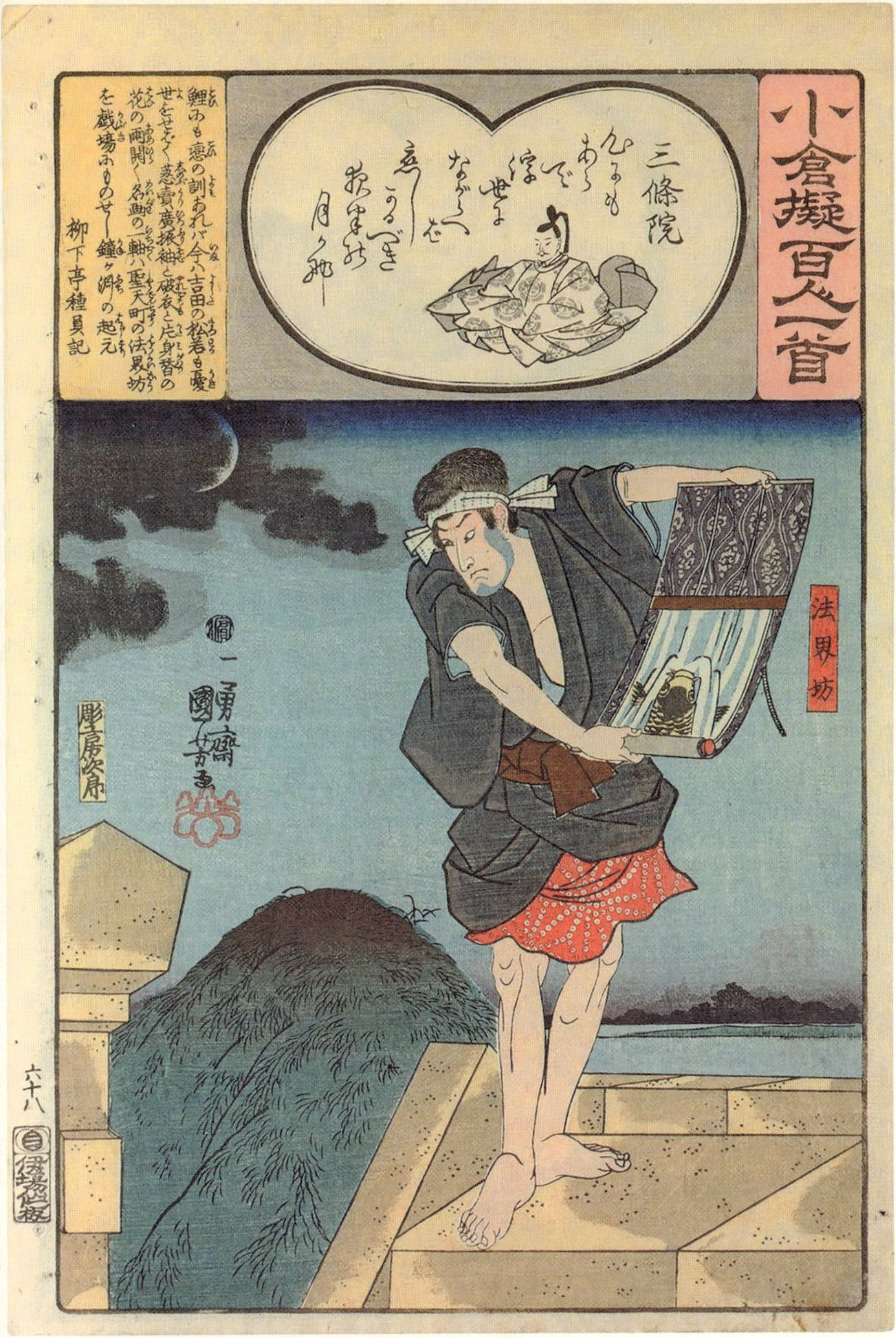

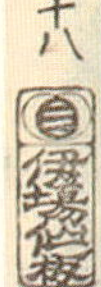

小倉擬百人一首
三條院
心にも
あらで
うき世に
ながらへば
こひしかるべき
夜半の月かな
鯉みも慈の訓あれば今ハ吉田の松若も憂
世をせそく慈賣廣振袖と破衣と忘身替の
花の兩開く名畫の一軸ハ聖天町の法界坊
を戯場ふものせ―鐘ヶ淵の起え
柳下亭種員記
法界坊
一勇齋國芳画
彫工房次郎
六十八

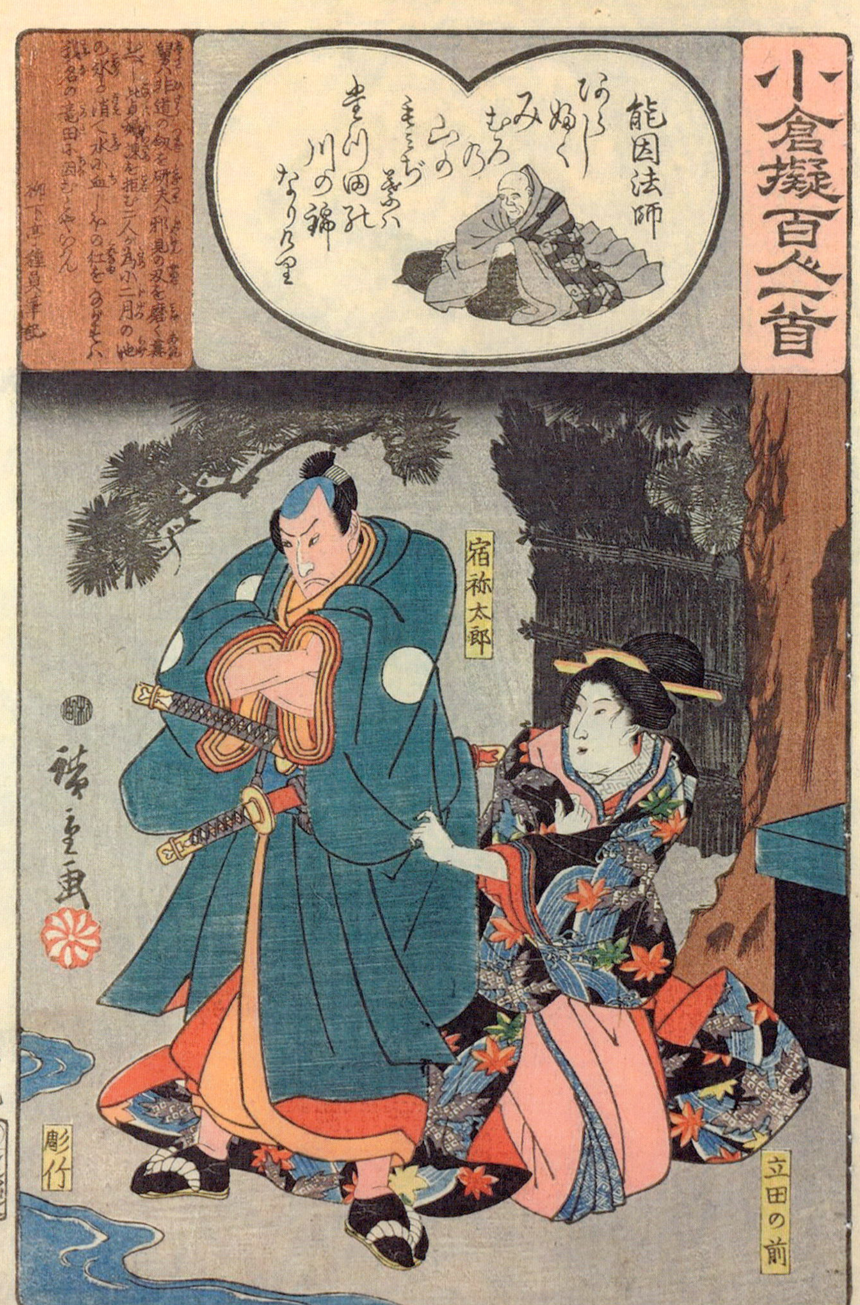
小倉擬百人一首
能因法師
あらし
ふく
み
むろ
の
山の
まきち
ゝきは
竜田の
川の錦
なりの里
宿祢太郎
立田の前
廣重画
彫竹
六十九
伊場仙板

69

The Priest Noin

Blown off Mount Mimuro
by stormy autumn winds—

it seems the maple leaves
have laid a rich red carpet
over the flowing Tatsuta.

嵐吹く
三室の山の
もみぢ葉は
龍田の川の
錦なりけり

arashi fuku

mimuro no yama no

momijiba wa

tatsuta no kawa no

nishiki nari keri

70

The Priest Ryosen

My solitude so great
I leave my simple cell to walk about,

but everywhere I look it is the same—
rusted leaves all scattered on the ground
in the gloom of autumn's dusk.

寂しさに
宿を立ち出て
眺むれば
いづこも同じ
秋の夕暮

sabishisa ni
yado wo tachi idete
nagamureba
izuko mo onaji
aki no yugure

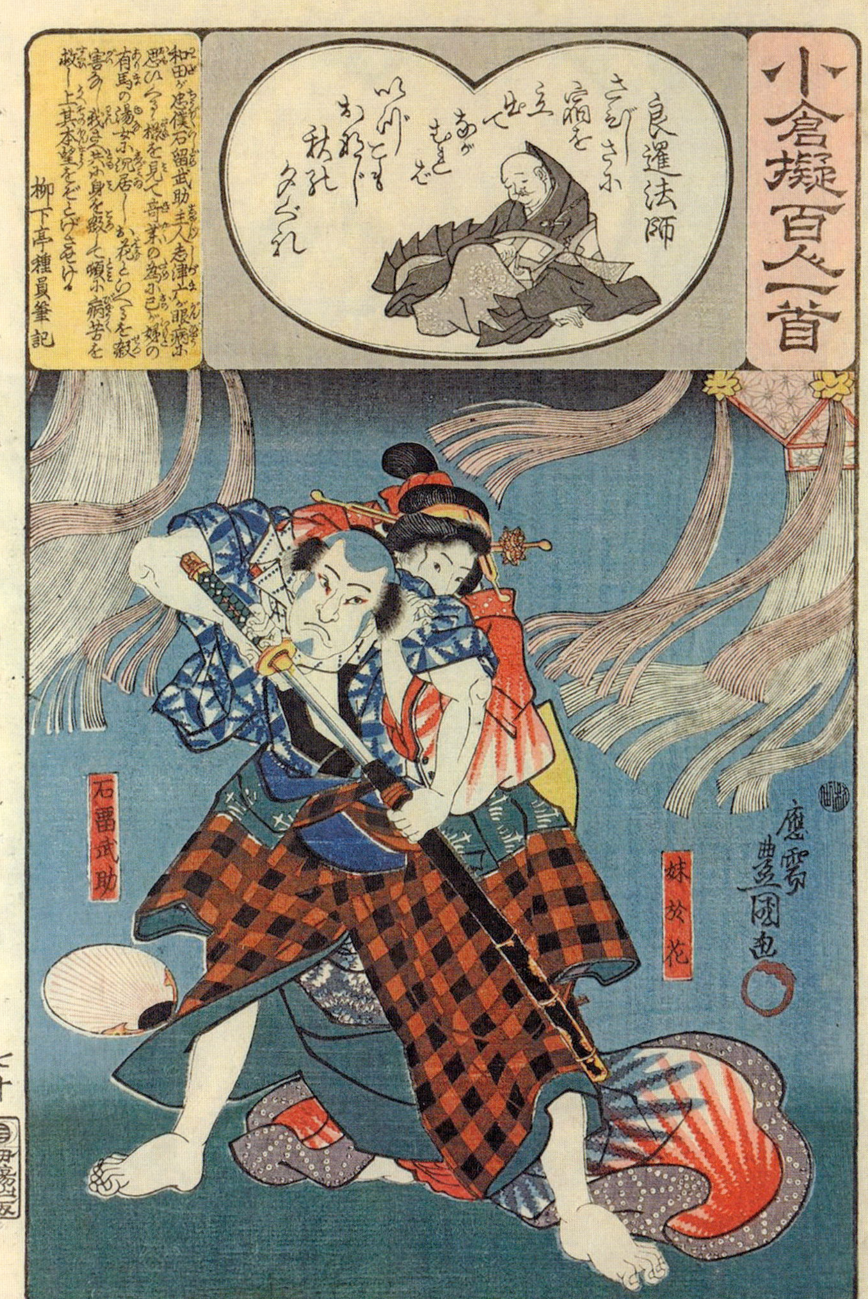

小倉擬百人一首
良暹法師
さびしさに
宿を立出て
ながむれば
いづこもおなじ
秋の夕ぐれ
和田が忠僕石留武助　主人志津太が眼病を
悪ひ〳〵樣を見て毒素の爲ひ己が姉の
有馬の湯女ふ沈居し　か樣とのくくを寂
害の　我さ共か身を蹴して頓ふ病苦を
救し上其本望をどとげきせけ
柳下亭種員筆記
石留武助
妹於花
應需
豊國画
七十
伊場仙板

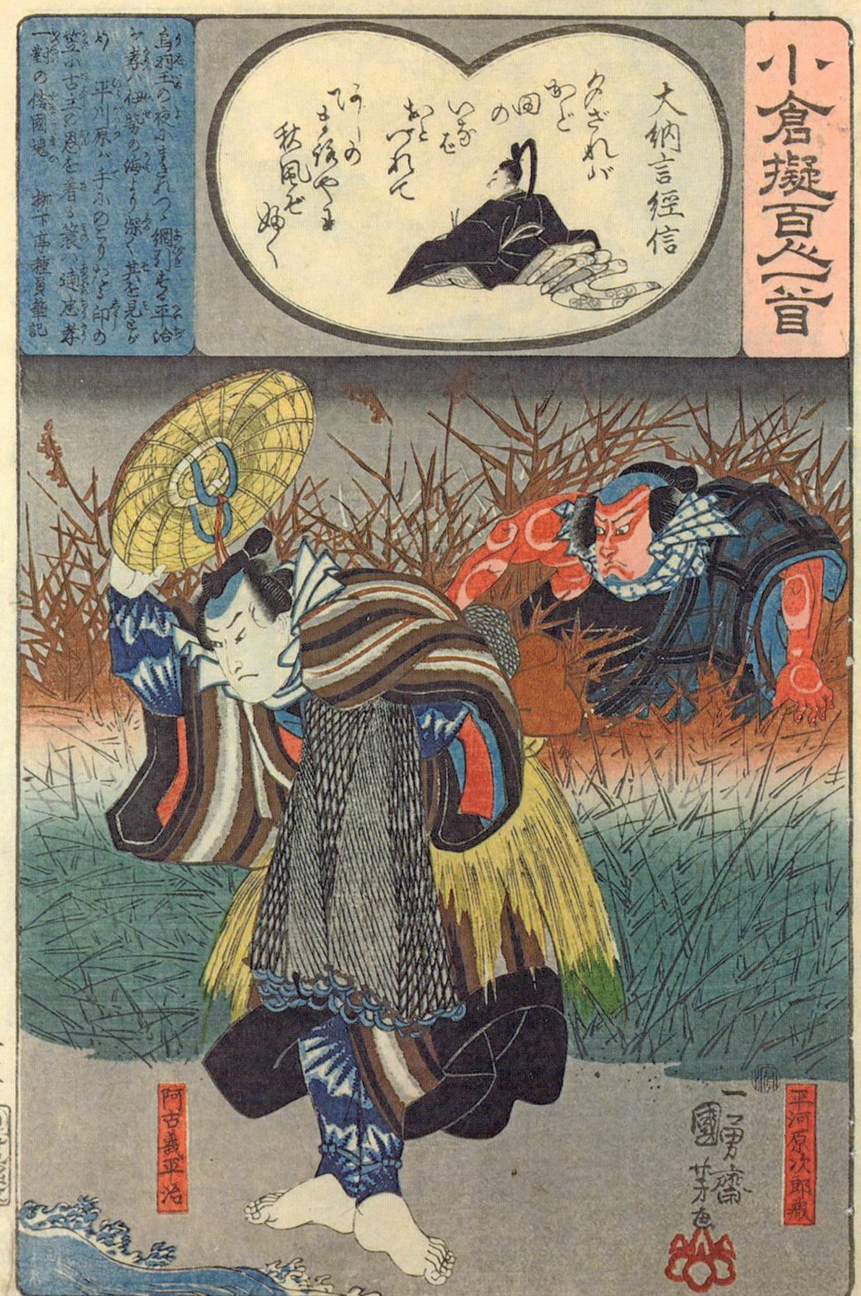
小倉擬百人一音
大納言経信
夕されば
門田の
稲葉
おとづれて
あしのまろやに
秋風ぞ吹く
七十一
阿古義平治
平河原次郎藏
一勇齋
國芳画

71

Minamoto no Tsunenobu

As dark descends,
a gentle autumn wind
whispers through the rice out in the fields,

comes to visit at my round reed hut
rustling its thatch.

夕されば
門田の稲葉
おとづれて
あしのまろやに
秋風ぞ吹く

yu sareba
kadota no inaba
otozurete
ashi no maroya ni
akikaze zo fuku

72

Lady Kii

I've listened to your high-sounding phrases,
inconstant as the waves that force themselves
upon Takashi—now go away.

You'll never sweep me off the beach
or drench my sleeves with salty spray.

音に聞く
高師の浜の
あだ浪は
かけじや袖の
ぬれもこそすれ

oto ni kiku
takashi no hama no
adanami wa
kakeji ya sode no
nure mo koso sure

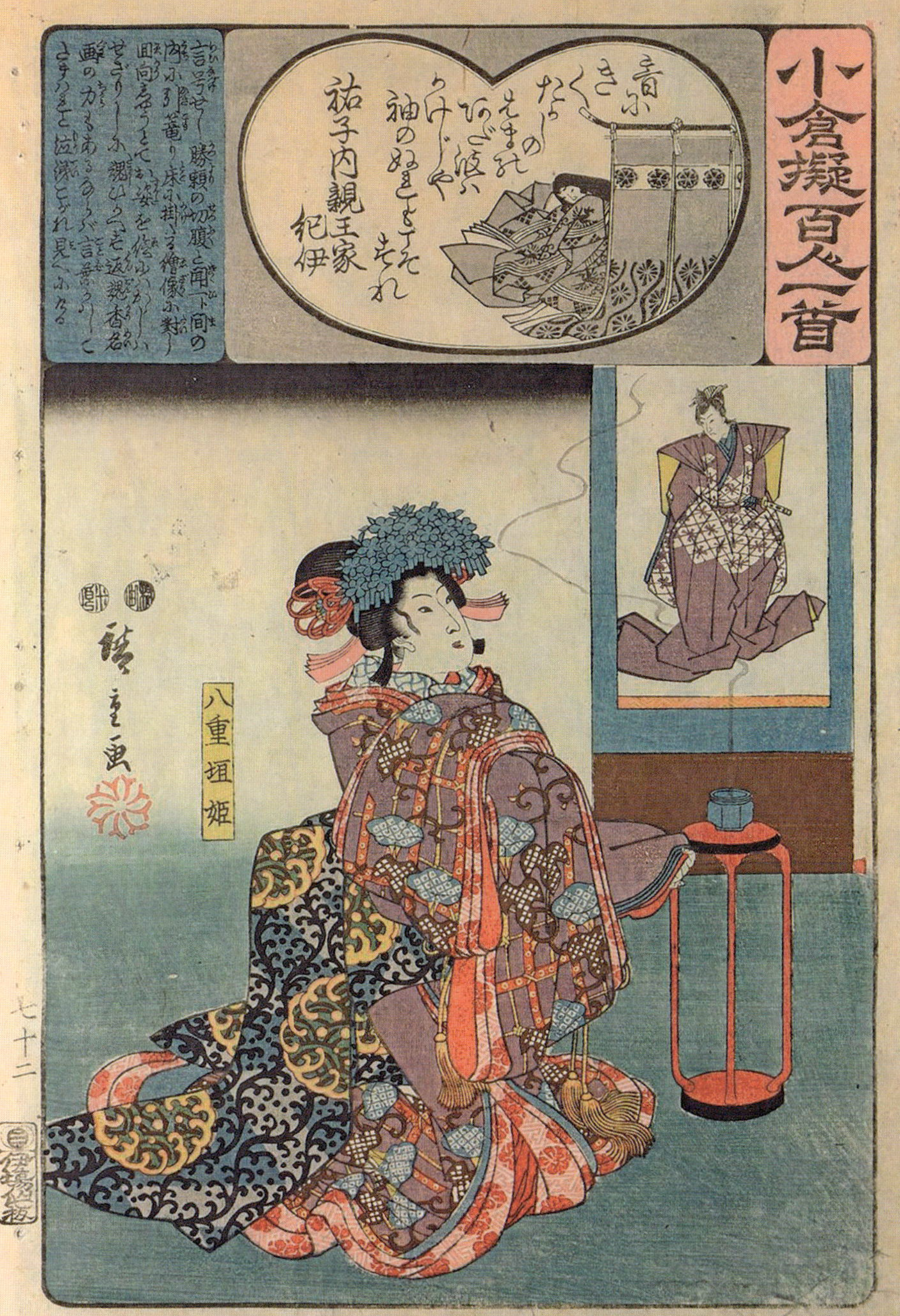
小倉擬百人一首

音にきく
たかしの
はまの
あだ浪は
かけじや
袖のぬれもこそすれ
祐子内親王家
紀伊

八重垣姫

広重画

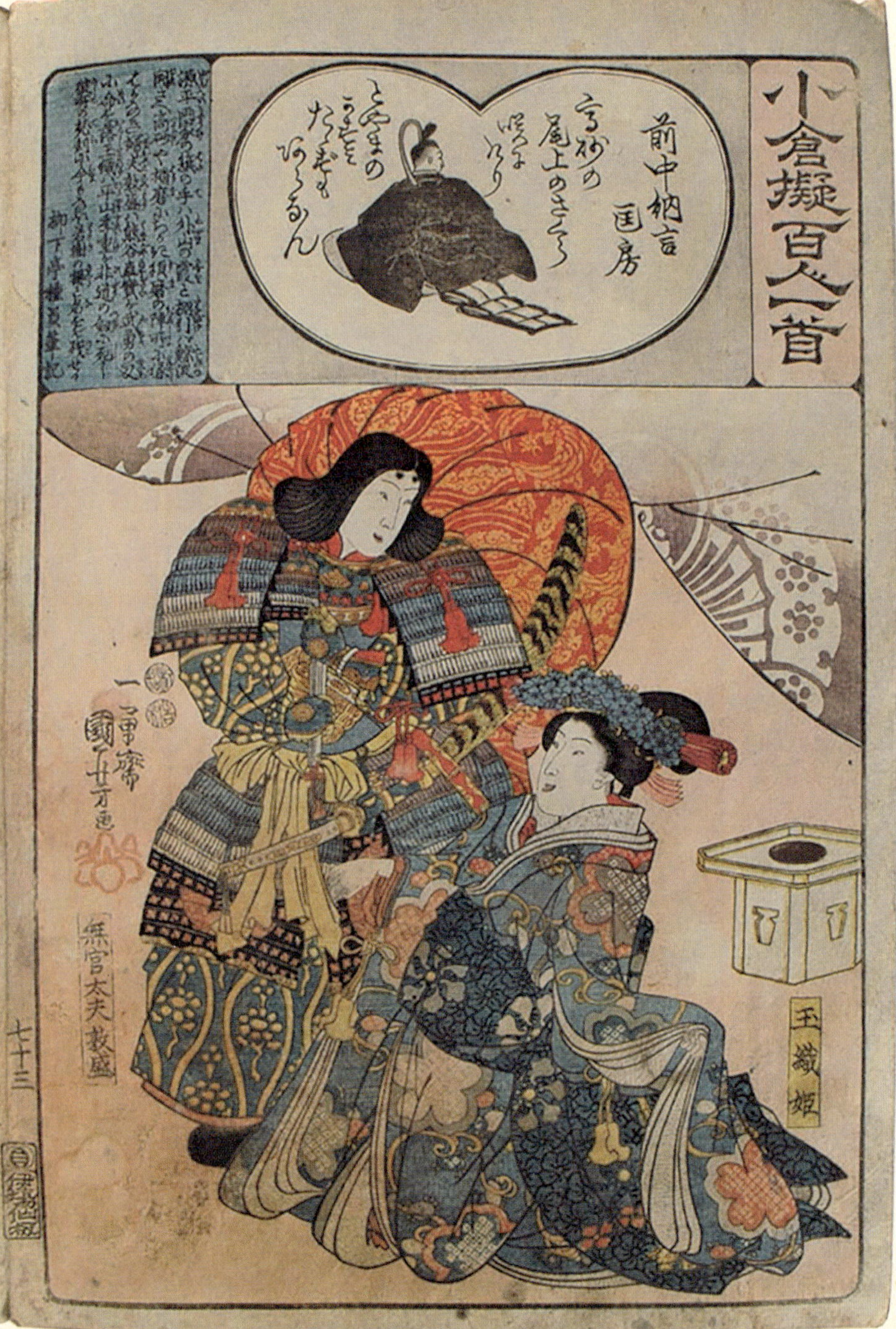
小倉擬百人一首
前中納言 匡房
高砂の
尾上のさくら
咲きに
けり
とやまの
かすみ
たゝずも
あらなん
一勇齋
國芳世万画
無官太夫敦盛
玉織姫
七十三

73

Oe no Masafusa

Below that mountain peak,
the cherries of its lower meadows
coming into bloom—

let's pray the mists arising from beneath
do not becloud our view.

高砂の
尾の上の桜
咲きにけり
外山の霞
立たずもあらなむ

takasago no
onoe no sakura
saki ni keri
toyama no kasumi
tatazu mo aranan

74

Minamoto no Toshiyori

Unsuspecting, I was shocked to feel
the bitter torrent of her scorn ferociously descend—

what was the Goddess thinking
to unleash Hatsuse's blasts upon me
when I only prayed for love?

うかりける
人を初瀬の
山おろし
はげしかれとは
祈らぬものを

ukari keru
hito wo hatsuse no
yama oroshi
hageshikare to wa
inoranu mono wo

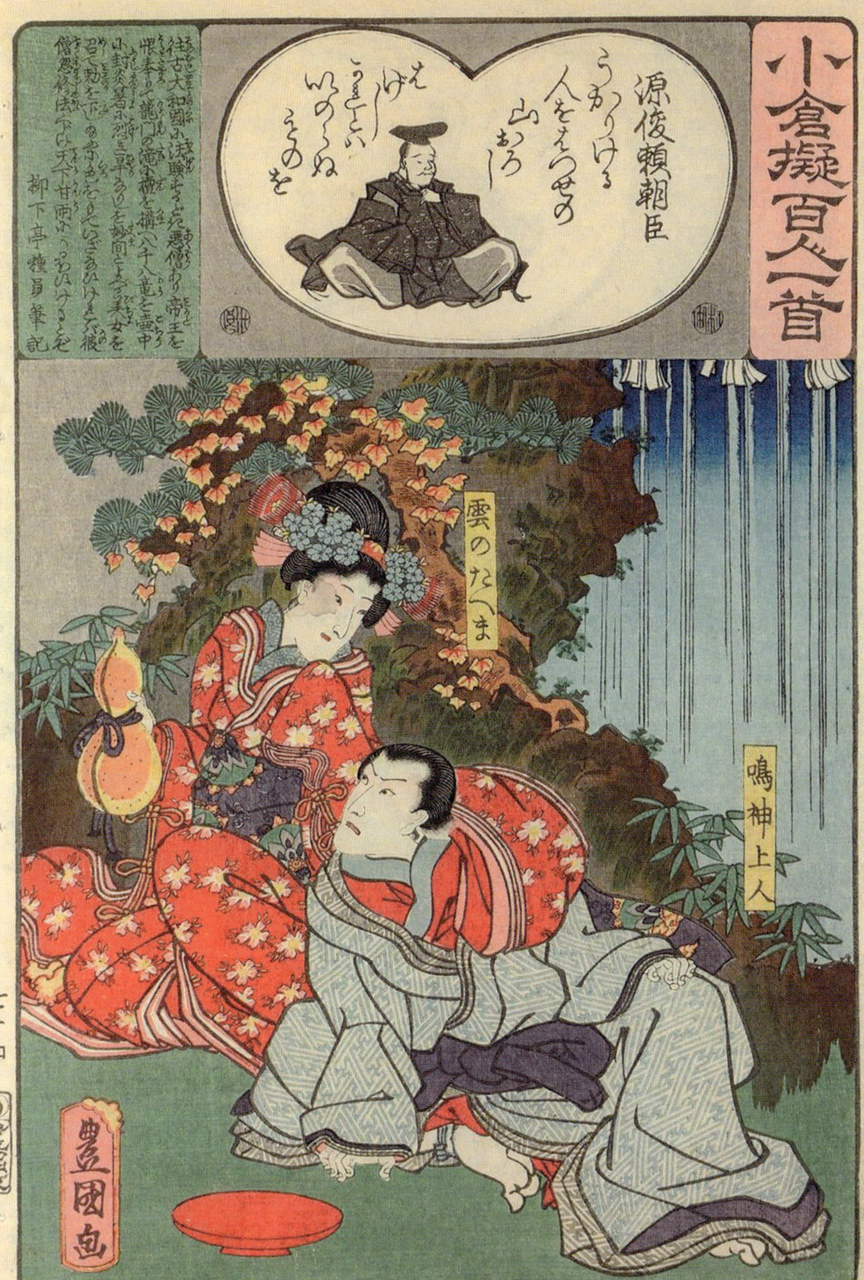

小倉擬百人一首
源俊頼朝臣
うかりける人をはつせの山おろし
はげしかれとはいのらぬものを
雲のたへま
鳴神上人
七十四
豊國画

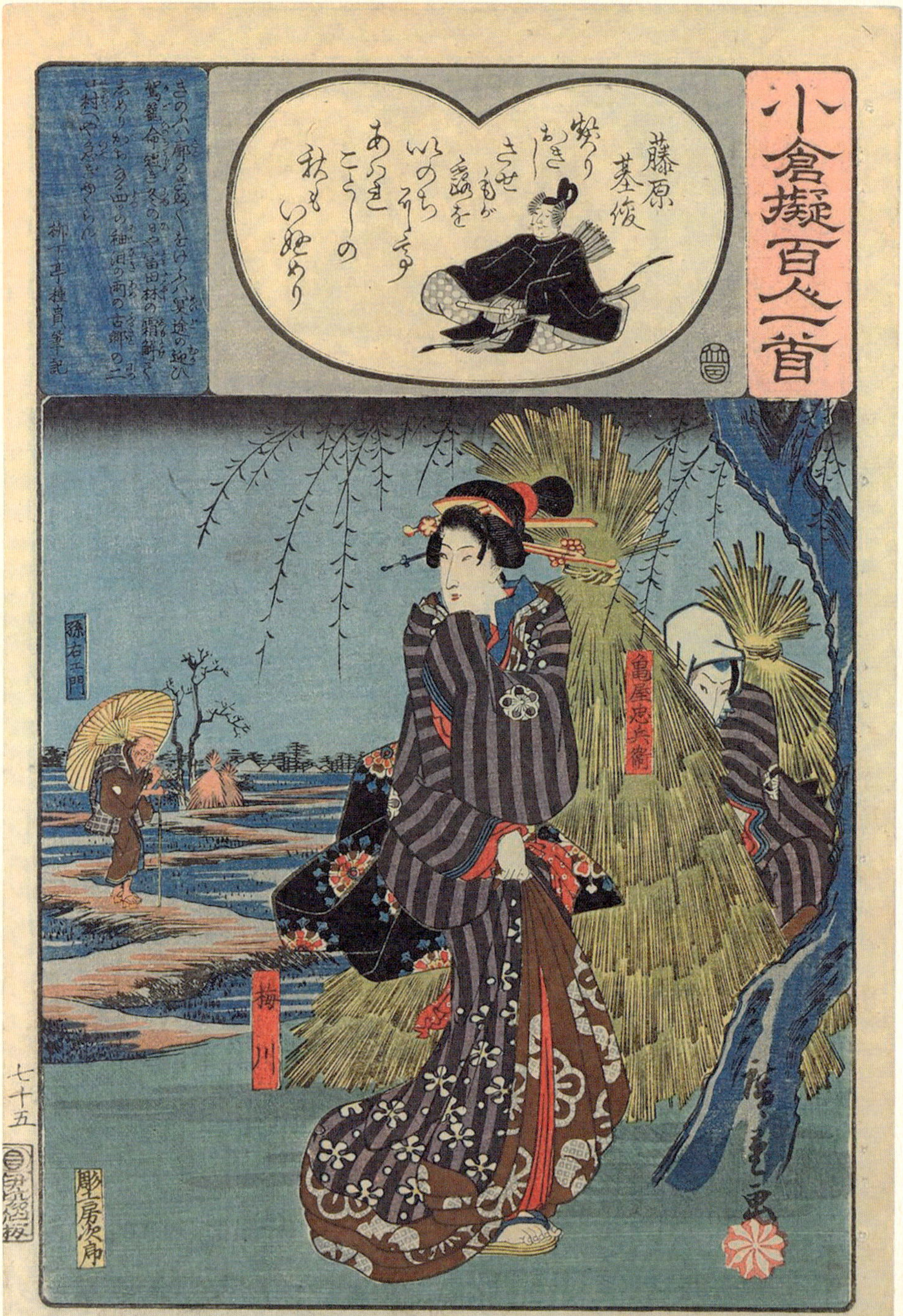

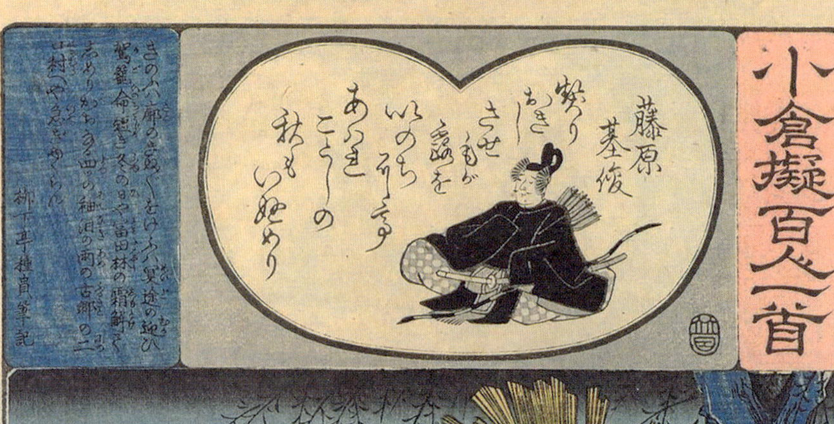
小倉擬百人一首
藤原
基俊
契りおき
させしもが
露をいのち
にて
あはれことしの
秋もいぬめり
柳下亭種員筆記
孫右衛門
亀屋忠兵衛
梅川
豊房次扉
七十五

75

Fujiwara no Mototoshi

I hung on your promise
As sasemo grass depends on autumn dew
for very life—

but the dew did not descend,
as this season too will shortly pass.

chigiri okishi
sasemo ga tsuyu wo
inochi ni te
aware kotoshi no
aki mo inumeri

76

Fujiwara no Tadamichi

Rowing out on the empty ocean
I look about
but cannot distinguish the horizon—

which is billowed cloud
and which is shining wave?

沖つ白波
雲居にまよふ
久方の
漕ぎ出でて見れば
わたの原

wata no hara
kogi idete mireba
hisakata no
kumoi ni mayou
okitsu shiranami

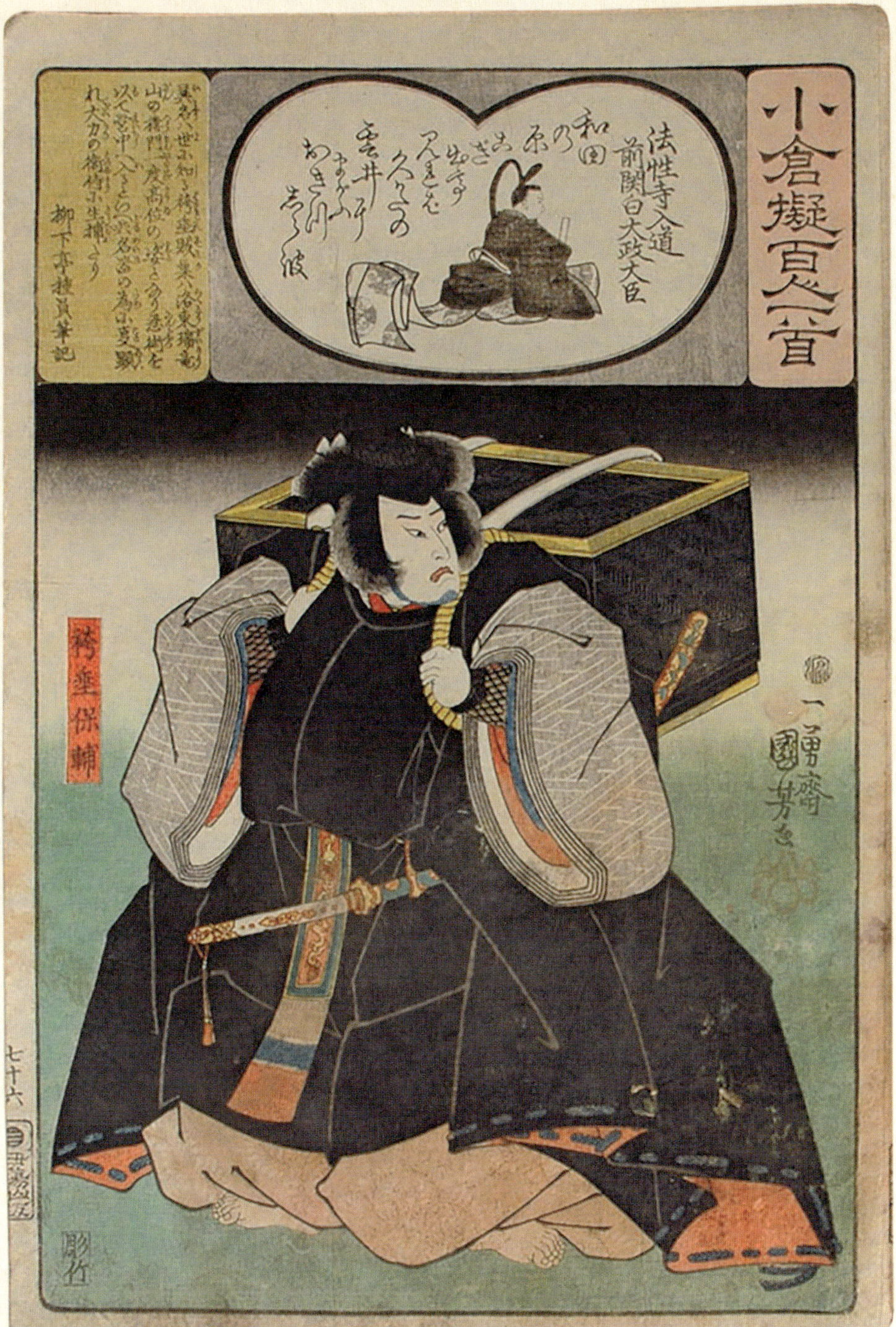

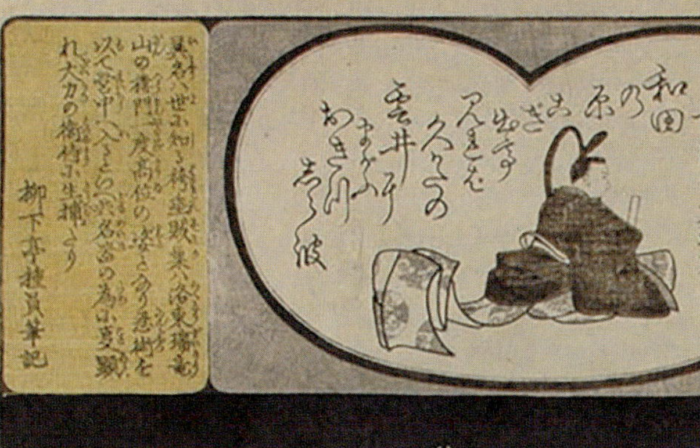

小倉擬百人一首

法性寺入道
前関白太政大臣

和田の原
こぎ出でて
みれば
ひさかたの
雲井に
まがふ
おきつ
しら波

袴垂保輔

一勇齋
國芳画

七十六

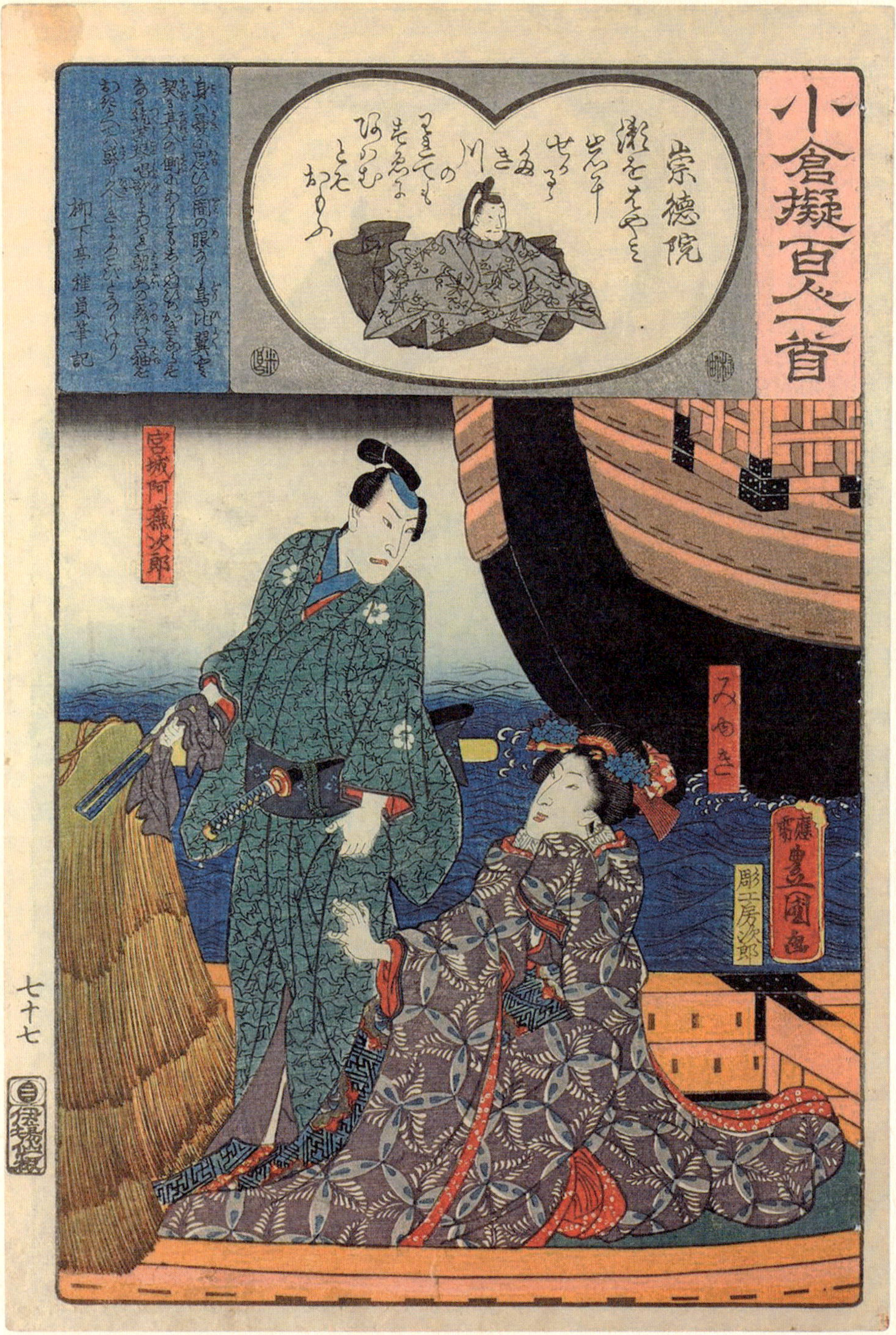

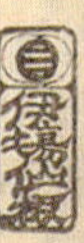

小倉擬百人一首

崇徳院

瀬をはやみ
岩にせかるる
滝川の
われても末に
あはむとぞ思ふ

身はうつせみの思ひの窓の眼う─鳥池翼
契る其人の断ふありとも
柳下亭 種員筆記

宮城阿蘇次郎

みゆき

応需 豊国画

彫工 房次郎

七十七

Retired Emperor Sutoku

Waters cascading down a mountain stream
are often split in two by boulders,
forcing them to flow in rivulets around.

Yet no matter how the streams are torn apart,
in the end they find a way, coming back together.

瀬を早み
岩にせかるる
滝川の
われても末に
逢はむとぞ思ふ

se wo hayami
iwa ni sekaruru
takigawa no
warete mo sue ni
awan to zo omou

78

Minamoto no Kanemasa

The plovers skipping nightly
to and from the island of Awaji
sadly cry—

and many times must waken
the Suma border guards.

淡路島
かよふ千鳥の
鳴く声に
幾夜寝覚めぬ
須磨の関守

awaji shima
kayou chidori no
naku koe ni
ikuyo nezamenu
suma no sekimori

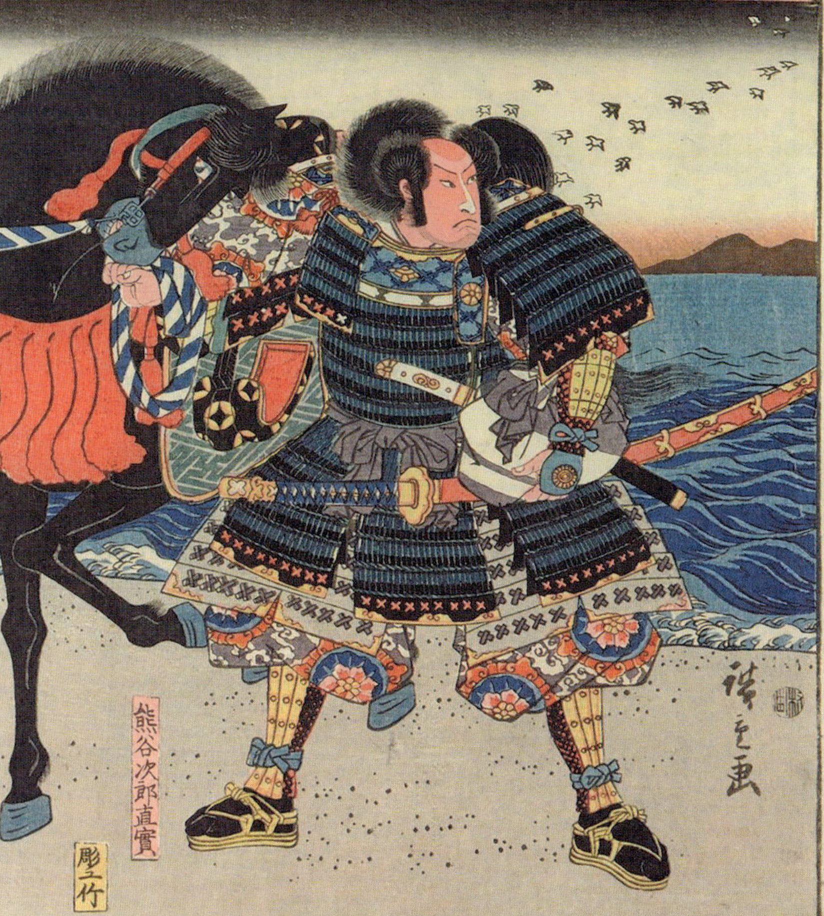

小倉擬百人一首

源兼昌
あはぢしま
かよふ
千鳥の
なく声に
いく夜ねざめぬ
須磨の関守

法がこの花の敦盛を是非なく討
も武門のあわひさ〳〵ふたけき
熊谷も悲歎の涙ふるゝふける
柳下亭種員筆記

七十八
伊場仙板

熊谷次郎直實

彫工竹

広重画

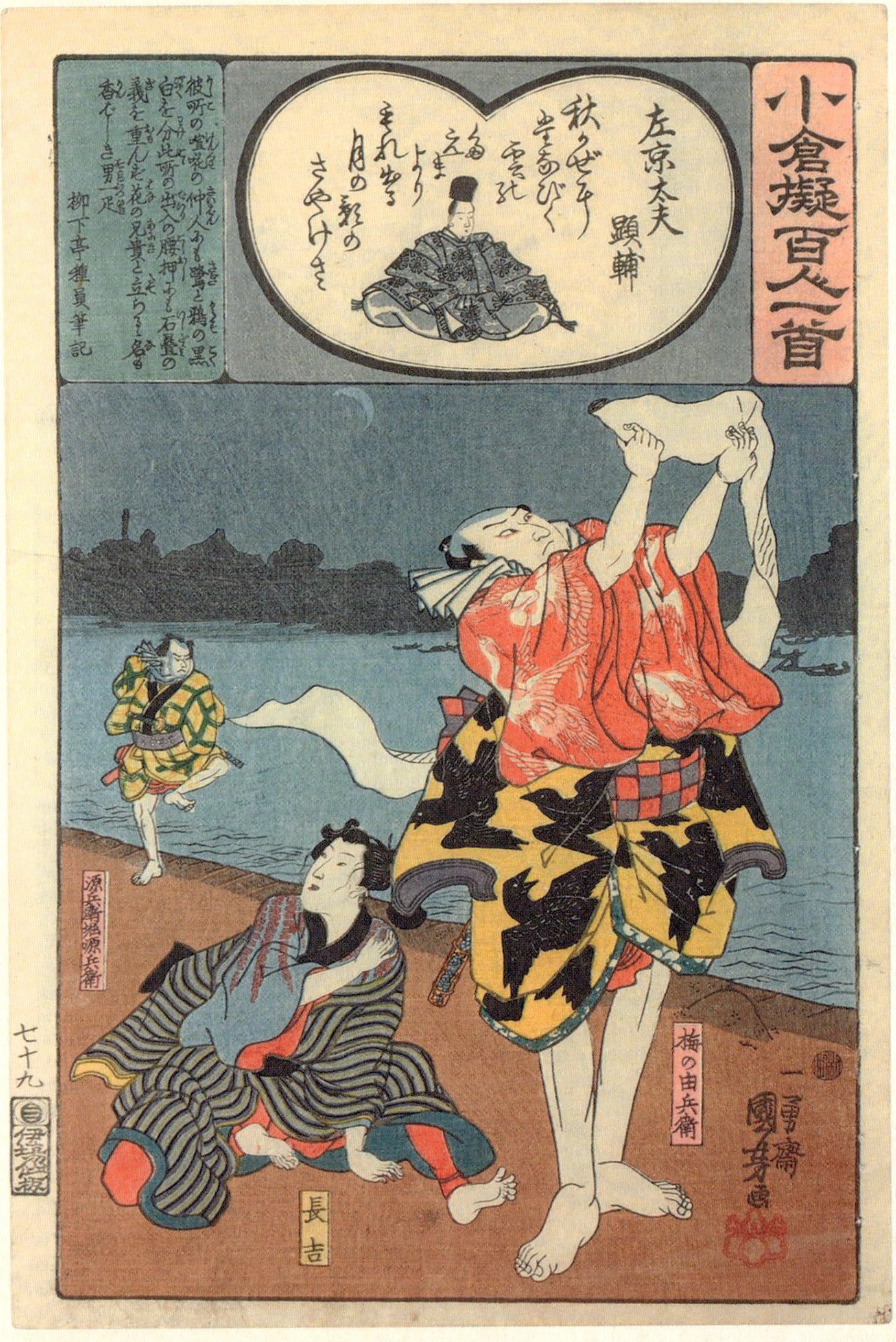

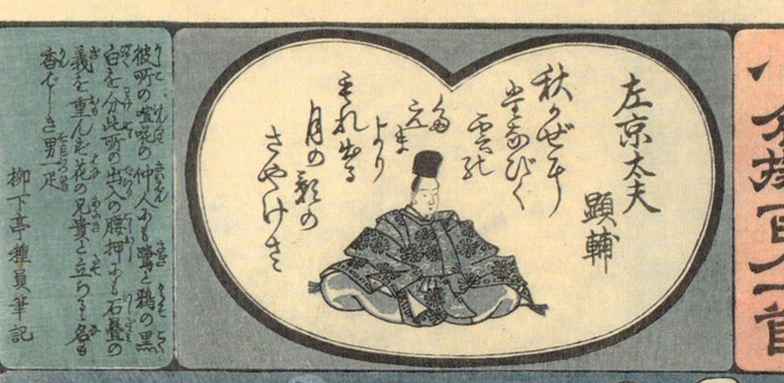

小倉擬百人一首

左京太夫　顕輔

秋風に
たなびく
雲の
たえま
より
もれ出づる
月の影の
さやけさ

彼の螢蛎の仲人をも譽と鶯の黒
白を分ち此所の出入の腰押もて石畳の
義を重んぞ花の兄貴と立る一名
酒ぐーと男一足
柳下亭種員筆記

源兵衛堀源兵衛
梅の由兵衛
長吉
一勇斎國芳画

七十九
伊場仙板

79

Akisuke

Lazy wisps of cloud linger about the sky
nudged gently by the autumn breeze—

but here and there a gap, and out from one of these
the hidden moon revealed clear and round,
illuminating both heaven and earth.

秋風に
たなびく雲の
絶え間より
もれ出づる月の
影のさやけさ

akikaze ni
tanabiku kumo no
taema yori
more izuru tsuki no
kage no sayakesa

80
Lady Horikawa

Brooding over his intentions.
Eternal—did he really mean it?

Thoughts and feelings in total disarray
like my long black hair strewn across the pillow
that morning he departed.

長からむ
心もしらず
黒髪の
みだれてけさは
ものをこそ思へ

nagakaran
kokoro mo shirazu
kurokami no
midarete kesa wa
mono wo koso omoe

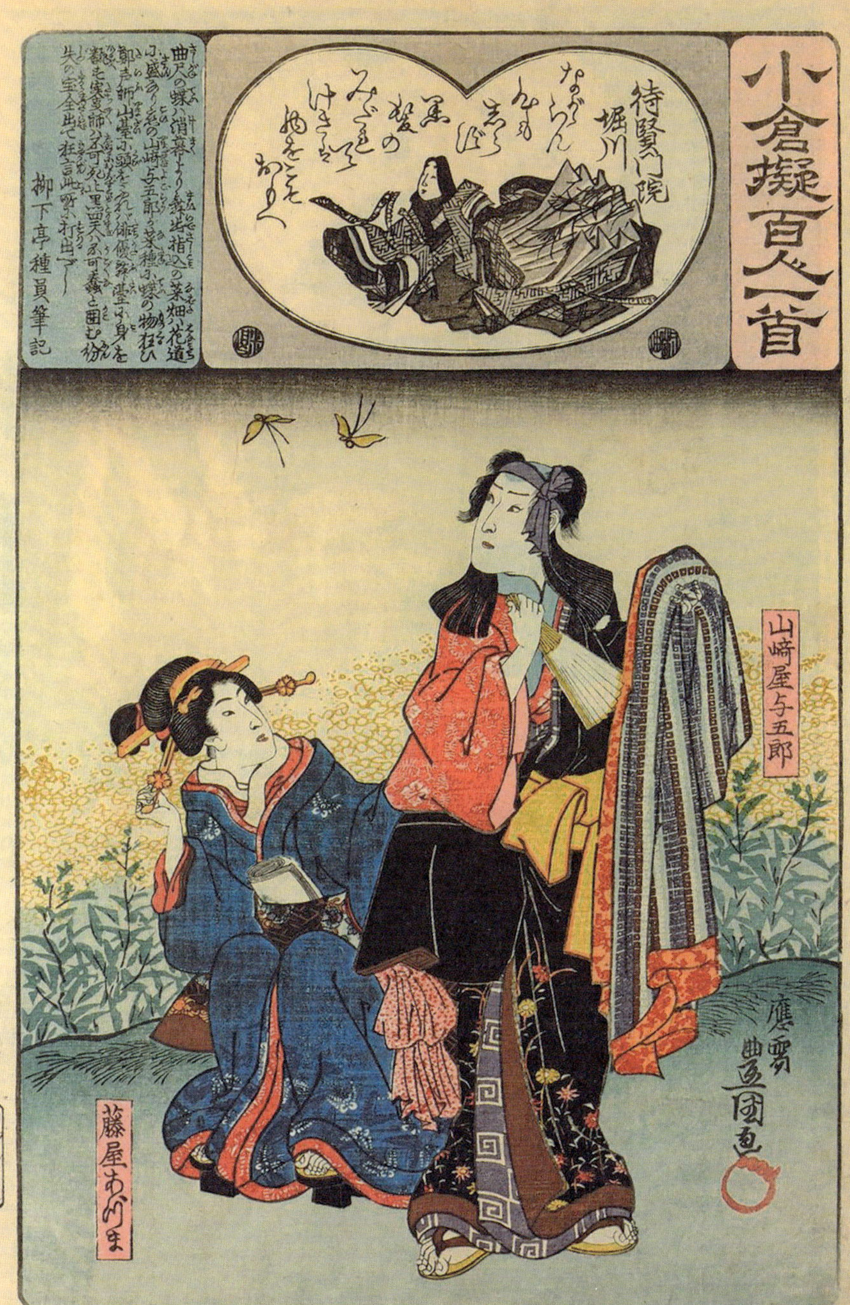

小倉擬百人一首
待賢門院堀川
ながからん心もしらず黒髪のみだれてけさは物をこそおもへ
山崎屋与五郎
藤屋あづま
應需 豊国画
八十

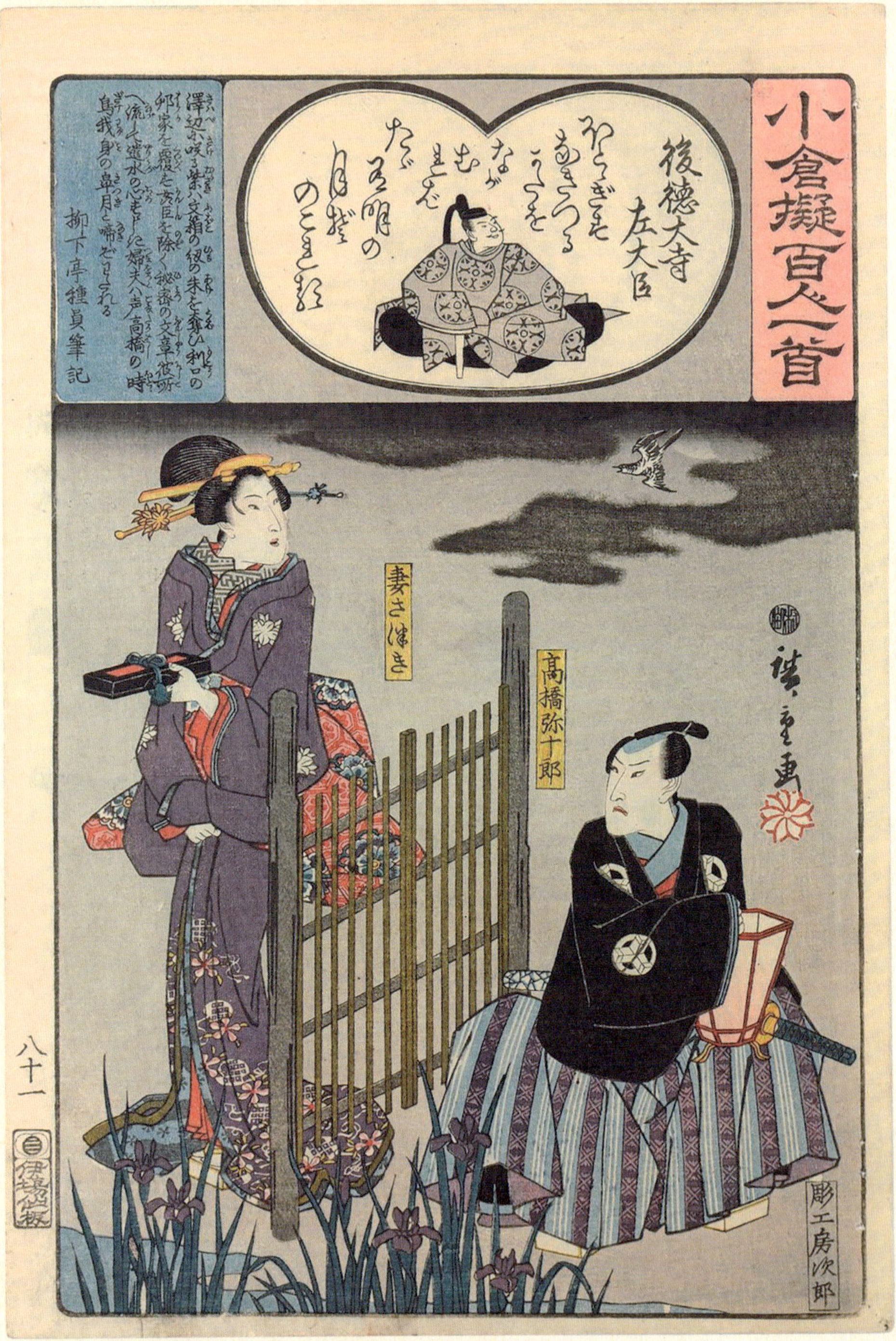

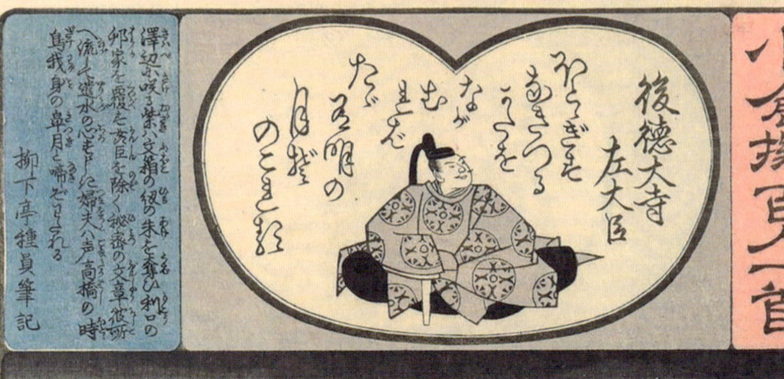

小倉擬百人一首

後德大寺左大臣

ほとゝぎす
なきつる
かたを
ながむれば
たゞ有明の
月ぞのこれる

澤辺に咲る紫は文絹の絞の朱を奪ひ利口の
郷家を覆ぞ亥巨を除く秘密の文章彼所
一流し遺水の心もとに婦夫ハ声ハ高橋の時
鳥我身の皐月と啼ぞらる

柳下亭種員筆記

妻さゆき

高橋弥十郎

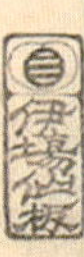

八十一

81

Gotoku Daiji Sanesada

I search the part of sky
from where the cuckoo's call came clear—

but only the morning moon
is lingering about.

ほととぎす
鳴きつる方を
眺むれば
ただ有明けの
月ぞ残れる

hototogisu
nakitsuru kata wo
nagamureba
tada ariake no
tsuki zo nokoreru

82

The Monk Doin

That life is but illusion
and thinking merely futile,
I do maintain—

but why then these tears
I cannot stop from falling?

思ひわび
さても命
はあるものを
憂きに堪へぬは
涙なりけり

omoi wabi
satemo inochi
wa aru mono wo
uki ni taenu wa
namida nari keri

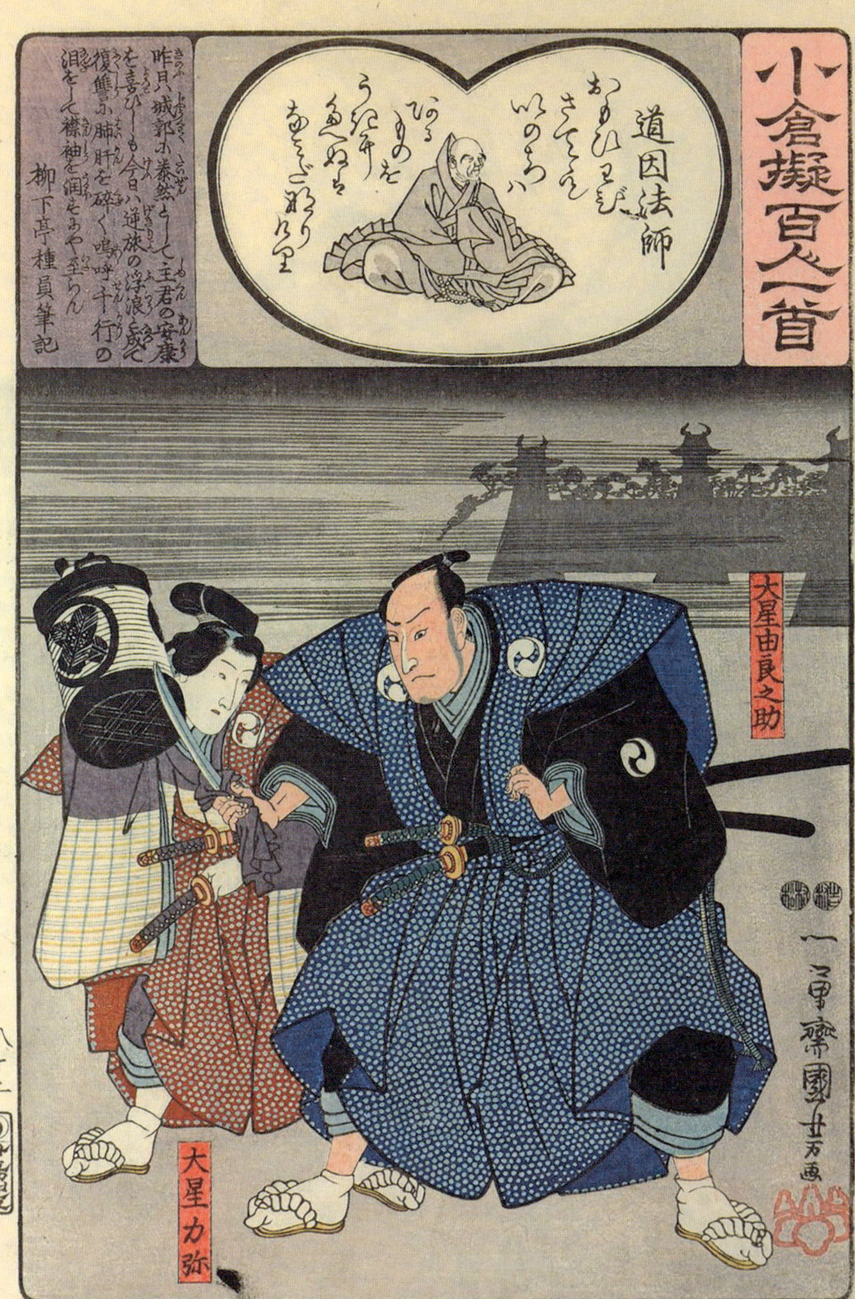
小倉擬百人一首
道因法師
おもひわび
さても命は
あるものを
うきにたへ
ぬは
涙なりけり
大星由良之助
大星力弥
一勇齋國芳画
八十二
伊場仙板

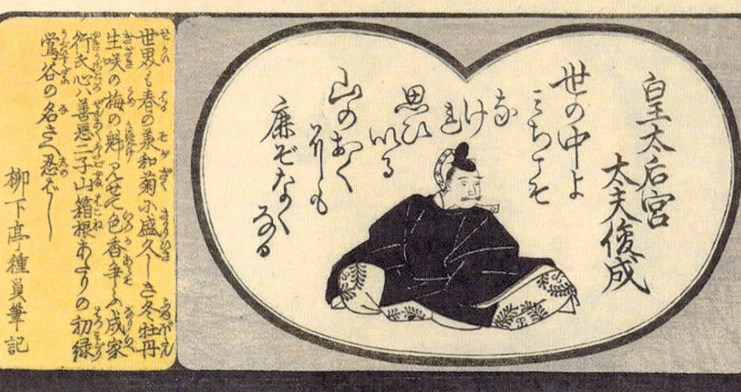

世界も春の兼和菊小盛久ーき冬牡丹
生咲の梅の料つゞせど色香幸ミ成家
竹氏心ハ善悪三子山箱根めぐりの初録
鶯名の名さ々忍ぶ
　　　柳下亭・種員筆記

八十三

83

Fujiwara no Toshinari

There is no road
to take me from this vale of tears—

for even here,
deep in mountain splendor, the deer cry out
as if lamenting their mortality.

世の中よ
道こそなけれ
思ひ入る
山の奥にも
鹿ぞ鳴くなる

yo no naka yo
michi koso nakere
omoi iru
yama no oku ni mo
shika zo naku naru

187

84

Fujiwara no Kiyosuke

I will survive and persevere—
these current agonies
becoming fond and secret memories

as early times of tribulation
now I lovingly recall.

ながらへば
またこの頃や
しのばれむ
憂しと見し世ぞ
今は恋しき

nagaraeba
mata konogoro ya
shinobaren
ushi to mishi yo zo
ima wa koishiki

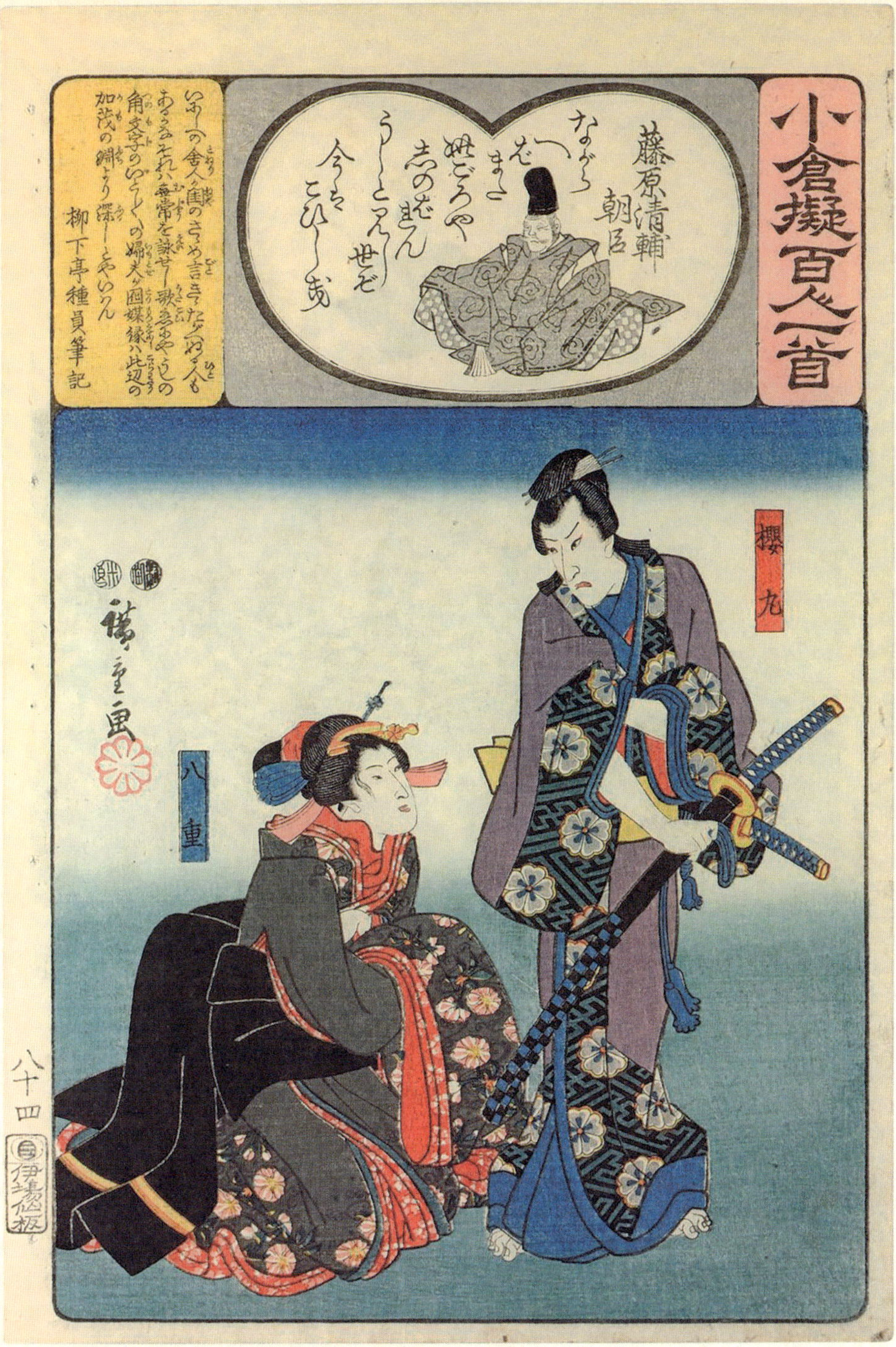

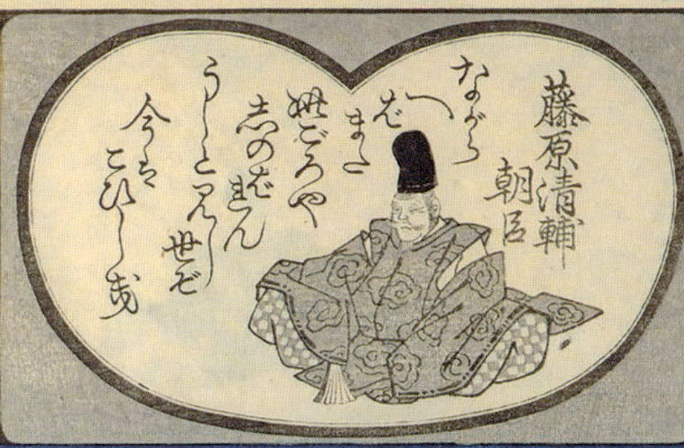
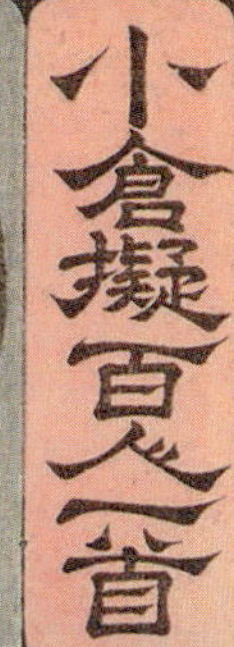
小倉擬百人一首
藤原清輔朝臣
ながらへば
またこのごろや
しのばれん
うしと見し世ぞ
今はこひしき
柳下亭種員筆記
櫻女
九
八重
廣重画
八十四
伊場仙板

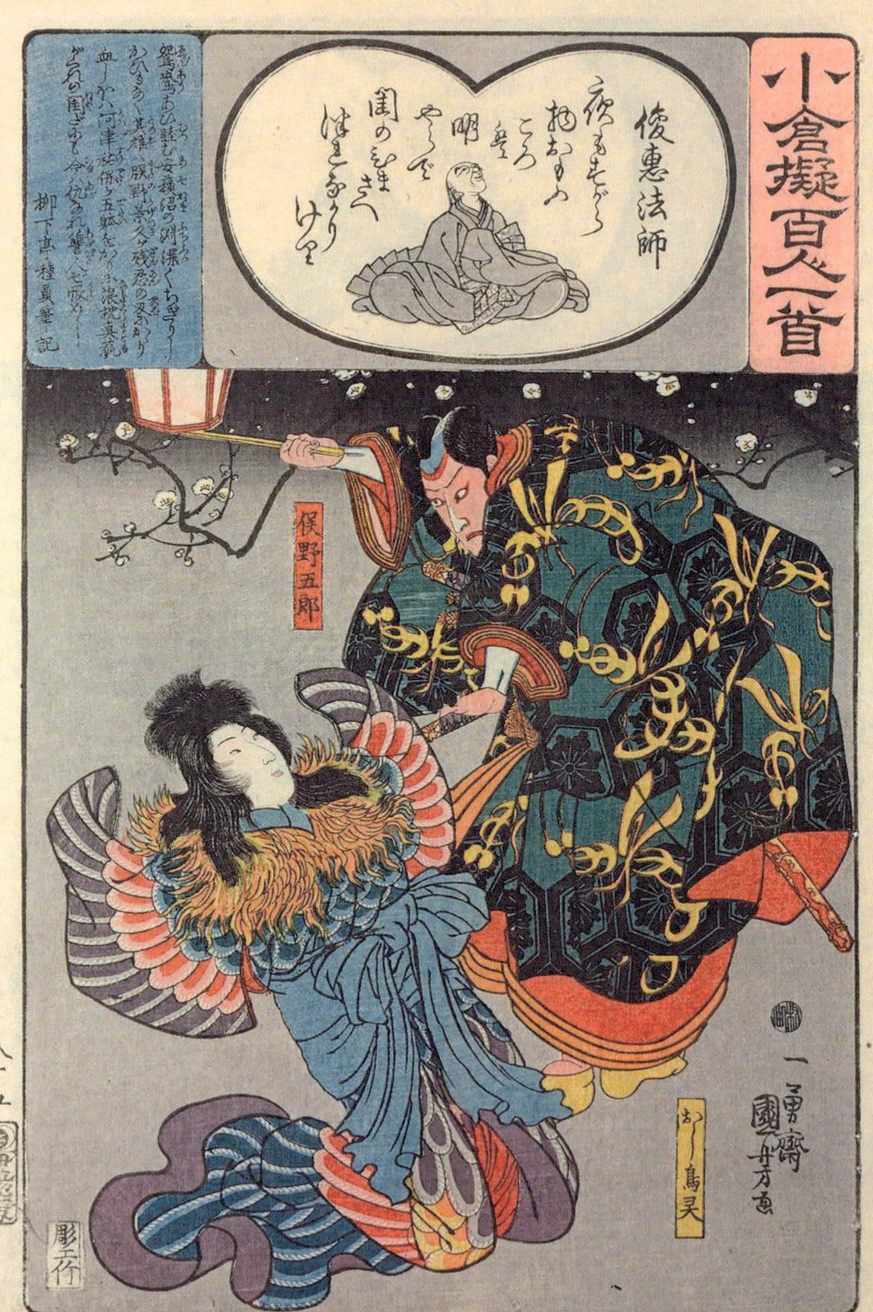
小倉擬百人一首

俊恵法師

夜もすがら
物思ふころは
明けやらで
閨のひまさへ
つれなかり
けり

俣野五郎

一勇齋國芳画

おし鳥夊

85

The Priest Shunye

I toss and turn all night
and ponder my obsession—

darkness that never ends.
Even the door's cruel crack
refuses me the light.

夜もすがら
もの思ふ頃は
明けやらぬ
閨のひまさへ
つれなかりけり

yo mo sugara
mono omou koro wa
ake yaranu
neya no hima sae
tsure nakari keri

86

The Priest Saigyo

The moon is not a dreary thing
that drives us into sullen thoughts
so do not call her so—

it's we who make sad faces,
we who shed the tears.

nageke tote
tsuki ya wa mono wo
omowasuru
kakochi gao naru
waga namida kana

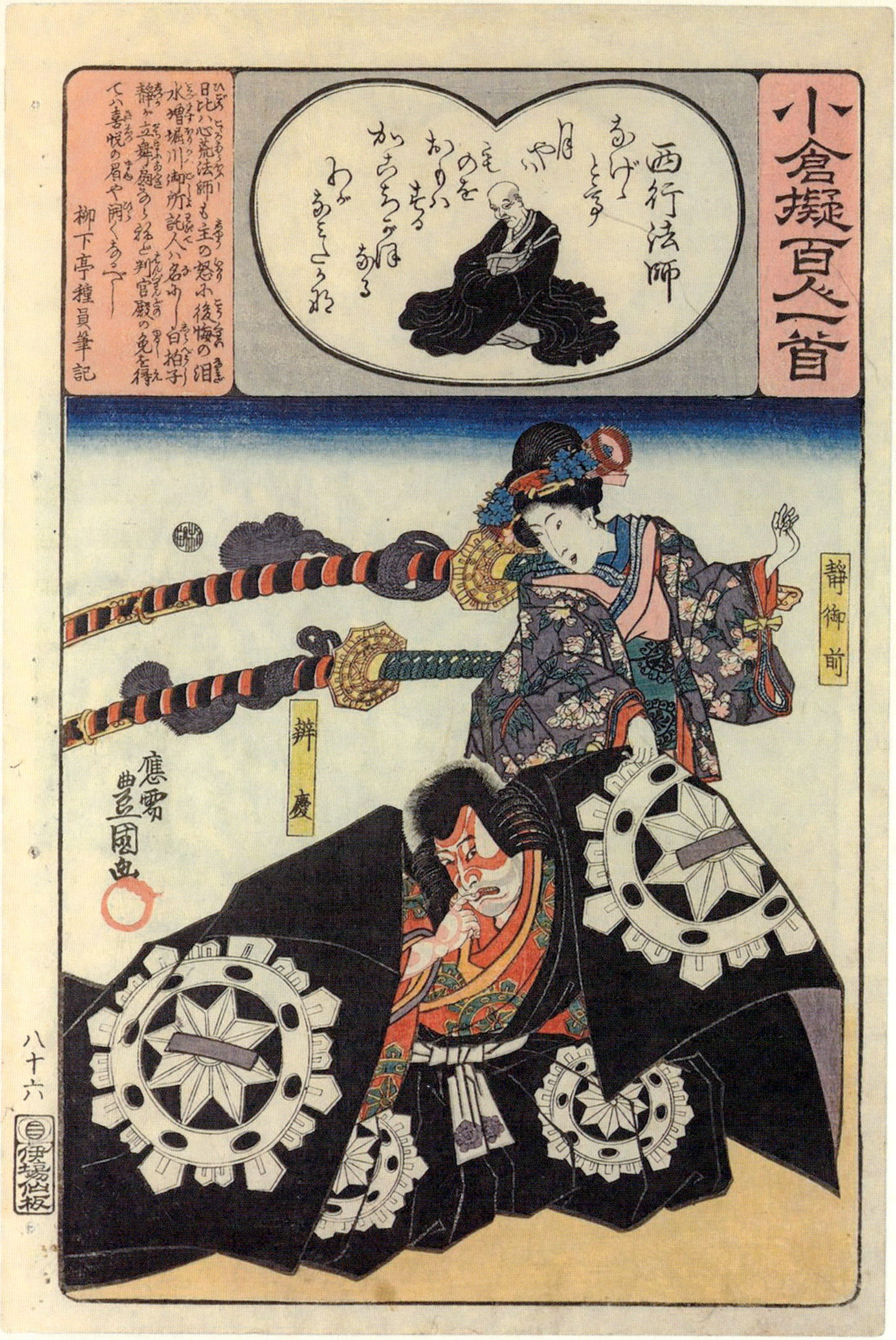

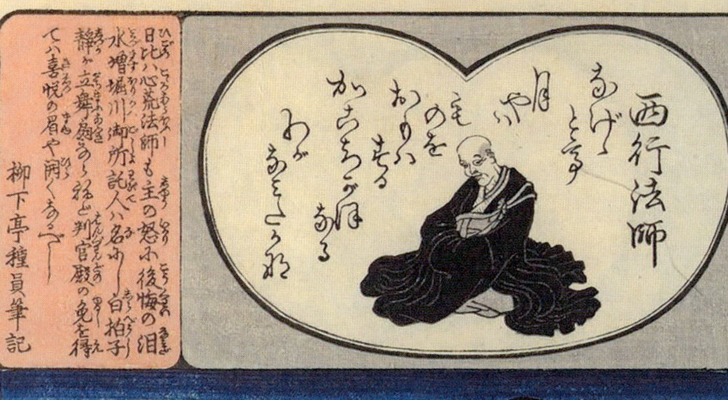

西行法師
嘆げとて
月やは
ものを
おもはする
かこちがほなる
わが涙かな

日比ハ心荒法師も主の怒ゐ後悔の泪
水増堀川御所託人ハ名めゝ白拍子
静ゕ立舞ゐ廻るゝゝ程ど判官殿の免を得
てハ喜悦の眉や開くあらゝゝ
柳下亭種員筆記

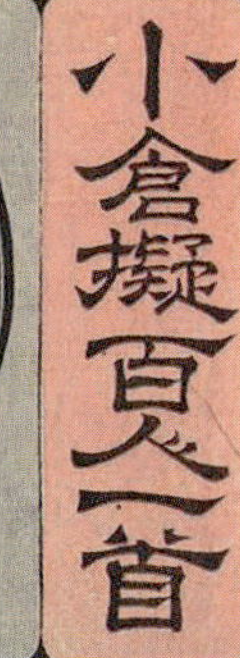

小倉擬百人一首

静御前
辨慶
應需
豊國画

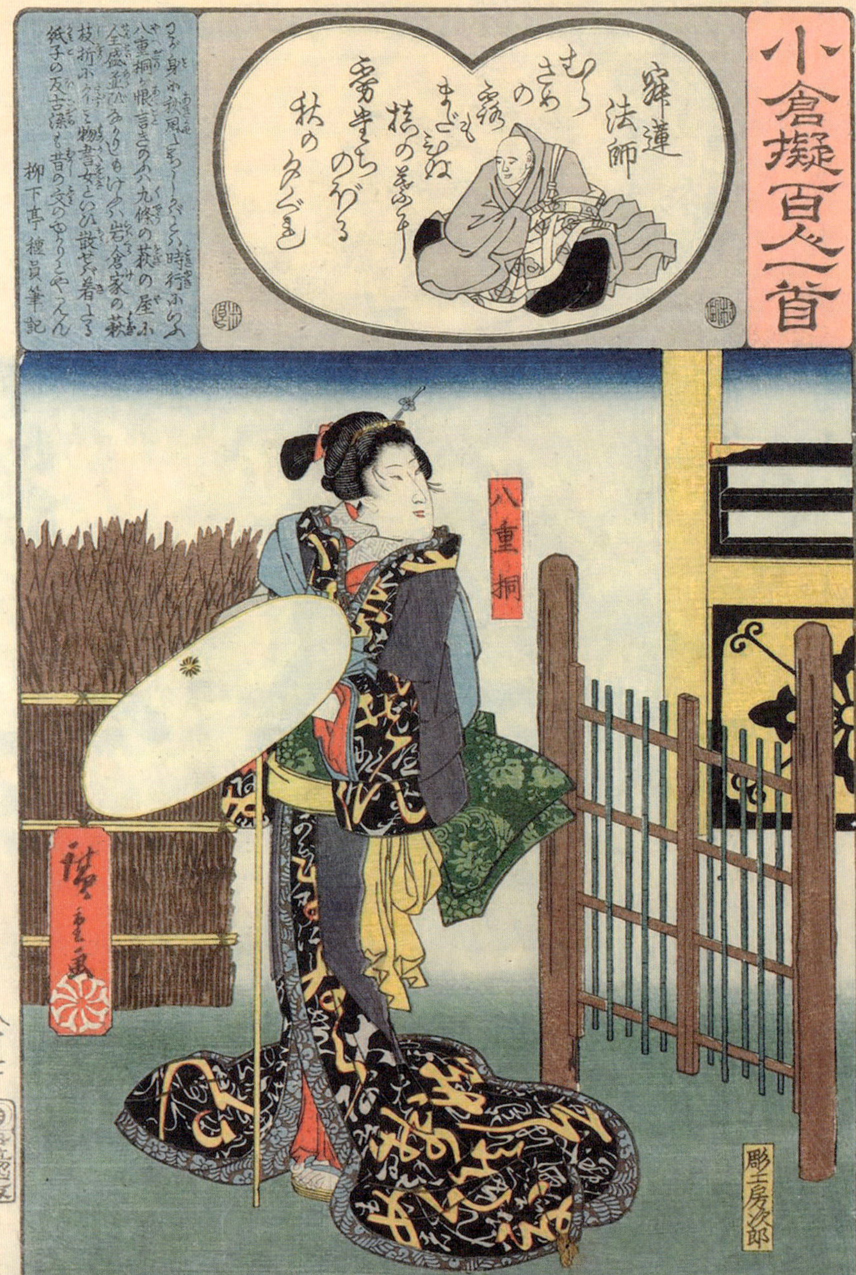
小倉擬百人一首

寂蓮法師

もらさぬ
さみしさ
まきの
露もまだひぬ
霧たちのぼる
秋の夕ぐれ

八重桐

廣重画

八十七

伊場仙板

彫工房次郎

柳下亭種員筆記

87

The Monk Jakuren

Passing local showers
leave behind a dew, still wet upon the leaves,
as mist arises from the saturated ground

covering the pine trees like a shroud
this autumn evening.

村雨の
露もまだひぬ
真木の葉に
霧立ちのぼる
秋の夕暮

murasame no
tsuyu mo mada hinu
maki no ha ni
kiri tachinoboru
aki no yugure

195

88

The Daughter of Toshitaka

Just a single night
short as the truncated stalks
at Naniwa Bay—

diving into waters marked too deep, I'm left no choice
but throw both body and soul across to him.

難波江の
芦のかりねの
ひと夜ゆゑ
みをつくしてや
恋わたるべき

naniwae no
ashi no karine no
hitoyo yue
mi wo tsukushite ya
koi wataru beki

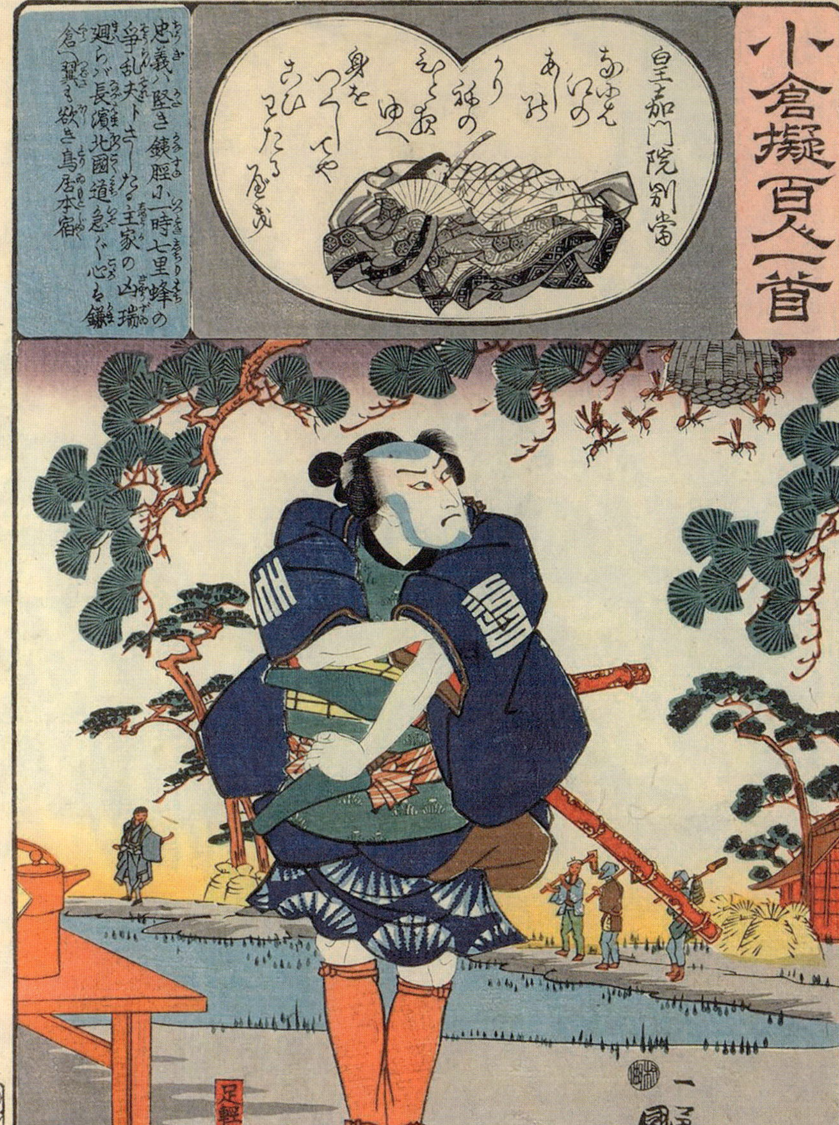

小倉擬百人一首

皇嘉門院別当
なにはえの
あしの
かりねの
ひとよゆゑ
身を
つくしてや
こひわたる
べき

忠義に堅き鏡脛小一時七里蜂の
争乱夫卜さ一な主家の凶瑞
廻らが長濱北國道急ぐ心を鎌
倉つ翼き敬き鳥居本宿

足軽市左門

一勇齋
國芳画

八十八

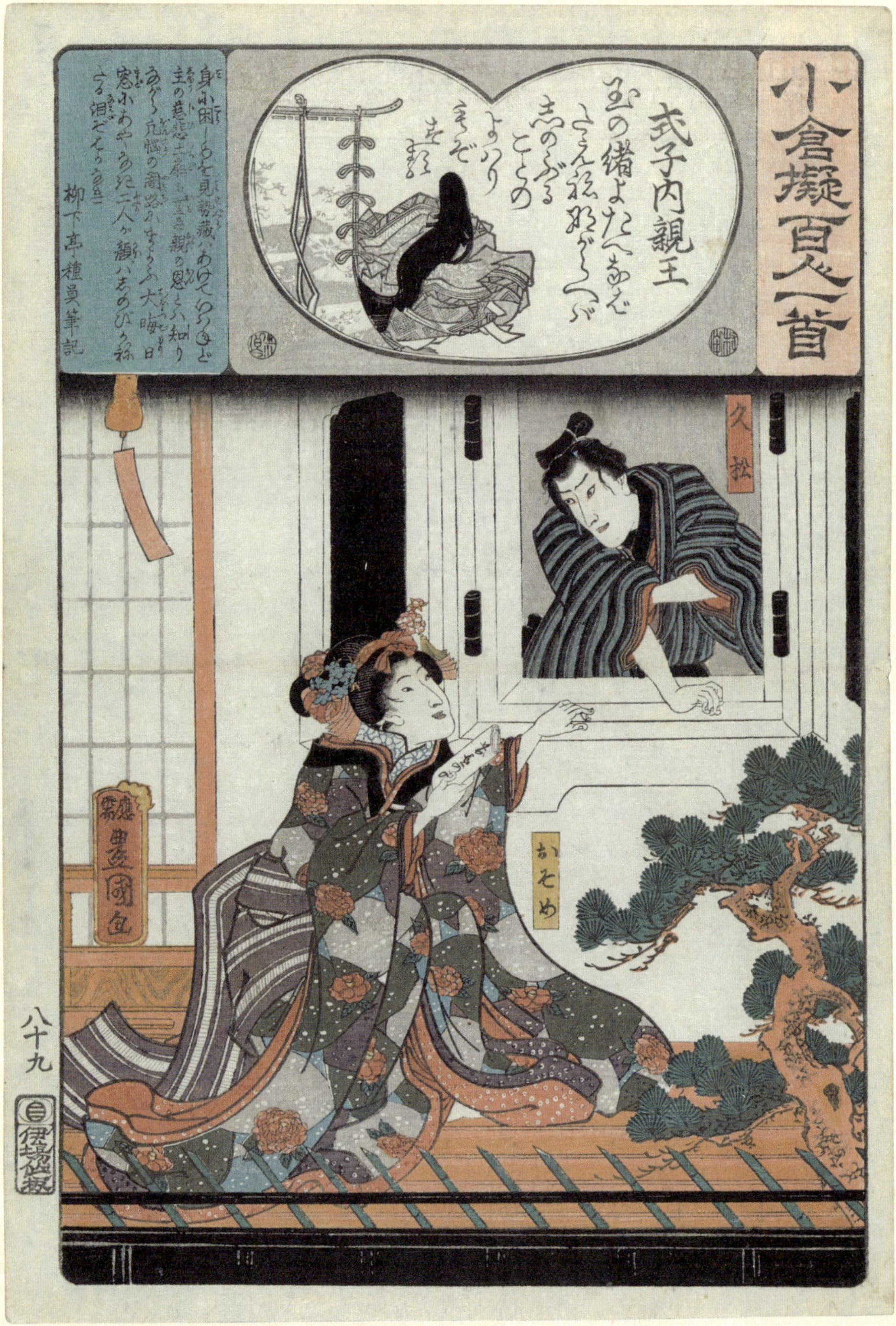

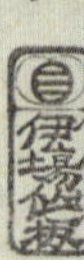

小倉擬百人一首
式子内親王
玉の緒よたえなばたえねながらへば忍ぶることのよはりもぞする
身も断りらを見勢蔵、あけそらうもど主の慈悲工藤らこ五三親の恩とふ知りあがらう冗惱の離路かまよるゐ大晦日窓ふあやうゐ兄二人ゞ瀬ハものびう稼らる泪ぞそうのあ【】
柳下亭種員筆記
久松
おそめ
應需 豊國画
八十九

89

Princess Shokushi

Like a rosary discarded
oh let me snap my string of days—

though outwardly I live,
within my heart is failing
from the shame I cannot bear.

玉
の
緒
よ
絶
え
な
ば
絶
え
ね
な
が
ら
へ
ば
忍
ぶ
る
こ
と
の
弱
り
も
ぞ
す
る

tama no o yo
taenaba taene
nagaraeba
shinoburu koto no
yowari mo zo suru

199

90

Princess Sukeko

You think that salty droplets
have no power
just because the spray-soaked sleeves
of divers off Ojima are unstained?

Here, let me show you mine!

見せばやな
雄島のあまの
袖だにも
濡れにぞ濡れし
色はかはらず

misebaya na
ojima no ama no
sode da ni mo
nure ni zo nureshi
iro wa kawarazu

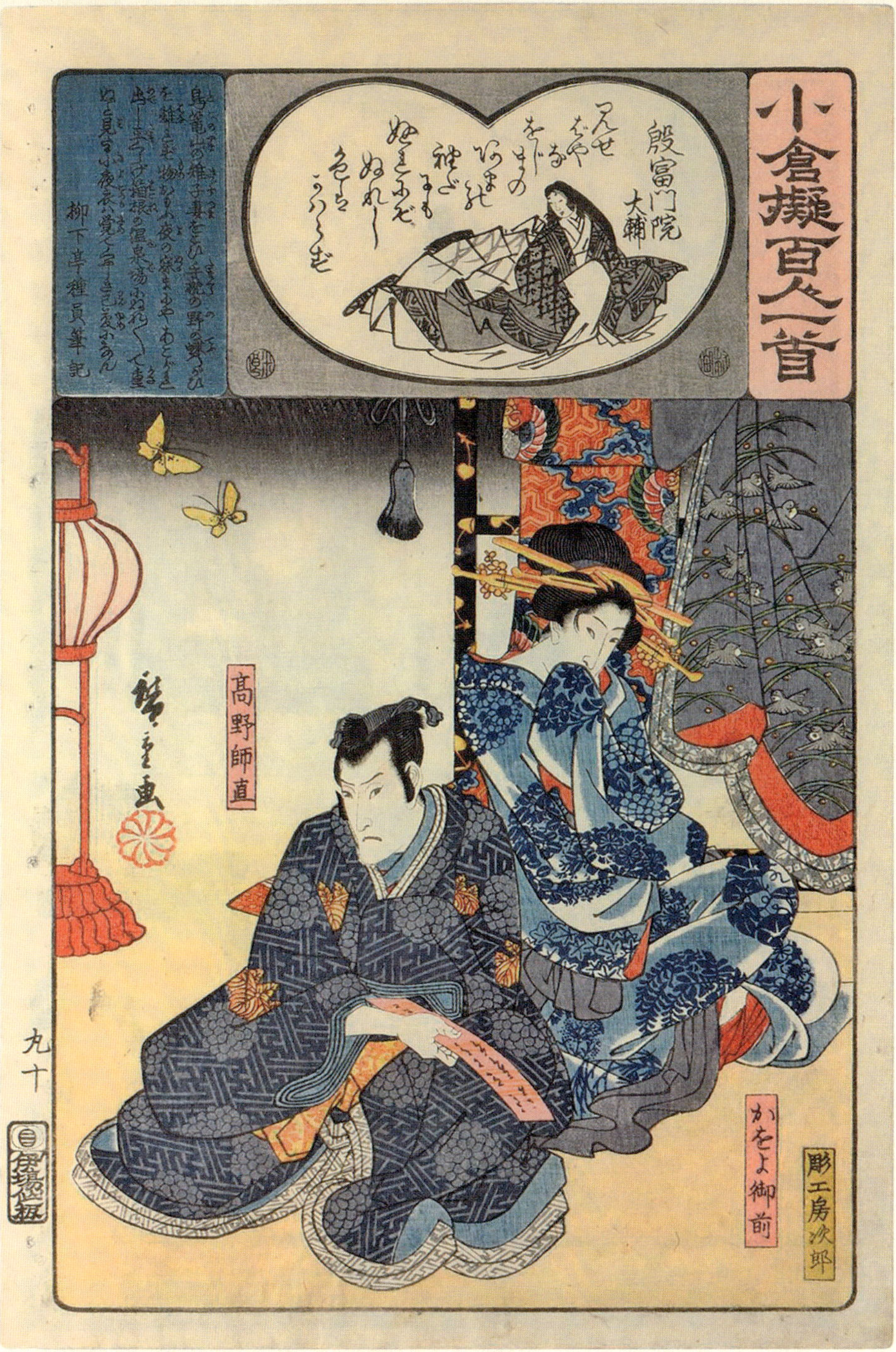

殷富門院大輔

見せばやな
雄島のあまの
袖だにも
ぬれにぞぬれし
色はかはらず

柳下亭種員筆記

高野師直

かをよ御前

彫工房次郎

廣重画

九十

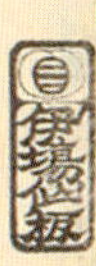

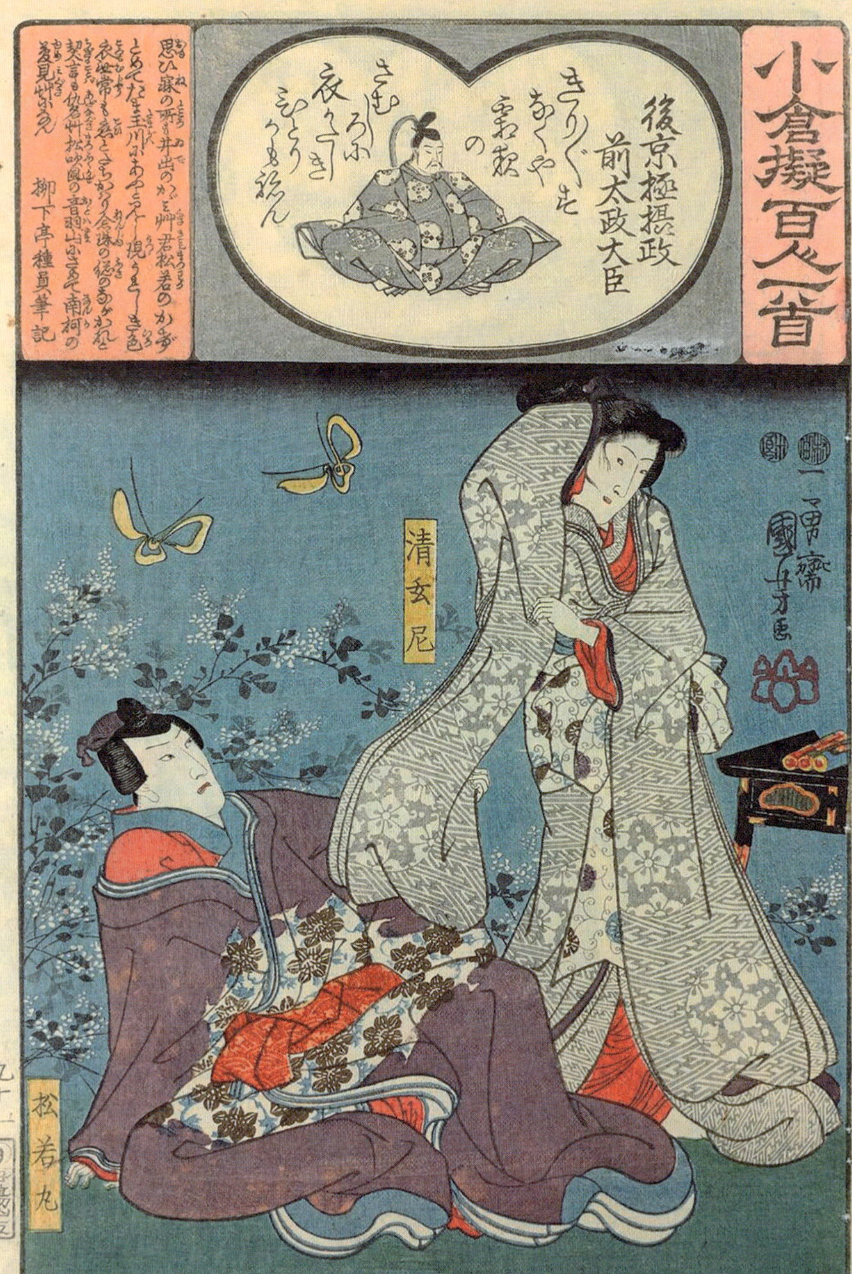

小倉擬百人一首
後京極摂政
前太政大臣
きりぎりす
なくや霜夜
の
さむしろ
衣かたしき
ひとりかもねん
柳下亭種員筆記
清玄尼
松若丸
九十一
一勇齋國芳画

91

Fujiwara no Yoshitsune

Clearly through the frosty air
a single cricket's crying may be heard—

awake I lie,
just one kimono
draped across my cold white bed.

きりぎりす
鳴くや霜夜の
さむしろに
衣かたしき
ひとりかも寝む

kirigirisu
naku ya shimo yo no
samushiro ni
koromo katashiki
hitori kamo nen

92

Lady Sanuki

My sodden sleeves
so like the sunken offshore rocks
you cannot see—

always drenched by salty spray,
impossible to dry.

waga sode wa
shiohi ni mienu
oki no ishi no
hito koso shirane
kawaku ma mo nashi

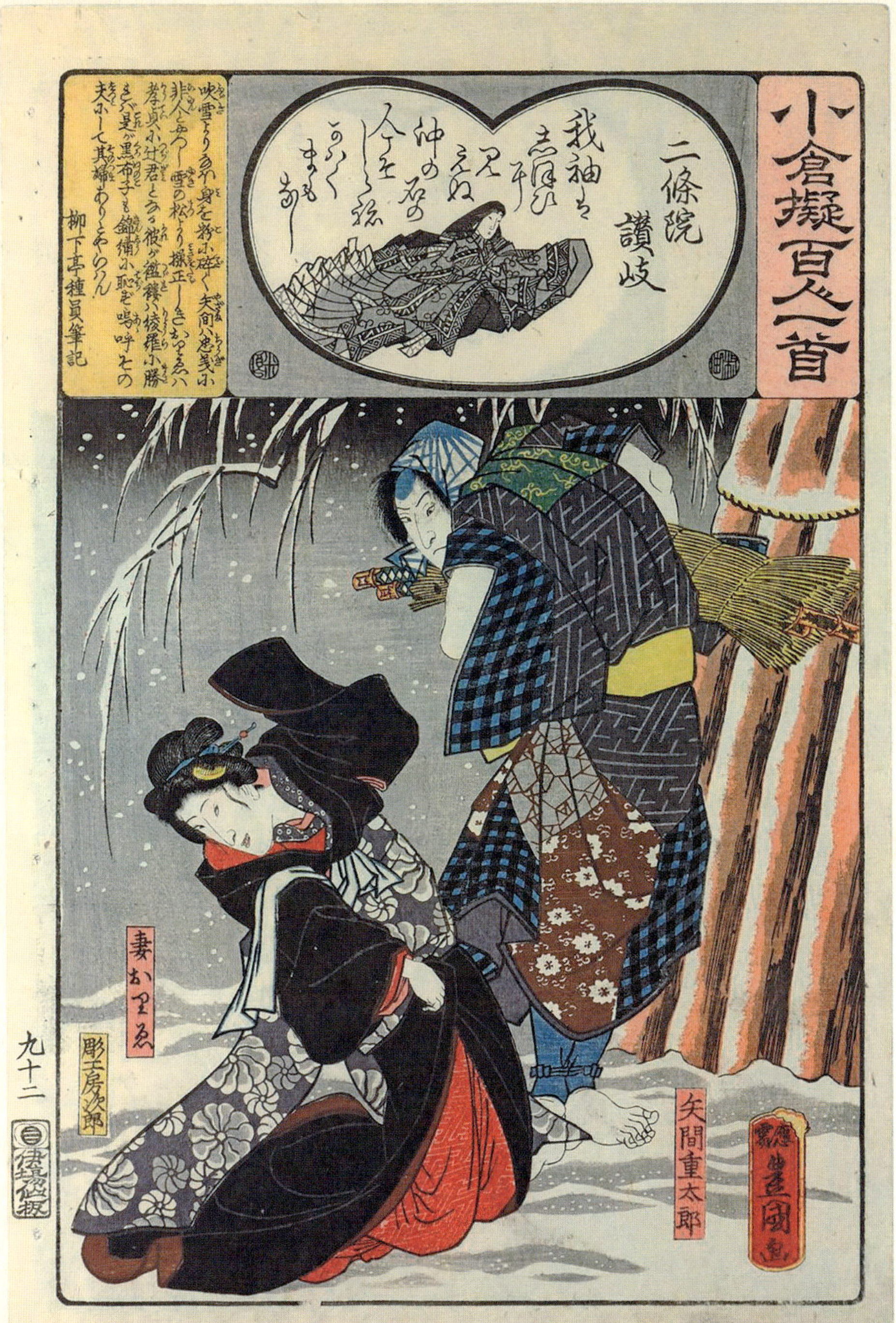

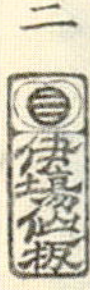

小倉擬百人一首

二條院 讃岐

我袖は
汐干に見えぬ
沖の石の
人こそしらね
かわくまも
なし

吹雪よりゆ糸身を教小砕く矢間八忠義小
非人と申つゝ雪の松よりゆ擬正しとおもへば
孝貞小辻君とつゝ彼ゲ鑑襪八棲羅小勝
さハ是が黒布子も錦繍小恥を鳴呼その
夫ふして其婦ありとやらりん
柳下亭種員筆記

妻お里ゑ

彫工房次郎

矢間重太郎

應需 豊國画

九十二

伊勢屋板

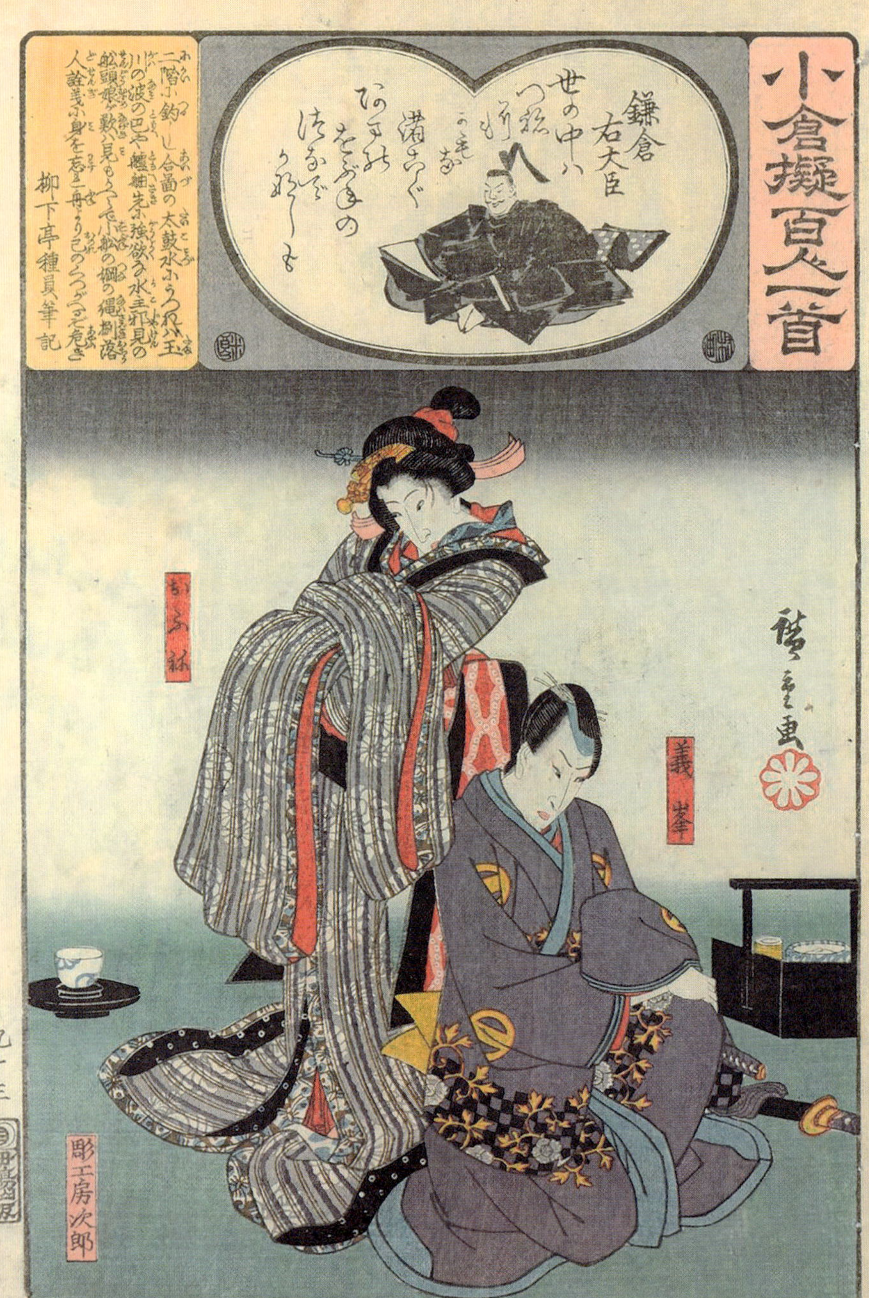
小倉擬百人一首
鎌倉右大臣
世の中は
つねにもがもな
渚こぐ
あまの小舟の
綱手かなしも
二階小釣り し合届の太鼓水ふう尺八玉
川の波の巴や艪袖先ふ強欲ふ水主邪見の
船頭娘が歎八見もう一て小松の棚の獨樹落
人詮義ふ身を忘二毎ようり己のくつぐつぞ危さ
柳下亭種員筆記
おそ松
義峯
廣重画
彫工房次郎
九十三

93

Minamoto no Sanetomo

Amid the troubles of this world,
I long for the safety of a peaceful harbor.

So sad to see, so close to shore
the diving boats these men are hauling,
towed by ropes they cannot steer.

世の中は
常にもがもな
渚漕ぐ
海土の小舟の
綱手かなしも

yo no naka wa
tsune ni mo ga mo na
nagisa kogu
ama no obune no
tsuna de kanashi mo

94

Masatsune

A visit to my old hometown—
autumn winds roll down from Mount Yoshino
as evening deepens in its chill.

No human voices heard above the howling wind,
just the sound of robes, being pounded out to dry.

み吉野の
山の秋風
小夜更けて
故郷寒く
衣うつなり

miyoshino no
yama no akikaze
sayo fukete
furusato samuku
koromo utsu nari

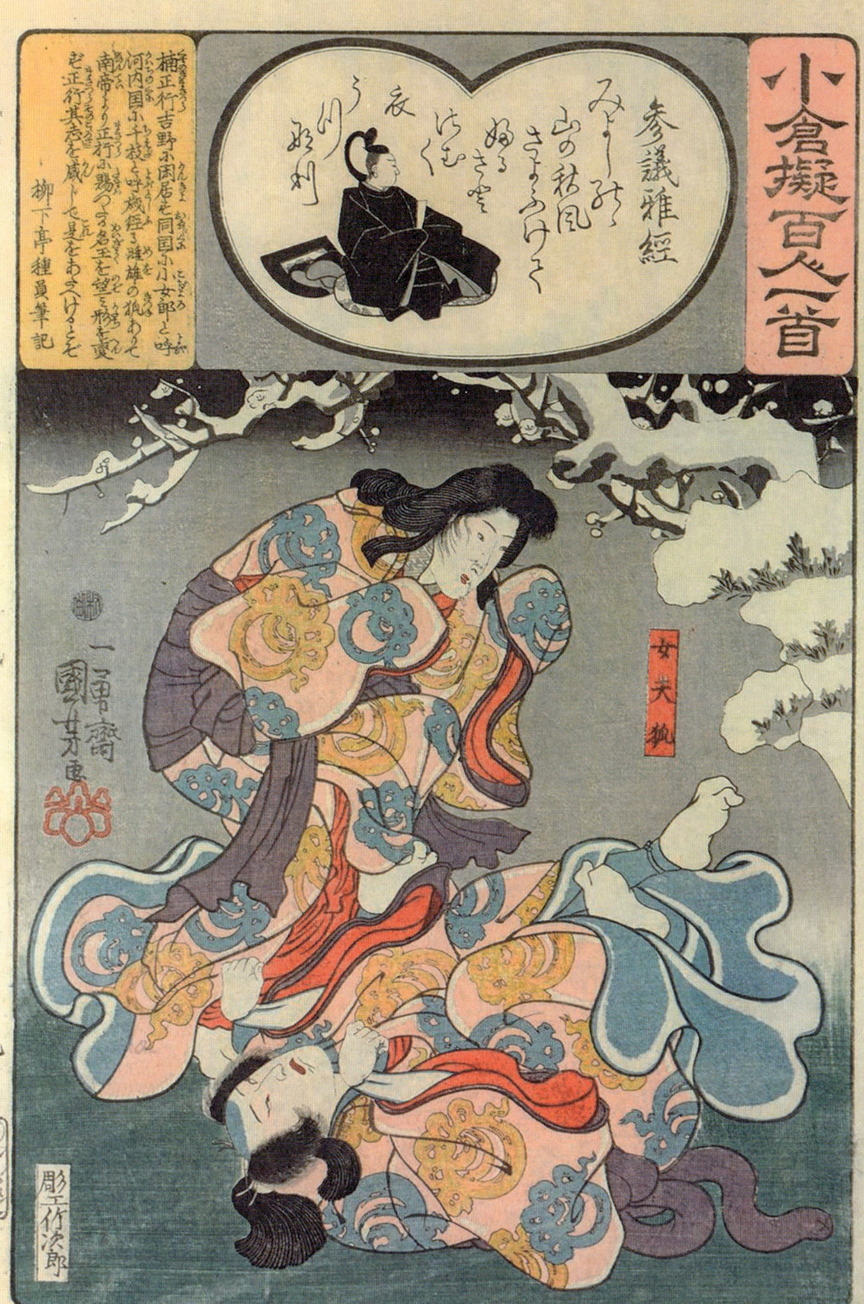
小倉擬百人一首
参議雅経
みよし野の
山の秋風
さよふけて
ふるさと
さむく
衣うつ
なり
女犬坊
一勇斎
國芳画
九十四
楠正行吉野に閑居を同国小々女郎と呼
河内国小十枝と呼蔵人雄の狐わせて
南帝より正行小賜つらの名王を望み形を裏
ぞ正行某志を威下て是をあさけるとぞ
柳下亭種員筆記
彫工竹次郎
伊場仙板

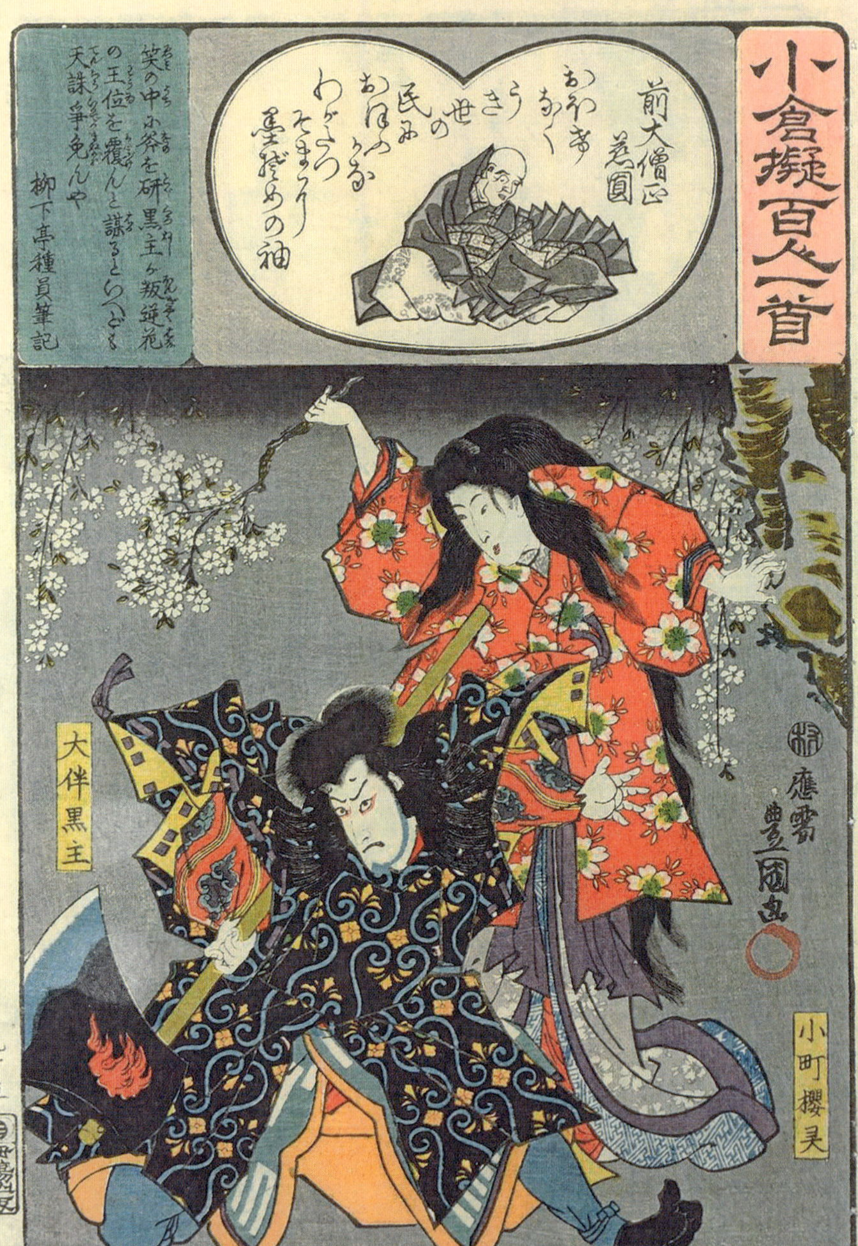
小倉擬百人一首

前大僧正慈圓

おほけなく
うき世の
民みの
おほふかな
わがたつ杣に
墨ぞめの袖

笑の中ふ斧を研黒主ゟ叛逆花
の王位を覆んと謀るらへども
天誅争免んや

柳下亭種員筆記

大伴黒主

小町櫻灵

應需
豊國画

九十五
伊場仙板

95

Former Archbishop Jien

Totally inadequate
to guide the people wandering
amid this wretched world—

I fold my ink-black sleeves in supplication,
retreating deep within the woods.

おほけなく
うき世の民に
おほふかな
わがたつ杣に
墨染めの袖

okenaku
ukiyo no tami ni
ou kana
waga tatsu soma ni
sumizome no sode

96

Saionji Kintsune

No, it is not snow
but scattered blossoms
strewn about the garden by a storm—

yet not just cherry blossoms suffer such a fate
but my poor body too, or so it seems.

花さそふ
嵐の庭の
雪ならで
ふりゆくものは
わが身なりけり

hana sasou
arashi no niwa no
yuki nara de
furi yuku mono wa
waga mi nari keri

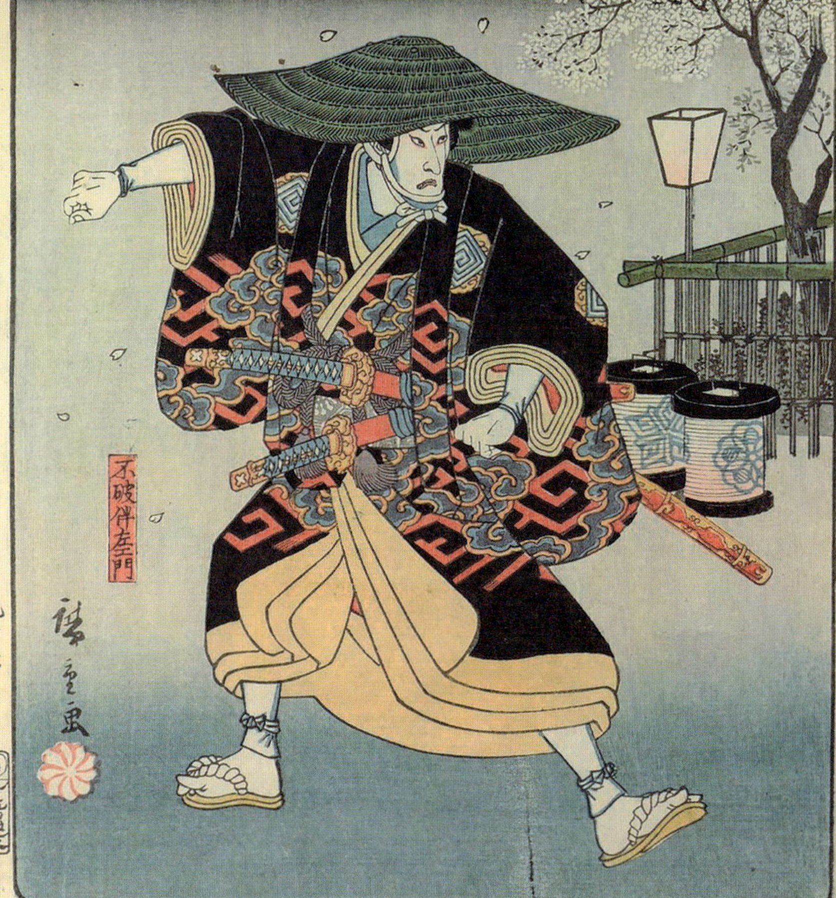

小倉擬百人一首

入道前大政大臣
花さそふ
あらしの庭の
雪ならで
ふりゆく
ものは
わが身
なりけり

「名古屋の浪宅不破伴小月もさして
雨をしのぐ軒場の破を見附と狂句彼ハ稲妻
を摸様ふつて丑の兆邪をあつ込是ハ三傘を
紋所ふりて旦の艶姿うるを如ぞ雲の電電
廓中燕何遊里の縁語るべ〜
柳下亭種員筆記

不破伴左衛門

廣重画

九十六

伊場仙板

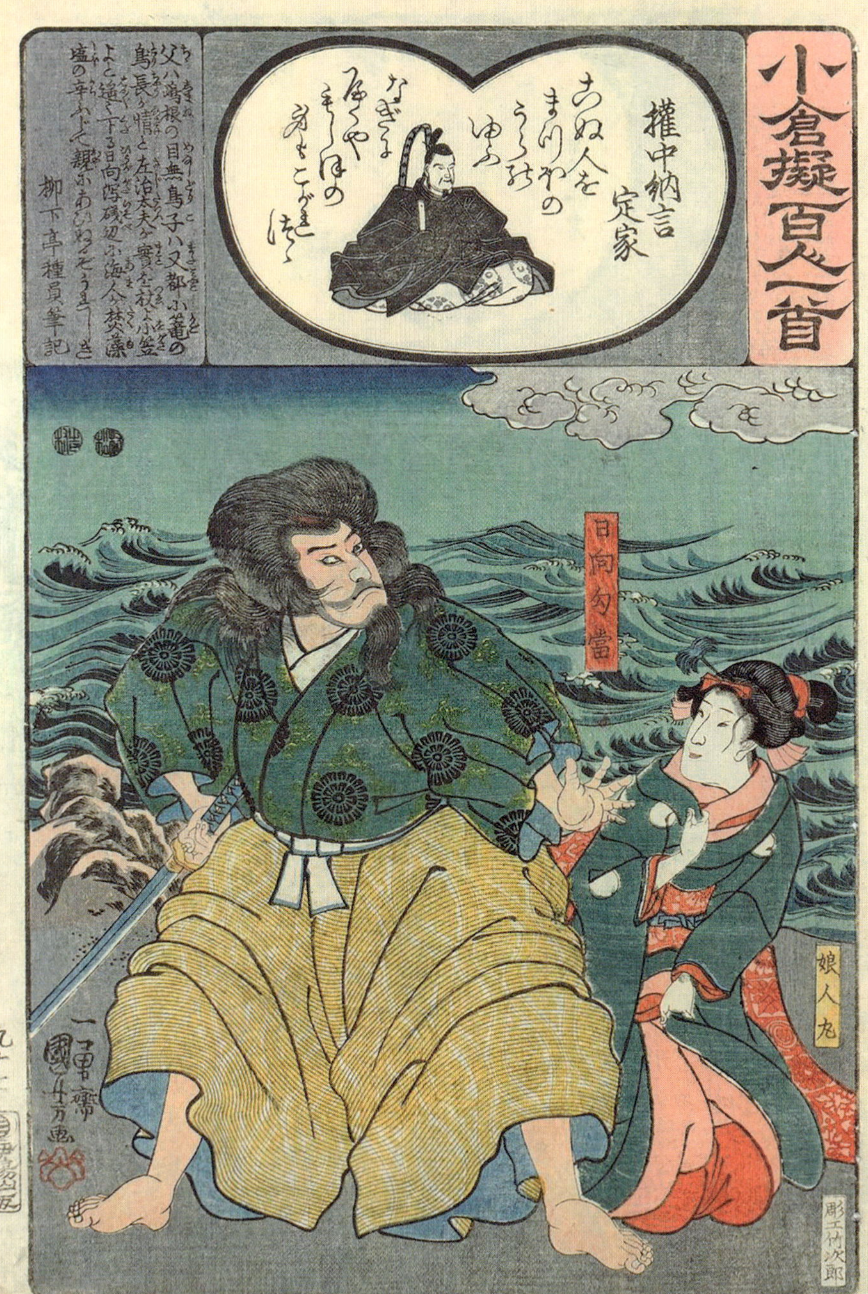
小倉擬百人一首

權中納言 定家

來ぬ人を
まつ帆の
うらの
ゆふ
なぎに
やくやもしほの
身もこがれつつ

父八瀬根の目無鳥子八都小菴の
鮎長り情と左治太夫分賣を秋小笠
よく遂て下る日向浮磯辺小海人焚藻
塩の辛ふじ親ふあ□ねそうまき□き
柳下亭種員筆記

日向勾當

娘人丸

九十七

一勇齋
國芳画

彫工竹次郎

97

Fujiwara no Teika

He does not come to visit here at Matsuo,
though night after night I anxiously await—

the evening might seem calm
but within, my heart just burns forever
like the salt vat's fire.

来ぬ人を
松帆の浦の
夕なぎに
焼くや藻塩の
身もこがれつつ

konu hito wo
matsuho no ura no
yunagi ni
yaku ya moshio no
mi mo kogare tsutsu

98

Fujiwara no Ietaka

A dying breeze disturbs the oaks
and causes them to flutter.
At Kamigamo it is twilight—

men perform their rituals in the stream
and remind me—summer still is with us.

風そよぐ
楢の小川の
夕暮は
みそぎぞ夏の
しるしなりける

kaze soyogu
nara no ogawa no
yugure wa
misogi zo natsu no
shirushi nari keru

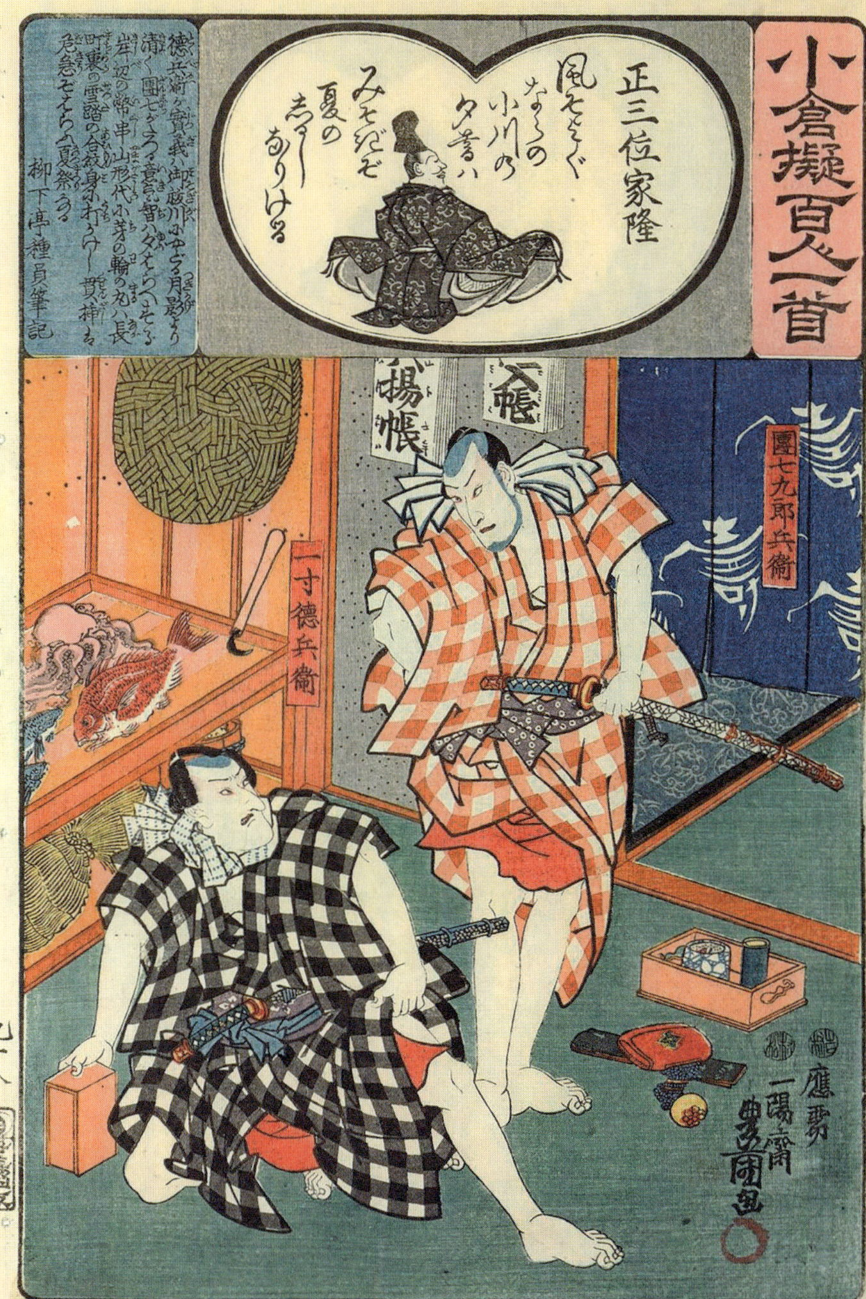

小倉擬百人一首
正三位家隆
風そよぐ
ならしの小川の
夕暮ハ
みそぎぞ
夏の志るし
ありける
一寸德兵衛
團七九郎兵衛
一陽齋豊國画
九十八

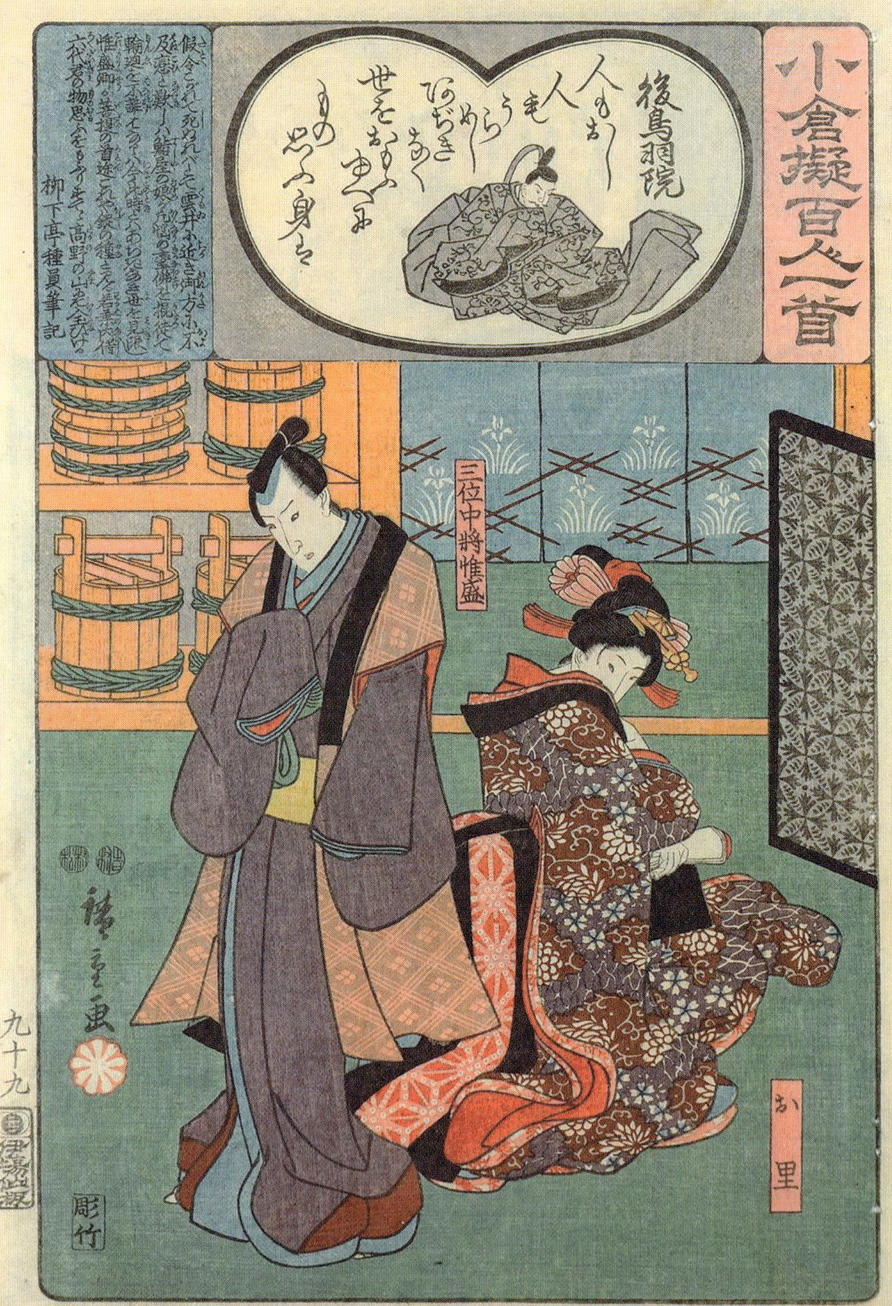
小倉擬百人一首

後鳥羽院
人もをし人もうらめしあぢきなく世をおもふゆゑにもの思ふ身は

三位中将惟盛

お里

柳下亭種員筆記

九十九

Retired Emperor Go-Toba

Some men I've met are noble—deserving better,
some men I've met malicious—deserving worse.

The more I think about the reasons,
the more my weariness increases—
I've lost my taste for all their machinations.

人も惜し
人も恨めし
あぢきなく
世を思ふ故に
もの思ふ身は

hito mo oshi
hito mo urameshi
ajiki naku
yo wo omou yue ni
mono omou mi wa

100

Retired Emperor Juntoku

Shinobu ferns have climbed so high,
their creeping vines now conceal the palace—
hundreds of its stones are strewn about.

Long gone the days
that place and I enjoyed together.

百敷や
古き軒端の
しのぶにも
なほあまりある
昔なりけり

momoshiki ya
furuki nokiba no
shinobu ni mo
nao amari aru
mukashi nari keri

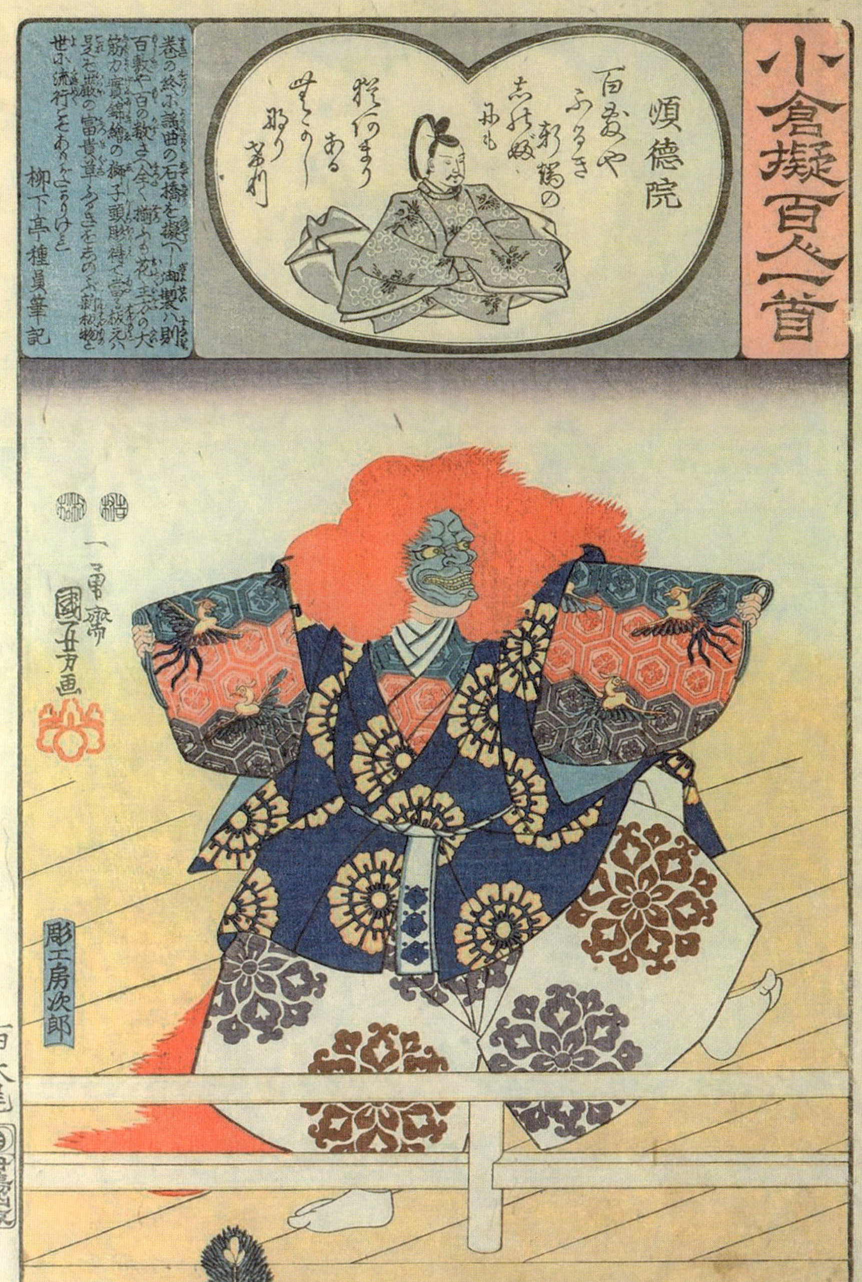
小倉擬百人一首
順徳院
百敷や
ふるき軒端の
しのぶにも
なほあまりある
昔なりけり
一勇斎
國芳画
彫工房次郎
柳下亭種員誌

Acknowledgements

THE TRANSLATIONS in this book had their beginnings some 47 years ago, during my Luce Scholarship year. Although many of the translations have changed since then, some have survived more or less intact. My encounter with Japanese literature and the Japanese language has been an ongoing affair throughout much of my life, and many people have provided guidance and assistance along the way.

John Nishimoto and Paul Nishijima sparked my interest in Japanese literature as we read together as undergraduates at the University of San Francisco. David Ferry of Wellesley College, one of the greatest teachers I have ever met, provided me with a sound understanding of the basics of poetry, not to mention welcome relief from the rigors of grad school while I was at MIT.

The Henry Luce Foundation through its Luce Scholars program funded my scholarship year (1977-1978), and especially my initial education in Japanese. Professor Makoto Nagao of Kyoto University is especially remembered for his kindness providing me with an institutional "home" during that year.

Professors Andrew Goble (University of Oregon) and the late Steve Salzberg (University of British Columbia, d. 2004) became close friends when we were together at Kyoto University's international student dormitory in Yamashina. During that time, we enjoyed long hours of entertaining and illuminating discussion regarding the nuances of certain Japanese expressions.

Two experienced translators who currently reside in Kyoto, Joseph Dreher and Stephen Horn, provided valuable assistance in discussing the complexities of translating and helping me locate scholarly resources.

Cathy Layne, my editor at Tuttle, was immensely helpful in providing stylistic guidance, spotting needed changes, and especially in helping to make the introduction clear and accessible to a non-scholarly audience.

I would like to thank the entire Takikawa family for their generosity and support. Miyuki, Harumi, and her husband Bill Dorrance welcomed me back into the family in 2015 with open arms. Karina's research skills and artistic talents helped me to understand many of the poems better.

Finally, of course, I owe an incalculable debt to Satsuki Takikawa, my co-translator for the senryu poems of They Never Asked, for her patience, her support, and her willingness to become my wife a mere 43 years after our first date.

—Michael Freiling

Illustration credits
Poems 1–20, 22, 23–31, 33–36, 38–39, 41, 44–53, 55–88, 90–100: © Trustees of the British Museum.
Poems 21, 24, 42: public domain.
Poems 23, 32, 37, 40, 43, 54, 89: Schenking van de Stichting Herwig-Kempers Kabuki Foundation.

"Books to Span the East and West"

Tuttle Publishing was founded in 1832 in the small New England town of Rutland, Vermont [USA]. Our core values remain as strong today as they were then—to publish best-in-class books which bring people together one page at a time. In 1948, we established a publishing outpost in Japan— and Tuttle is now a leader in publishing English-language books about the arts, languages and cultures of Asia. The world has become a much smaller place today and Asia's economic and cultural influence has grown. Yet the need for meaningful dialogue and information about this diverse region has never been greater. Over the past seven decades, Tuttle has published thousands of books on subjects ranging from martial arts and paper crafts to language learning and literature—and our talented authors, illustrators, designers and photographers have won many prestigious awards. We welcome you to explore the wealth of information available on Asia at www.tuttlepublishing.com.

Published by Tuttle Publishing, an imprint of Periplus Editions (HK) Ltd.

www.tuttlepublishing.com

Copyright @2025 Periplus Editions (HK) Ltd.

All rights reserved. No part of this publication may be reproduced or utilized in any form or by any means, electronic or mechanical, including photocopying, recording, or by any information storage and retrieval system, without prior written permission from the publisher.

Library of Congress Cataloging-in-Publication Data in process

ISBN 978-4-8053-1923-9

29 28 27 26 25
10 9 8 7 6 5 4 3 2 1   2503CM

Printed in China

TUTTLE PUBLISHING® is a registered trademark of Tuttle Publishing, a division of Periplus Editions (HK) Ltd.

Distributed by:

North America, Latin America & Europe
Tuttle Publishing
364 Innovation Drive, North Clarendon
VT 05759-9436 U.S.A.
Tel: 1 (802) 773-8930
Fax: 1 (802) 773-6993
info@tuttlepublishing.com
www.tuttlepublishing.com

Japan
Tuttle Publishing
Yaekari Building, 3rd Floor
5-4-12 Osaki, Shinagawa-ku
Tokyo 141-0032
Tel: (81) 3 5437-0171
Fax: (81) 3 5437-0755
sales@tuttle.co.jp
www.tuttle.co.jp

Asia Pacific
Berkeley Books Pte. Ltd.
3 Kallang Sector #04-01
Singapore 349278
Tel: (65) 6741-2178
Fax: (65) 6741-2179
inquiries@periplus.com.sg
www.tuttlepublishing.com